The Fine Art of Political Wit

Leon A. Harris

THE FINE ART OF
POLITICAL WIT

*being a Lively Guide to the Artiſtic
Invective, Elegant Epithet, and Poliſhed
Impromptus as well as the Gallant
and Graceful Worldly Wit of various
Britiſh & American Politicians
from the 18th Century through our own
Days of Grace. A Handbook for
Piercing the Political Epidermes
of Opponents.*

BELL PUBLISHING COMPANY
NEW YORK

Manufactured in United States of America

This book is for
RUTH SPENCE

Contents

ILLUSTRATIONS

ACKNOWLEDGMENTS

Most of the politicians quoted in this book who are now alive were tape-recorded by the author in interviews on both sides of the Atlantic. The views on the uses, the dangers and the importance of wit in politics expressed by Adlai Stevenson, Barry Goldwater, Hubert Humphrey, Harold Wilson, Clement Attlee, and the others are, therefore, not the studied expressions of speech writers and press agents but the spontaneous responses of the leading politicians of our day.

Much of what is quoted in this book is taken from the *Congressional Record* and from *Hansard*. However, although *Hansard* may not be changed except for reporting errors, this is not the case with the *Congressional Record*. Members of the American Congress may, and do, delete entirely things they have said and, therefore, many things actually said in the Congress are not in the *Record*. Much in this book is the best recollection of contemporaries of the speakers, either recounted to the author or taken from memoirs. If the recollection of a Lord Attlee or an Adlai Stevenson is not absolutely correct, the author has nevertheless felt as the Abbé Raynal did about Benjamin Franklin, that he would rather recount some men's stories than other men's truths.

In the Bibliography are listed those books particularly useful in studying this facet of political life. Especially helpful were Edward Boykin, *The Wit and Wisdom of Congress* (Funk & Wagnalls); Colin Coote, *Sir Winston Churchill, a Self-Portrait* (Eyre & Spottiswoode); Michael Foot, *Aneurin Bevan* (Atheneum); Max Hall, *Benjamin Franklin and Polly Baker* (University of North Carolina Press); Emmanuel Hertz, *Lincoln Talks* (Viking Press); André Maurois, *Disraeli* (Appleton); Hesketh Pearson, *Dizzy* (Harper & Bros.); Samuel Rosenman, *Working with Roosevelt* (Harper & Bros.); Carl Sandburg, *Abraham Lincoln* (Harcourt, Brace); and Geoffrey Williams and Charles

Roetter, *The Wit of Winston Churchill* (Max Parrish).

While it is not possible to acknowledge all of the assistance I received in the preparation of this book, I want to thank the following for their kind help, at the same time absolving them from any of my errors: Mrs. C. P. Aberg; Mr. Sam Acheson; The Rt. Hon. The Earl Attlee; Mr. Wilbur J. Bender; Mr. Simon Michael Bessie; The Rt. Hon. Nigel Birch; The Lord Bossom; The Hon. Clive Bossom; Congressman Emanuel Celler; Mr. George Christ; Mr. Clark Clifford; The Rt. Hon. W. F. Deedes; Senator Everett M. Dirksen; The Rt. Hon. James Chuter Ede; Senator Sam J. Ervin, Jr.; Mr. Mark Ethridge; Mr. Luther Evans; Mr. James Farley; The Hon. Michael Foot; Professor Frank Freidel; Mr. John George; The Hon. Charles Leslie Hale; Mr. Max Hall; Mr. D. B. Hardeman; Mrs. Joan Hardin; Mrs. Lucile Harris; Mr. Brooks Hays; Mr. David Holland; Senator Hubert H. Humphrey; the late Jack Hyman; Mr. Thomas A. Knight; Mr. Arthur Krock; Mr. Myrick Land; The Lord Mancroft; The Hon. Sir Gerald D. N. Nabarro; The National Broadcasting Company-TV; Miss Lynn Nesbit; Mr. Paul Porter; Mr. Kenneth Rose; Judge Samuel I. Rosenman; Mr. Pierre Salinger; Professor Arthur Schlesinger, Jr.; The Rt. Hon. Emanuel Shinwell; Mr. Theodore Sorensen; Mrs. Ruth Spence; Ambassador Adlai Stevenson; Marina Svetlova; The Hon. Jeremy Thorpe; Mr. Decherd Turner, Jr.; Mr. William S. White; and The Rt. Hon. James Harold Wilson.

I also wish to thank the Dallas Public Library, the Widener Library, the Houghton Library, the Library of Congress, the British Museum, the New York Public Library, and the Library of the House of Commons for their many courtesies. And most especially, my wife, for all her help and patience.

Introduction

Ballads, *bon mots*, anecdotes, give us better insight into
the depths of past centuries than grave and voluminous
chronicles. "A Straw," says Selden, "thrown up into the
air will show how the wind sits, which cannot be learned
by casting up a stone."   Emerson, *Journals*

In America there have been periods when wit by politicians
was out of fashion with the electorate; and American politicians from Lincoln to Adlai Stevenson have been criticized for their use of wit. Particularly in the years since
World War II, when America has been faced with a
frustrating multiplicity of problems that could be neither
easily understood nor simply solved, politicians, as a group,
have tended to be more pious and less witty. This is strange,
because in America, as in Great Britain, every citizen
prides himself on having a sense of humor. In fact, it is
usually safer to question a man's intelligence, probity, ancestry, or politics than to question his sense of humor. Yet
in recent years in America, politicians have been advised—
and for the most part have taken the advice—to avoid wit,
especially on controversial subjects.

It may or may not be unimportant that many of the major
sponsors of television programs try zealously to avoid anything that may result in angry letters from viewers, no
matter how psychologically upset the complaining viewers
may be. But when politicians began using television and
sought the advice of "television experts" in this new medium
and these experts advised the same banality and conformity
for politicians as for soap flakes and cosmetics programs, a
disservice was done to democracy. A political election involves, or at least should involve, a controversy between

men with conflicting ideas on what government should be
and do. And wit has historically often been both an effective tool for explaining ideas and an effective weapon for
attacking opponents.

There have been numberless eulogies written in the last
fifteen years on the death of wit in American politics, and
most of them include Senator Thomas Corwin's advice to
Garfield: "Never make people laugh. If you would succeed
in·life, you must be solemn, solemn as an ass. All great
monuments are built over solemn asses." Even the greatest
political wits in Great Britain and the United States have
always been aware of the dangers of being witty. Disraeli
wrote, "Men destined to the highest places should beware
of badinage . . . an insular country subject to fogs, and with
a powerful middle class, requires grave statesmen."

No American politician was ever more criticized for his
use of wit than was Lincoln. One of the bitterest of many
anti-Lincoln cartoons appeared in *Harper's Weekly* in
1863. It showed Columbia asking accusingly, "Where are
my fifteen thousand sons murdered at Fredericksburg?"
Lincoln replies, "This reminds me of a little joke . . ."
When Lincoln was criticized by his own Secretary of the
Treasury, the vain and pompous Salmon Chase, for telling
stories at his Cabinet meetings, Lincoln replied: "They say
I tell a great many stories; I reckon I do, but I have found
in the course of a large experience that common people,
take them as they run, are more easily informed through
the medium of a broad and humorous illustration than in
any other way, as to what the hypercritical few may think,
I don't care." Many great leaders, from Jesus Christ to
John F. Kennedy, have had this same point of view.

A case for political invective is harder to make. One can
only observe that it seems always to have existed, and
therefore presumably will continue to exist. From the
Greek Olympic Games through today's televised prize-

fights, spectator citizens have enjoyed watching a good fight. Political opponent-baiting has, on occasion, surpassed in popularity even badger-baiting, as in the case of the Lincoln-Douglas debates. If a do-good basis is needed to justify political abuse, it may be well to remember that all kinds of organizations, from the AFL-CIO and League of Women Voters in America to the Hansard Society in Great Britain, are anxious to increase the interest of the average citizen in politics; and history seems to indicate that verbal assault in the political arena increases interest.

In every election year in the United States and Great Britain, we hear a great many words spoken by politicians. It is to be hoped that some of the pomposity, piety, and nonsense will be cleared away by wit and also that speeches may occasionally be enlivened by some interesting invective, as historically has been the case in both countries. If wit does nothing else but lighten the tensions that abound in election years, it serves a real purpose. But besides this, real wit, like real poetry, sometimes goes clearly to the heart of the matter and concisely presents real issues. It is impossible to be witty vaguely or generally, hypocritically or pompously. In the 1960's some politicians choose to run against Khrushchev, as in the past some British politicians ran against Bonaparte, or as Big Bill Thompson of Chicago used to run against the King of England. There have always been some, however, who run on real issues and state their case and the case against their opponents with both clarity and wit.

Had President Kennedy, the greatest American political wit since Lincoln, not been killed, the debates in the 1964 presidential campaign would have been the wittiest since the Lincoln-Douglas debates. In the last four years Kennedy had almost single-handedly revived the taste in America for wit from its politicians. Whether this renaissance of wit begun by the late President will continue remains to be seen.

This book includes only the invective and wit of British and American politicians, and none of that of countless journalists, professional comedians, cartoonists, and authors. Any book that addresses itself to the use of wit and abuse by politicians must of necessity be selective. For example, the choice of Richard Brinsley Sheridan as the witty British politician of the eighteenth century has eliminated a chapter on the bons mots of John Wilkes. It was Wilkes who said in reply to the Earl of Sandwich's prediction that he would die either upon the gallows or of venereal disease, "That depends, my lord, whether I embrace your principles or your mistress."

Limiting the book to British and American politicians has, of course, also meant leaving out many political wits such as Prince Talleyrand. When told that the chief of Napoleon's secret police, Fouché, had a profound contempt for human nature, it was Talleyrand who replied, "Of course, he is much given to introspection." And in reply to the statement that consciences were to be found in the Upper Chamber, the Prince said, "Ah, yes, many, many consciences. Semonville, for example, has at least two." Limiting the book to a period from the eighteenth century through today has also precluded using any of the great political wit and abuse from earlier times, as when Demosthenes said to General Phocian, "The Athenians will kill you some day when they are in a rage," and Phocian replied, "And you some day when they are in their senses."

In politics, as in most areas of life, there are some constants (hunger, poverty, greed, courage, loyalty), and differences are usually differences of degree or style rather than differences of kind. In assembling this book, the recurrence of the same subjects in political wit from decade to decade and between the two countries has been striking.

For example, it is the similarities between David Lloyd George's and Huey Long's appeals for the votes of the poor that are interesting rather than the differences of accent or syntax. Both were eloquent and effective because both really understood the needs and fears of the poor. Both were elected and re-elected on the universal appeal of "Every man a king" and "a country fit for heroes." (Whether the legal fees collected by Huey Long's law firm from corporations wanting to do business in Louisiana were less moral than Lloyd George's wholesale selling of peerages is a nice question, but one for another book.)

Often, the politician's joke is not on his opponent but on the electorate itself, and often comes to light only many years later, if at all. Such jokes are at first known only to, and enjoyed by a few insiders. An example of this was a stratagem of Huey Long's, whose sense of humor and sense of politics were inseparable. Always a real friend of the Negro, for the very practical reason that he wanted the Negro vote, Long was once approached by some Negro leaders who pointed out that although a majority of the patients in the Charity Hospital were Negroes, there were no Negro nurses. Long promised to correct this, but warned the Negroes that they might not like his method. Some days later, Long announced he was making an inspection of the hospital, and drove out surrounded by police outriders with their motorcycles roaring and their sirens screaming. He was, as always, followed by reporters, for whom the Kingfish invariably provided good copy. After inspecting the hospital, when he was asked what he thought, Long exploded: "It's a Gawd-damn disgrace! That hospital's full of niggers being tended by nice white girls! It's a Gawd-damn disgrace, and I won't stand for it!" Needless to say, the hospital soon rectified the disgrace and so, thirty-five years ago, long before civil rights became fashionable, Governor Long was working for them in the only way possible in Louisiana and in that day. One wonders whether privately he laughed more at the racists, whom he had circumvented, or at the liberals, who labeled him a bigot. Certainly the Negroes were laughing with him.

In some of the chapters of this book a few of the serious words of politicians have been quoted along with their wit and invective as a reminder that they are all of a piece. Many of these politicians were witty on subjects about which they had the most serious feelings. The wit and sense of humor of Benjamin Disraeli or Franklin D. Roosevelt are as important as their courage and vision in any attempt seriously to understand them. During the Civil War Lincoln said, "I laugh because I must not cry. That is all. That is all."

The wit of politicians flourishes in a democratic society, but not in a tyranny. Although a despot may sometimes make jokes freely and in public about himself or about his subordinates, the subordinates do not retort in kind. President Kennedy once said: "Mr. Khrushchev himself, it is said, told the story a few years ago about the Russian who began to run through the Kremlin, shouting, 'Khrushchev is a fool. Khrushchev is a fool.' He was sentenced, the Premier said, to twenty-three years in prison, 'three for insulting the party secretary, and twenty for revealing a state secret.'" We know, however, no jokes by Mikoyan or Gromyko about Khrushchev.

Some books try to define and explain wit and humor. This book does not. It gives many and varied examples of the wit of politicians, and merely suggests that if wit gives a special vitality to wisdom that makes it more comprehensible or memorable, then it is valuable. Invective may be only another tool of politics. But wit, surely, is more than a mere tool with which to attack an opponent, relieve a tense political atmosphere, or put things in proper perspective. It is a blessing. Wit may not be so noble as courage, nor so elevating as faith. However, as it is given to man and not to other animals to know that he thinks and to laugh, so to men of wit is given that special felicitous perception of the comical, the ludicrous, and the absurd and that special insight which sees new associations between ideas and words not usually seen. So wit may lead in politics, as in other areas of human life, to wisdom and courage and perhaps even uphold if not lead to faith.

The Fine Art of Political Wit

I

Richard Brinsley Sheridan

Those who cannot miss an opportunity of saying a good thing . . . are not to be trusted with the management of any great question.

William Hazlitt, *Characteristics*

As has been the case with many great English wits, Richard Brinsley Sheridan was Irish. Although he is remembered today as the author of the ultimate in elegant eighteenth century English comedy, *The School for Scandal,* he was thought of during his lifetime as the greatest parliamentary wit and orator England had ever produced.

Born in Dublin where his father was the actor-manager of the theater, Sheridan was sent to Harrow in 1762 at the age of eleven, where he proved to be a poor and lazy scholar. He had an unhappy time at this school whose students were mainly sons of the aristocracy and where he was teased unmercifully for being the son of an actor. The only known attempt at wit by Sheridan while he was at Harrow was his reply to a comment on his father made by the son of a prominent London physician: " 'Tis true my father lives by pleasing people, but yours lives by killing them."

Throughout his life Sheridan sought to dissociate himself from the theater in the minds of his contemporaries, which was particularly difficult since he was both the greatest dramatist of his day and because during most of his adult life he was closely associated with and derived most of his income from the Drury Lane Theatre, of which he was the major shareholder. His extravagance in dress, in entertainment, and in gambling, which kept him constantly in debt, as well as his prominence as a Whig member of the House of Commons, were all part of his constant effort to be thought a "gentleman" rather than a theatrical person.

After graduating from Harrow, Sheridan joined his family in Bath, where he met and fell in love with the beautiful sixteen-year-old Elizabeth Linley. After an extraordinary series of romantic adventures with her, which included fighting two duels, eloping in a great storm, hiding her in a nunnery in France, a secret and illegal marriage near Calais, and the usual interdiction of both families against the lovers ever seeing each other again, they were finally legally married in 1773.

In spite of the fact that he was penniless and that his wife was the most sought-after singer in England and could have earned them large sums, Sheridan forbade her to sing in public after their marriage. Having suffered enough for being "a player's son," he was resolved not to be known as "a singer's husband." In spite of his great desire to be a "gentleman" and only because he had to earn money in order to eat, he turned to the theatre and with great success. In 1775 *The Rivals* was produced, and by 1776 he and a group of his friends were able to buy the Drury Lane Theatre from Garrick. By 1780 he had both earned enough money and sufficiently "arrived" in society to turn to politics, and he entered the House of Commons as a Whig Member from Stafford.

His maiden speech was expected to be brilliant and the former playwright was listened to with unusual attention. Afterward, when he asked his friend Woodfall in the reporters' gallery what he thought of it, he was told: "I am sorry to say I do not think this is your line. You had much better have stuck to your former pursuits." After a pause,

Sheridan replied, "It is in me, however, and by God it shall come out." The truth was that in his first few months in the House, Sheridan, who was to become the greatest Parliamentary speaker in a generation that included such masters as Pitt, Burke, and Fox, took himself too seriously. He not only refrained from any display of humor himself but also criticized its use by other Members, especially Courtenay, until the latter finally observed, "The honorable Member seems to be inimical to mirth and wit in any house but his own."

However, Sheridan could not long suppress his natural good humor. One day in the House, which had long been plagued by a Member who constantly interrupted every speaker with cries of "Hear, hear!" Sheridan rose and, in a speech, asked rhetorically, "Where oh where shall we find a more foolish knave or a more knavish fool than this?" When from the usual bench Sheridan heard the shout of "Hear, hear!" he turned and, amidst the general laughter of the House, thanked the honorable gentleman for the answer to his question.

When a very long-winded Member stopped in the middle of a lengthy oration to take a glass of water, Sheridan immediately rose to a point of order. Asked by the Speaker what the point of order could be, he replied, "I think, sir, that it is out of order for a windmill to go by water."

A good political joke often has many reincarnations. Nearly two hundred years later, when Governor Adlai Stevenson of Illinois welcomed to Chicago the 1952 Democratic Convention that was to nominate him for the Presidency, he used the same joke in alluding to the water-drinking members of the Republican Convention he had welcomed a few weeks earlier.

Anyone who has in preparing his taxes tried to understand the American tax structure with its hundreds of exceptions, exemptions, and amendments will share Sheridan's feelings expressed in his speech on the Perfume Tax. "In the recent administration acts for taxation have multiplied so excessively that the Justices of the Peace who administer them must often have puzzled their wise heads, especially as the bills have been drafted so carelessly, that session after, session they came up for amendment and explanation." Indeed, Sheridan went on, they reminded him of "The House That Jack Built." "First there comes the act imposing the tax; next comes an act to amend the act for imposing the tax; then comes an act to explain the act that amended the act imposing the tax; and next an act to remedy the defects of the act for explaining the act that amended the act; and so on *ad infinitum*. This tax bill is like a ship built in a dockyard, which put to sea on the first voyage before it was discovered that they had forgotten the rudder. After every voyage it revealed some new defect that had to be remedied; it had to be caulked, then to be new-planked; then to be new-rigged; then to be careened, and after all these expensive alterations, the vessel was obliged to be broken up and rebuilt. In fact, every recent bill has gone through as many transformations as a butterfly's egg before it emerges as a butterfly."

In attacking Pitt's Cabinet, Sheridan pointed out that one member, Dundas, held three posts in the Cabinet at one time. "If as has been stated, that gentlemen would serve their country, without at the same time serving themselves," Sheridan said, "we certainly have at present a most gentlemanly administration; and one gentleman, Mr. Secretary Dundas, is three times as much a gentleman as any of them, for he has three places." Having thus been made a laughingstock in the House, Dundas, then very recently married, rose and very seriously explained that his situation was not to be envied—every morning when he got up and every night when he went to rest, he had a task to perform almost too great for human powers. Sheridan immediately rose again to say that he himself would be happy to relieve Dundas from the fatigues of the Home Office.

Of this same Dundas, Sheridan once said in debate in the House, "The right honorable gentleman is indebted to his memory for his jests and to his imagination for his facts." Sheridan had a reputation for brilliant impromptus, and his offhand and careless manner of delivery seemed to fulfill Sidney Smith's definition of wit, "in a midwife's phrase, a quick conception and an easy delivery." In truth, however, Sheridan worked as hard on his wit as some men do on their solemnities. He wrote: "A true-trained wit lays his plan like a general—foresees the circumstances of the conversation—surveys the ground and contingencies—and detaches a question to draw you into the palpable ambuscade of his ready-made joke."

Asked about his use of humor in the House, Sheridan said, "I found that four fifths of the House were composed of country squires and great fools; my first effort, therefore, was by a lively sally, or an ironical remark to make them laugh; that laugh effaced the recollection of what had been urged in opposition to my view of the subject from their stupid pates, and then I whipped in an argument, and had all the way clear before me."

Sheridan's political independence, which was both his glory and one of the chief reasons for his downfall, was such that he would use his wit even against his own party. Once, when the Whigs were defeated on a very unpopular bill of which Sheridan himself had not approved, he said he had often heard of people knocking their brains out against a wall, but never before knew of anyone building a wall expressly for the purpose.

Except for two very brief periods, Sheridan spent his entire parliamentary career in opposition, which psychologically suited him. During this career of over twenty-five years, two causes that he embraced completely disinterestedly brought down upon him the anger of many of his best friends: Catholic Emancipation and better treatment for Ireland. He opposed what was euphemistically called a bill for the preservation of peace in Ireland, and pooh-poohed fears of an insurrection there. He pointed out that after all the alarm, "nine taylors and one pike had been discovered in a back garret in Tooley Street in the Borough." When a speaker who preceded him suggested firm and cruel suppression of the Irish, saying there could be no strife where there was no opposition, Sheridan replied, "True, just as there can be no rape where there is no opposition."

No legislation moved Sheridan more strongly than any attack on or restriction of the press and its freedom. In the debate on May 30, 1799, concerning refusal of permission to newspapers to publish on Sundays, Sheridan said, in answer to Lord Belgrave, "in the law, as it at present exists; there is an exception in favor of selling mackerel, on the Lord's Day; but would the Noble Lord recollect that people might think stale news as bad as stale mackerel." Although he could joke on the subject, he could also be eloquently serious, as in 1810 when he said, "Give them a corrupt House of Lords; give them a venal House of Commons; give them a tyrannical Prince; give them a truckling court, —and let me have an unfettered press; I will defy them to encroach a hair's breadth upon the liberties of England."

Not only a great wit, Sheridan was also a master of invective, and his most famous example was a five-hour speech against Warren Hastings, the Governor-General of India, and his alleged maltreatment of the Begums, or princesses, of Oude in 1787. When Sheridan finished, the House adjourned because even Pitt recognized that they were "under the wand of the enchanter." Pitt said further, "that it surpassed all the eloquence of ancient and modern times and possessed everything that genius or art could furnish to agitate or control the human mind." Burke said the Begum speech was "the most astounding effort of eloquence, argument and wit united, of which there was any record or tradition." Fox said, "All that I have ever heard, all that I have ever read, when compared with it, dwindles into nothing and vanishes like vapour before the sun." And Lord Byron in his diary called it "the very *best* oration ever conceived or heard in this country."

In spite of this acclaim, no full copy of this most famous of all of Sheridan's attacks exists. How much of the tremendous effect was in the delivery, the gestures, the voice, the timing of this consummate orator, we cannot know, but this short excerpt will give an idea of the style of Sheridan's invective: "The public capacity of Mr. Hastings exhibits no proof that he has any just claim to . . . greatness. We see nothing solid or penetrating, nothing noble or magnanimous, nothing open, direct, liberal, manly, or superior, in his measures or his mind. All is dark, insidious, sordid and insincere. Wherever he has option in the choice of his objects, or his instruments, he instinctively settles on the worst. His course is one invariable deviation from rectitude. And the only trace or vestige of system descernible in the whole of a dozen years' administration is that of 'acting without any.' The serpent may as well abandon the characteristic obliquity of his motion for the direct flight of an arrow, as he can excuse his purposes with honesty and fairness. He is all shuffling, twisting, cold and little. There is nothing open or upright, simple or unmixed. There is by some strange, mysterious predominance in his vice, such a prominence as totally shades and conceals his virtues. There is, by some foul, unfathomable, physical cause in his mind, a conjunction merely of whatever is calculated to make human nature hang its head with a sorrow or shame. His crimes are the only great thing about him, and these are contrasted by the littleness of his motives. He is at once a tyrant, a trickster, a visionary, and a deceiver. He affects to be a conquerer and law-giver, an Alexander and a Caesar; but he is no more than a Dionysius and a Scapin. . . . He reasons in bombast, prevaricates in metaphor, and quibbles in heroics."

When Hastings was finally brought to trial in Westminster Hall in 1794, Sheridan spoke for four days to a great audience, and concerning the "protection" Hastings had given the allies of Great Britain, he said, "They send all their troops to drain the products of industry, to seize all the treasures, wealth and prosperity of the country. Like a vulture with her harpy talons grappled into the vitals of the land, they flap away the lesser kites, and they call it protection. It is the protection of the vulture to the lamb."

But, significantly, the best-remembered words today are not Sheridan's long flights of invective, but his quips. During the Warren Hastings speech he had referred to the "luminous author of *Decline and Fall*," and when this was later repeated to him and he was asked why he had flattered Gibbon, he answered, "'Luminous'! Oh, of course, I meant voluminous."

Told that if he continued to drink so much wine and spirits he would destroy the coat of his stomach, Sheridan replied, "Well, then, my stomach must just digest in its waistcoat."

Informed that his opponents were speaking ill of him because he favored a certain tax bill his party was about to force through the House, he said, "Well, let them. It is but fair that they should have some pleasure for their money."

Meeting George Rose coming out of St. Margaret's, Sheridan asked, "Any mischief on foot, George, that you have been at church?" "No; I have been getting a son christened; I have called him William Pitt." "William Pitt!" cried Sheridan. "A rose by any other name would smell as sweet."

The dominant political figure of Sheridan's time was, of course, William Pitt, and everything about him made him Sheridan's natural and worthy opponent. The brilliant and aristocratic son of a prominent father, Pitt entered the House before he was twenty-two, became Tory Prime Minister at twenty-three, and was in power in the Tory ministries during most of the time that Sheridan was in the Whig Opposition.

Although Sheridan had opposed British interference in the French Revolution, he was both militant and adamant against the ambitions of Napoleon, and in debate in 1802 he made fun of Pitt on two points. Although after a long tenure in the Ministry, Pitt had now left it, Sheridan maintained he still controlled it, and compared Pitt's long sitting on the Treasury Bench to Theseus, who "When Hercules pulled him off, he left all the sitting part of the man behind him." In this same speech Sheridan ridiculed Pitt's attitude toward Napoleon, who had described England as "a nation of shopkeepers," and Pitt's conviction that France would come around to being more like England, which is not too dissimilar from the attitude of some British politicians today that Russia, if left alone or encouraged, will become like Britain and the United States. Pitt had said in effect that war must be avoided at all costs and that sooner or later Napoleon would be satisfied and settle down. In reply Sheridan said, "But let France have colonies! Oh, yes! Let her have a good trade, that she may be afraid of war, says the Learned Member . . . that's the sure way to make Buonaparte love peace. He has had, to be sure, a military education. He has been abroad, and is rather rough company; but if you put him behind the *counter* a little, he will mend exceedingly. When I was reading the Treaty, I thought of all the names of foreign places, viz. Pondicherry, Chandenagore, Cochin, Martinico, etc., all *cessions*. Not they . . . they are all so many *traps* and *holes* to catch this

silly fellow in, and make a merchant of him! I really think
the best way upon this principle would be this: Let the mer-
chants of London open a public subscription, and set him
up at once. I hear a great deal respecting a certain *statue*,
about to be erected to the Right Honorable Gentleman
now in my eye (Mr. Pitt), at a great expense. Send all that
money over to the First Consul, and give him, what you
talk of so much, *capital*, to begin trade with. I hope the
Right Honorable Gentleman over the way will, like the
First Consul, refuse a statue for the present, and postpone
it as a work for posterity. There is no harm, however, in
marking out the place. The Right Honorable Gentleman is
musing, perhaps on what square, or place, he will choose
for its erection. I recommend the *Bank of England*. Now
for the material. Not gold: no, no! ... He has not left enough
of it. I should, however, propose *pâpier-maché* and old
bank notes!"

Earlier, in 1796, Sheridan had characterized the Bank as
a demure matron playing the coquette with the Minister.
"Last year much was said in the newspapers about the con-
nexion between the Chancellor of the Exchequer and the
Bank. It was asserted that the banns had been forbidden.
The conduct of the right honorable gentleman, indeed,
showed that he cultivated the alliance on account of the
lady's dowry, and not for the comfort of her society. At
first, the affair seemed to wear the appearance of a penitent
seduction; but now it has degenerated into a contented
prostitution. The country wishes to forgive the indiscretion,
on the hopes of amendment; but what had produced the
infatuation was not easy to conjecture, unless the right
honorable gentleman had given the old lady love-powder.
The hey-day of the blood was over; but the rankness of
passion had not subsided, for the dear deceiver was taken
again into favor and the ruin he had occasioned was forgotten."

Although most of Sheridan's mots were his own, he was not above borrowing. His reference to Theseus and Hercules in connection with Pitt was originally used by Gilbert Wakefield in a letter to Fox. Fox had read it to Sheridan a few minutes before the debate. Another time in the House, Sheridan had risen when the Address of Thanks on the Peace (with France) was moved, to say, "This, sir, is a peace which every one will be glad of, but no one can be proud of"—which exact comment had been made that same day to Sheridan by Sir Philip Francis on his way to the House with Sheridan. (It does not measure up to the comment of John Wilkes, who said of the peace, which Pitt's father had achieved by the wholesale purchase of votes in Parliament, "It is certainly the peace of God, for it passeth understanding.") For his comment that "half the debt of England has been incurred in pulling down the Bourbons, and the other half in setting them up," Sheridan was indebted to Sir Arthur Pigott. But although he was not above plagiarism himself, he criticized it in Pitt. Commenting on Pitt's India bill in 1788, Sheridan said it was "nothing more than a bad plagiarism from Mr. Fox's; disfigured, indeed, as gipsies do stolen children, in order to make them pass for their own."

In 1800, in the debate on the suspension of *habeas corpus*, Sheridan, as usual, spoke in opposition, and criticized the burdens imposed by the Tories on the people. He told a story about a man named Patterson who had a shop in Manchester and had painted on his cart "Pitt and Patterson." As it was known that Patterson had no partner in his business, he was asked why he put the name of Pitt on his cart, since the latter had no share in the business. According to Sheridan, the apocryphal tradesman replied, "Ah, he has indeed no share in the business, but a very large share in the profits of it."

Pitt himself was not without wit. Once when he was

reading a document sent by a body of London volunteers who offered to enlist but wanted many exceptions, he came to a clause stating that one condition of their enlistment was that they never be required to leave England. At that point, Pitt wrote in the margin, "except in the case of actual invasion." Nor was Pitt loath to make fun of Sheridan. On seeing Sheridan's play *Pizarro,* which is really nothing but patriotic bombast, Pitt was asked how he liked it. Forgetting perhaps his earlier expressed admiration for the Begum speech, he replied, "If you mean what Sheridan wrote, there is nothing new in it, for I heard it all long ago in his speeches on the Hastings trial."

When Pitt proposed his Sinking Fund in the House of Commons, Sheridan opposed it, saying that at present it was clear that there were no purpose and means and that indeed the only means that suggested themselves to him were a loan of a million pounds, which would enable Pitt to say "with the person in the comedy 'If you won't lend me the money, how can I pay you?'"

Even when one would least have expected ready wit from Sheridan, he showed it. One night he came to the House drunk, and Pitt, who saw the state he was in, suggested postponing the discussion of a matter in which he knew Sheridan was interested, "in consideration of the peculiar state of the honourable Member."

Immediately Sheridan rose and said that in the history of the House but one instance of the disgraceful conduct insinuated by the honorable Member had occurred. There was only one example of Members having entered that House in a state of temporary disqualification for its duties, and that example, however discreditable to the parties, could not perhaps be deplored, as it had given rise to a pleasant epigram. The honorable Member on the Treasury Bench (Pitt) would correct him if he misquoted the words. Two gentlemen, the one blind drunk, the other seeing

RICHARD BRINSLEY SHERIDAN

Benj. Franklin

double, staggered into the House, arm in arm, and thus communicated their parliamentary views to each other:

> "I can't see the Speaker,
>   Pray, Hal, do you?"
> "Not see the Speaker, Bill!
>   Why I see *two*."

The subjects of this epigram had been Henry Dundas and William Pitt.

How far Sheridan had come from his days at Harrow may be illustrated by some of his quips against various peers who were now his intimate friends. Once, while walking in St. James's Street, Sheridan met two royal dukes and was asked by one, "I say, Sherry, we have just been discussing whether you are a greater fool or rogue. What is your opinion?" Taking each by the arm, Sheridan replied, "Why i' faith, I believe I am between both."

Lord Lauderdale, who was often the butt of Sheridan's jokes, once said, on hearing a story of Sheridan's, that he must immediately tell it to a friend, wherewith Sheridan said to him gravely, "For God's sake don't, my dear Lauderdale; a joke in your mouth is no laughing matter." And on another occasion Sheridan said, on entering a room full of friends, "By the silence that prevails I conclude that Lauderdale has been making a joke."

Sheridan had become the boon drinking companion and closest friend and adviser of the profligate Prince of Wales, and was considered to be a sort of Gay Eminence. He even dared to make fun of the future King George IV, who was in the habit of taking credit for all good things that happened in England. After a summer of extraordinarily fine weather, Sheridan said, "What His Royal Highness most particularly prides himself upon, is the late excellent harvest."

There are many examples of how his sense of humor served Sheridan in his political campaigns, but none more characteristic than the time he was coming up to town in one of the public coaches to canvass the electors of Westminster when his opponent there was Paull. Sheridan discovered that there were two electors of Westminster in the coach when one asked the other to whom he would give his vote, and the answer came, "To Paull, certainly; for, though I think him but a shabby sort of fellow, I would vote for anyone rather than Sheridan."

"Do you know Sheridan?" asked the other elector.

"Not I, sir, nor should I wish to know him," was the reply.

Sheridan said nothing, and the conversation stopped; but when the party alighted for breakfast Sheridan called aside the elector who had asked the first question and said, "Pray who is that very agreeable friend of yours? He is one of the pleasantest fellows I have ever met with, and I should be glad to know his name."

"His name is Mr. Richard Wilson; he is an eminent lawyer, and resides in Lincoln's Inn Fields."

When breakfast was finished, the passengers returned to the coach and Sheridan began a conversation on the law. "It is a fine profession," he said. "Many may rise from it to the highest eminence in the state; and it gives vast scope to the display of talent; many of the most virtuous and noble characters recorded in our history have been lawyers. I am sorry, however, to add that some of the greatest rascals have also been lawyers; but of all the rascals of lawyers I ever heard of, the greatest is one Wilson, who lives in Lincoln's Inn Fields."

"I am Mr. Wilson," said the lawyer.

"I am Mr. Sheridan."

Wilson not only laughed at the joke but also helped Sheridan in his campaign for Westminster. In this campaign an episode occurred indicating that Sheridan had changed from the snubee to the snob. Paull, who was Sheridan's opponent, was the son of a tailor, and he said of the brilliant uniform and decorations of Sir Samuel Hood, who was campaigning for the second seat from Westminster, "If I chose, I might have appeared before the electors with such a coat myself." "Yes, and you might have made it, too," Sheridan replied.

There are, of course, many examples of Sheridan's wit in connection with the theater. Once, when the playwright Cumberland attended a performance of *The School for Scandal* with his family, and his children laughed delightedly, Cumberland pinched them, saying: "What are you laughing at, my dear little folks? You should not laugh, my angels, there is nothing to laugh at! Keep still, you little dunces." When this was reported to Sheridan, he said, "It was ungrateful of Cumberland to have been displeased with his children for laughing at my comedy, for when I went to see his tragedy I laughed from beginning to end."

Of a prominent judge who slept through much of Sheridan's play *Pizarro,* the author said, "Poor fellow, I suppose he fancied he was on the bench."

Having been told that the editor Gifford boasted of his power to confer and distribute literary reputation, Sheridan said, "I think he has done it so profusely as to have left none for himself."

When Rogers said to Sheridan concerning the great actress, "Your admiration of Mrs. Siddons is so high that I wonder you never made open love to her," Sheridan replied, "To her! To that magnificent and appalling creature! I should as soon have thought of making love to the Archbishop of Canterbury."

Pretending to defend the lawyer Clifford, who constantly abused and attacked him, Sheridan said, "I hardly expect you will believe me, but I pledge you my word that once if not twice, but most assuredly once, I did meet him in the company of gentlemen."

Sir Lumley Skeffington said at the time a play of his was to be produced at Covent Garden, that it would "make Drury Lane a splendid desert." His play failed, and soon afterward he had a friend show a new play of his to Sheridan, hoping to have it produced at the Drury Lane. "No! No!" Sheridan exclaimed, "I can't agree to connive at putting his former threat into effect."

At the time in the history of English politics when party loyalty was beginning to become an important element (one of the things that most obviously differentiates English politics from American), Sheridan continued to set more store by his independence. Although he was both a friend and admirer of Fox, he often voted against his fellow Whigs, and though he was the Prince's best friend, he made it clear that he would not have the royal mark on him. Sheridan best expressed his feelings in his *Eulogium on the Death of Mr. Fox*, in answer to the insinuation that he was about to retire from seeking the seat from Westminster because it would bring upon him the disapproval of the Ministry in which he held office: "To such insinuations I shall scorn to make any other reply than a reference to the whole of my past political life. I consider it as no boast to say that any one who has struggled through such a portion of life as I have, without acquiring an office, is not likely to abandon his principles to retain one when acquired. To be at all capable of acting on principle, it is necessary that a man should be independent: and for independence the next best thing to that of being very rich is to be very poor. Independence, however, is not allied to wealth, to birth, to rank, to power, to titles, or to honours. Independence is in the mind of a man, or it is nowhere. . . . No minister can expect to find in me a servile vassal. No minister can expect from me the abandonment of any principle I have avowed, or any pledge I have given. I know not that I have hitherto shrunk in place from opinions I have maintained in opposition. Did there exist a minister of different cast from any I know existing, were he to attempt to exact from me a different conduct, my office should be at his service tomorrow. Such a ministry might strip me of a situation, in some respects of considerable emolument, but he could not strip me of the proud conviction that I was right; he could not strip me of my own self-esteem; he could not strip me, I think, of some portion of the confidence and good opinion of the people."

Indeed, Sheridan was almost fanatic in his determination to prove his independence, and among the Whigs earned the reputation of being untrustworthy. Of the Prince he never requested anything for himself (though he did accept appointment as Receiver-General of the Duchy of Cornwall), and late in his life, when he needed help desperately, he so often refused it from the Prince as to earn his displeasure.

Sheridan's son Tom inherited both his feeling for independence and his wit. When the boy decided to seek a seat in the Commons, he said to his father: "I think that many men who are called great patriots in the House of Commons are great humbugs. For my own part, if I get into Parliament, I will pledge myself to no party; but write upon my forehead in legible characters, 'To be let.'"

"And under that, Tom," his father suggested, "write 'unfurnished.'"

Tom also inherited his father's chronic lack of funds. Told by his father that he ought to take a wife, Tom asked, "Whose wife, sir?" After Tom's marriage, and at a time when Sheridan was angry with his son, he met him and said he had made his will and cut him off with a shilling. Tom said he was sorry, but asked, "You don't happen to have the shilling about you now, sir, do you?"

Once when Tom was completely out of money, and complained to his father, Sheridan suggested, "Try the highway."

Tom answered: "I have, but I made a bad hit. I stopped a caravan full of passengers, who assured me they had not a farthing, for they all belonged to the Drury Lane Theatre and could not get a single penny of their salary."

On a similar occasion when Tom was at his father's cottage near Hounslow Heath (which was infested with highwaymen), he again asked his father for money, was told there was none, and then said he absolutely had to have some. "If that is so," said Sheridan, "you will find a case of loaded pistols upstairs and a horse ready saddled in the stable; the night is dark, and you are within half a mile of Hounslow Heath."

"I understand what you mean," Tom replied, "but I tried that last night. Unluckily I stopped Peake, your treasurer, who told me that you had been beforehand with him and robbed him of every sixpence in the world."

There is no doubt that Sheridan's love for Tom was genuine, but it is also true that he knew the political value of being a family man, particularly since Sheridan had the reputation of being a great rake. He was, therefore, both sincere and politic when he said, in speaking of his son in 1806 on the hustings of Westminster, "I would ask no greater distinction than for men to point at me and say, 'There goes the father of Tom Sheridan.'"

Whether or not the eighteenth century was more immoral than our own, it was, at least, more frank and less surreptitious and hypocritical. This view from the top may be a symbolic example. As Queen Caroline lay dying, she urged her husband, George II, to marry again. The King replied, "No, I shall take mistresses," to which the Queen answered, "Oh, my God, that doesn't make any difference."

Although Sheridan was no more of a rake than most of

his contemporaries, because he was both so prominent and so prone to make jokes about his drinking, his betting, his infidelities, and especially about his debts, an exaggerated picture of these has come down to us. In debt to all the moneylenders of London, Sheridan once said, on being told that the lost tribes of Israel had been found, "I am glad to hear it, as I have nearly exhausted the other ten."

He was asked, "How is it that your name has not an O prefixed to it? Your family is Irish, and no doubt illustrious."

"No family has a better right to an O than our family, for in truth we owe everybody."

On the night of February 24, 1809, the House was sitting, their business being Mr. Ponsonby's motion on the Conduct of the War, when the House was suddenly illuminated by a blaze of light and debate was interrupted. Then word came that the Drury Lane Theatre was on fire. A motion was made to adjourn, but Sheridan said, with great calm, "Whatever might be the extent of the private calamity, I hope it will not interfere with the business of the country." He then left the House and witnessed the complete destruction of his property as he sat drinking at the Piazza Coffeehouse. As he watched the blaze, a friend remarked on the coolness and fortitude with which he bore his misfortune. Sheridan replied, "A man may surely be allowed to take a glass of wine by his own fireside."

In 1812 Sheridan failed in the General Election to gain his seat in the Commons for Stafford, and this, coupled with the destruction of his theater, completed his ruin. Sheridan was offered a seat by the Prince Regent; but, having always been his own man in the House, he refused, even though he knew that he would lose his immunity from arrest for debt if he left the Commons. His last words spoken in Parliament in 1812 are worthy to be compared to Churchill's during World War II. "Yet, after the general subjugation and ruin of Europe, should there ever exist an independent historian to record the awful events that produced this universal calamity, let that historian have to say,—'Great Britain fell, and with her fell all the best securities for the charities of human life, for the power and the honor, the fame, the glories and the liberties, not only of herself, but of the whole civilized world.'"

Sheridan was imprisoned for debt in the spring of 1815, and even though his friends obtained his release almost immediately, the effect on the man who prided himself on being a "gentleman" cannot be exaggerated. As he lay on his deathbed in 1816, another sheriff's officer arrested him for debt and was about to carry him off again to the spunginghouse, but was deterred by Sheridan's doctor, who said he would die on the way and that he personally would pursue the bailiff for murder.

Sheridan died a few days later, on Sunday, the seventh of July, at the age of sixty-five, but the bailiffs did not cease to pursue him even after his death. As his body lay in state in Great George Street, awaiting burial in Westminster Abbey, a bailiff disguised as a mourner was admitted to have a last look. Once entered, he served the corpse with a warrant arresting it in the King's name for a debt of five hundred pounds. Only when Mr. Canning and Lord Sidmouth each satisfied the bailiff with a check for two hundred and fifty pounds did he release the body, so that the funeral could proceed.

It was a funeral as splendid as Sheridan could have wished. He was buried in the Poets' Corner (though he would have preferred to lie next to Fox), and the Abbey was filled with royal dukes, earls, lords, and bishops. It was such a great array that it caused a French newspaper to comment, in contrasting Sheridan's last years of poverty with the splendor of his funeral, "France is the place for a man of letters to live in, and England the place for him to die in."

II

Benjamin Franklin

Wit consists in knowing the resemblance of things which
differ, and the difference of things which are alike.
Madame de Staël, *Germany*

On April 15, 1747, gentlemen reading their copies of the
General Advertiser in the clubs and coffee houses of eighteenth century London found in this leading daily newspaper an article entitled "The Speech of Miss Polly Baker."
From it they learned of the recent trial "at *Connecticut*
near *Boston*" of this unfortunate lady, who was charged for
the fifth time with having a bastard child. Miss Baker's
moving and intelligent speech to the Court was reproduced
in its entirety. She points out that "I am a poor unhappy
Woman, who have no Money to fee Lawyers to plead for
me," but her reasoning and eloquence exceed any which a
paid advocate could have provided. Polly freely admits her
crime against the existing law, but says: "I take the Liberty
to say, That I think this Law, by which I am punished, is
both unreasonable in itself, and particularly severe with
regard to me, who have always lived an inoffensive Life in
the Neighborhood where I was born, and defy my Enimies
(if I have any) to say I ever wrong'd Man, Woman or
Child."

Polly movingly refers to her seduction, which must have
reminded the readers in Hogarth's London of similar fictional fallen ladies such as Daniel Defoe's *Moll Flanders*
and Polly Peachum in John Gay's *The Beggar's Opera*. "I

defy any Person," says Polly, "to say, I ever refused an Offer of that Sort: On the contrary, I readily consented to the only Proposal of Marriage that ever was made me, which was when I was a Virgin; but too easily confiding in the Person's Sincerity that made it, I unhappily lost my own Honour, by trusting to his; for he got me with Child, and then forsook me: That very Person you all know; he is now become a Magistrate of this Country; and I had Hopes he would have appeared this Day on the Bench, and have endeavoured to moderate the Court in my Favour; then I should have scorn'd to have mentioned it; but I must now complain of it, as unjust and unequal, That my Betrayer and Undoer, the first Cause of all my Faults and Miscarriages (if they must be deemed such) should be advanc'd to Honour and Power in the Government, that punishes my Misfortunes with Stripes and Infamy."

But Polly is far too proud to name her now-prominent seducer. Instead, she defends herself saying, "I have brought Five fine Children into the World, at the Risque of my Life; I have maintain'd them well by my own Industry, without burthening the Township, and would have done it better, if it had not been for the heavy Charges and Fines I have paid." She then asks logically, "Can it be a Crime (in the Nature of Things I mean) to add to the Number of the King's Subjects, in a new Country that really wants People? I own it, I should think it a Praiseworthy, rather than a punishable Action."

Polly wonders aloud whom she can really have offended. "I have debauched no other Woman's Husband, nor enticed any Youth; these Things I never was charg'd with, nor has any one the least Cause of Complaint against me, unless, perhaps, the Minister, or Justice, because I have had Children without being married, by which they have missed a Wedding Fee." But she points out that even her defrauding these gentlemen of their fee was not her fault.

"I appeal to your Honours. You are pleased to allow I don't want Sense; but I must be stupified to the last Degree, not to prefer the Honourable State of Wedlock, to the Condition I have lived in. I always was, and still am willing to enter into it; and doubt not my behaving well in it, having all the Industry, Frugality, Fertility, and Skill in Oeconomy, appertaining to a good Wife's Character."

She then denounces bachelors as the real culprits, saying, "if you, Gentlemen, must be making Laws, do not turn natural and useful Actions into Crimes, by your Prohibitions. But take into your wise Consideration, the great and growing Number of Batchelors in the Country, many of whom from the mean Fear of the Expences of a Family, have never sincerely and honourably courted a Woman in their Lives; and by their Manner of Living, leave unproduced (which is little better than Murder) Hundreds of their Posterity to the Thousandth Generation. Is not this a greater Offence against the Publick Good, than mine? Compel them then, by Law, either to Marriage, or to pay double the Fine of Fornication every Year. What must poor young Women do, whom Custom have forbid to solicit the Men, and who cannot force themselves upon Husbands, when the Laws take no Care to provide them any; and yet severely punish them if they do their Duty without them."

Polly even has the temerity in defending herself to expound her own theology. "If mine, then, is a religious Offense, leave it to religious Punishments. You have already excluded me from the Comforts of your Church-Communion. Is that not sufficient? You believe I have offended Heaven, and must suffer eternal Fire: Will not that be sufficient? What Need is there, then, of your additional Fines and Whipping? I own, I do not think as you do; for, if I thought what you call a Sin, were really such, I could not presumptuously commit it. But, how can it be believed, that Heaven is angry at my having Children, when to the little done by me towards it, God has been pleased to add his Divine Skill and admirable Workmanship in the Formation of their Bodies, and crown'd it, by furnishing them with rational and immortal Souls. Forgive me, Gentlemen, if I talk a little extravagantly on these Matters; I am no Divine."

It is on this religious note and with increasing pride that Polly ends her address, stating she has done "the Duty of the first and great Command of Nature, and of Nature's God, *Encrease and Multiply*. A Duty, from the steady Performance of which, nothing has been able to deter me; but for its Sake, I have hazarded the Loss of the Publick Esteem, and have frequently endured Publick Disgrace and Punishment; and therefore ought, in my humble Opinion, instead of a Whipping, to have a Statue erected to my Memory."

Although there is nothing in the newspaper story indicating that Polly's wish for a statue in her honor came true, her words produced an even more extraordinary result. The article states that Polly's speech influenced the Court to dispense with her punishment, and induced one of her judges to marry her the next day.

Polly Baker's speech was reprinted widely in other London newspapers and magazines, and also in Edinburgh and Dublin. When some of these had arrived by sail in the American colonies, the speech appeared in Boston, New York and Annapolis journals. Also, throughout Europe Polly's speech was printed and reprinted and much discussed. In England it was written about at length by the deist, Peter Annet, but it was in the 1770's in France that Polly's speech had the greatest popularity. She was characterized as a revolutionary heroine who dared to speak out against her oppressors and against their arbitrary and unjust laws and in favor of Reason and Nature. Her speech made "la Philosophe Polly" the darling of the Abbé Raynal.

Her fame and her cry for political justice and freedom spread as far as the court of Catherine the Great.

The most remarkable thing of all about Polly Baker is that she was a complete hoax. She was the invention of the only internationally known American of his day, Benjamin Franklin. Dr. Franklin was, in the eyes of the French, the very embodiment of those things for which Polly cried, Reason, Nature, Liberty and Equality. The fifteenth child of a poor Boston soap and candle maker, he had become, by means of his own hard work and genius, a highly respected and prosperous printer, scientist, author, inventor, businessman, and politician. In the words of John Adams who neither liked nor approved of Franklin, "his reputation was more universal than that of Leibnitz or Newton, Frederick or Voltaire, and his character more beloved and esteemed than any or all of them." This extraordinary respect for Franklin was demonstrated by the reaction to his confession of the Polly Baker hoax. Franklin described to Thomas Jefferson the meeting at which he told the Abbé Raynal that Polly was a fraud. Raynal in his enormously influential and best-selling book had treated Polly's story as an historic event of serious importance, yet, when he heard from Franklin's own mouth that she was imaginary, Raynal had immediately replied, "Oh, very well, Doctor, I had rather relate your stories than other men's truths."

Jefferson's own wit and tact were demonstrated when he was asked by a lady of the French Court if he had come to take Dr. Franklin's place. The Virginian replied that he was Dr. Franklin's successor, but that no one could take his place.

During his whole life, Franklin's favorite method of expressing his extraordinary wit was by the elaborate and skillful perpetration of literary frauds. At sixteen when he was apprenticed to his brother James, he successfully brought off his first one. James Franklin printed what he assumed to be the letters of a country widow. In reality they were Franklin's now famous "Silence Dogood" papers. At the age of twenty-four he wrote and published in Philadelphia the "true" story of another trial of his own invention, this time one for witchcraft allegedly at Mount-Holly, New Jersey.

The funniest and most famous of all his frauds was in his almanac, where, as "Poor Richard" Saunders, he predicted the hour and minute of the death of a rival almanac maker, Titan Leeds, to the amusement of all except Mr. Leeds himself. Most of Franklin's hoaxes were written. These include his anonymous account of "the grand Leap of the Whale in that Chace up the Fall of Niagara" published in London in the *Public Advertiser* in 1765 and his anti-British propaganda in the form of a fictitious report of the scalping of 1062 Americans by Indians acting for George III, published anonymously in 1782. But occasionally his hoaxes were oral. The most remembered was his reading aloud in London supposedly from the Book of Genesis, when he was in fact reciting a fictional Biblical chapter of his own invention. Franklin's chapter extolled toleration, describing how the Lord rebuked Abraham for thrashing a stranger who refused to worship.

Polly Baker was the example of Franklin's wit which most directly influenced politics, especially French politics leading to the French Revolution. The whole story is told by Max Hall in his fascinating book, *Benjamin Franklin and Polly Baker*. Another hoax of Franklin, written as he was dying in 1790, addressed itself to the growing political problem in America concerning slavery. Franklin had early in his life owned and sold slaves, but by the end of it he had become the President of the Pennsylvania Society for Promoting the Abolition of Slavery, and the Relief of Free Negroes Unlawfully Held in Bondage. This Society memorialized the first House of Representatives of the United

States on February 12, 1789, urging that body to discourage traffic in slaves. The Congressional Committee to which the memorial was referred reported that Congress had not the authority to interfere in the internal affairs of the states and one of the speeches to that effect quoted in the *Federal Gazette* was by Congressman James Jackson of Georgia. Franklin, writing anonymously on March 23, 1790, sent this letter to the *Federal Gazette*, which they printed.

"Sir,

"Reading last night in your excellent Paper the speech of Mr. Jackson against their meddling with the Affair of Slavery, or attempting to mend the condition of the Slaves, it put me in mind of a similar One made about 100 Years since by Sidi Mehemet Ibrahim, a member of the Divan of Algiers, which may be seen in Martin's Account of his Consulship, anno 1687." Scholars searching for the *Account* of the fictional Mr. Martin have, of course, been as unsuccessful as those seeking to find the source of Franklin's fictional chapter of Genesis. Franklin then went on to refer to a sect he called "Erika," which he meant to correspond to the Quaker abolitionist group in Pennsylvania.

"It was against granting the Petition of the Sect called *Erika*, or Purists, who pray'd for the Abolition of Piracy and Slavery as being unjust. Mr. Jackson does not quote it; perhaps he has not seen it. If, therefore, some of its Reasonings are to be found in his eloquent Speech, it may only show that men's Interests and Intellects operate and are operated on with surprising similarity in all Countries and Climates, when under similar Circumstances."

Franklin then proceeds with his invented African speech which parodies brilliantly both the style and content of Jackson's pro-slavery speech. At that point in our history Americans despised the Algerian pirates and were especially incensed by their taking of Christian slaves. This

made particularly ironic Franklin's putting into the mouth
of his fictitious Algerian potentate the same justifications
for capturing and keeping Christian slaves as were being
used by American slaveowners in Franklin's own day to
justify their keeping Negro slaves.

"The African's Speech, as translated, is as follows.

" '*Allah Bismillah, etc. God is great, and Mahomet is his
Prophet.*

" 'Have these *Erika* considered the Consequences of
granting their Petition? If we cease our Cruises against the
Christians, how shall we be furnished with the Commodi-
ties their Countries produce, and which are so necessary
for us? If we forbear to make Slaves of their People, who
in this hot Climate are to cultivate our Lands? Who are to
perform the common Labours of our City, and in our
Families? Must we not then be our own Slaves? And is
there not more Compassion and more Favour due to us as
Mussulmen, than to these Christian Dogs? We have now
above 50,000 Slaves in and near Algiers. This Number, if
not kept up by fresh Supplies, will soon diminish, and be
gradually annihilated. If we then cease taking and plundering the Infidel Ships, and making Slaves of the Seamen and
Passengers, our Lands will become of no Value for want
of Cultivation; the Rents of Houses in the City will sink
one half; and the Revenues of Government arising from its
Share of Prizes will be totally destroy'd! And for what? To
gratify the whims of a whimsical Sect, who would have
us, not only forbear making more Slaves, but even to
manumit those we have.

" 'But who is to indemnify their Masters for the Loss?
Will the State do it? Is our Treasury sufficient? Will the
Erika do it? Can they do it? Or would they, to do what
they think Justice to the Slaves, do a greater Injustice to
the Owners? And if we set our Slaves free, what is to be
done with them? Few of them will return to their Coun-

tries; they know too well the greater Hardships they must there be subject to; they will not embrace our holy Religion; they will not adopt our Manners; our People will not pollute themselves by intermarrying with them. Must we maintain them as Beggars in our Streets, or suffer our Properties to be the Prey of their Pillage? For men long accustom'd to Slavery will not work for a Livelihood when not compell'd. And what is there so pitiable in their present Condition? Were they not Slaves in their own Countries?' "

Franklin then proceeded to have fun, first at the expense of the European governments and then at the expense of the Americans who advanced "Christian" arguments for the keeping of Negro slaves. " 'Are not Spain, Portugal, France, and the Italian states govern'd by Despots, who hold all their Subjects in Slavery, without Exception? Even England treats its Sailors as Slaves; for they are, whenever the Government pleases, seiz'd and confin'd in Ships of War, condemn'd not only to work, but to fight, for small Wages, or mere Subsistence, not better than our Slaves are allow'd by us. Is their Condition then made worse by their falling into our Hands? No; they have only exchanged one Slavery for another, and I may say a better; for here they are brought into a Land where the Sun of Islamism gives forth its Light, and shines in full Splendor, and they have an Opportunity of making themselves acquainted with the true Doctrine, and thereby saving their immortal Souls. Those who remain at home have not that Happiness. Sending the Slaves home then would be sending them out of Light into Darkness.

" 'I repeat the Question, What is to be done with them? I have heard it suggested, that they may be planted in the Wilderness, where there is plenty of Land for them to subsist on, and where they may flourish as a free State; but they are, I doubt, too little dispos'd to labour without Compulsion, as well as too ignorant to establish a good government, and the wild Arabs would soon molest and destroy or again enslave them. While serving us, we take care to provide them with every thing, and they are treated with Humanity. The Labourers in their own Country are, as I am well informed, worse fed, lodged and cloathed. The condition of most of them is therefore already mended, and required no further Improvement. Here their Lives are in Safety. They are not liable to be impress'd for Soldiers, and not forc'd to cut one another's Christian Throats, as in the Wars of their own Countries. If some of the religious mad Bigots, who now teaze us with their silly Petitions, have in a Fit of Blind Zeal freed their Slaves, it was not Generosity, it was not Humanity, that mov'd them to the Action; it was from the conscious Burthen of a Load of Sins, and Hope, from the supposed Merits of so good a Work, to be excus'd Damnation.' "

In Franklin's day, as before and since, men quoted Chapter and Verse to prove the virtue of their actions, however selfish. His imaginary Moslem was adept in this too. " 'How grossly are they mistaken in imagining Slavery to be disallowed by the Alcoran! Are not the two Precepts, to quote no more, *"Masters, treat your Slaves with kindness; Slaves serve your Masters with Cheerfulness and Fidelity."* clear Proofs to the contrary? Nor can the Plunderings of Infidels be in that sacred Book forbidden, since it is well known from it, that God has given the World, and all that it contains, to his faithful Mussulmen, who are to enjoy it of Right as fast as they conquer it. Let us then hear no more of this detestable Proposition, the Manumission of Christian Slaves, the Adoption of which would, by depreciating our Lands and Houses, and thereby depriving so many good Citizens of their Properties, create universal Discontent, and provoke Insurrections, to the endangering of Government and producing general Confusion. I have therefore no doubt, but this wise Council will prefer the Comfort and Happiness of a whole Nation of true Believers to the Whim of a few *Erika,* and dismiss their Petition.'

"The Result was, as Martin tells us, that the Divan came to this Resolution; 'The Doctrine, that Plundering and Enslaving the Christians is unjust, is at best *problematical;* but that it is the Interest of this State to continue the Practice, is clear; therefore let the Petition be rejected.'

"And it was rejected accordingly.

"And since like Motives are apt to produce in the Minds of Men like Opinions and Resolutions, may we not, Mr. Brown, venture to predict, from this Account, that the Petitions to the Parliament of England for abolishing the Slave-Trade, to say nothing of other Legislatures, and the Debates upon them, will have a similar Conclusion? I am, Sir, your constant Reader and humble Servant, Historicus"

And so Dr. Benjamin Franklin, less than four weeks from his death, spent his last days using his brilliant wit and biting ridicule in an attempt to resolve that political problem which was temporarily to destroy the Union he had helped to found. The diversity of his genius made him the closest approach to a Leonardo that America has yet produced. But when he died on April 17, 1790, the epitaph he had written for himself reminded his friends that he thought of himself mainly as a printer and man of letters.

The body of
Benjamin Franklin, printer,
(Like the cover of an old book,
Its contents worn out,
And stript of its lettering and gilding)
Lies here, food for worms!
Yet the work itself shall not be lost,
For it will, as he believed, appear once more
In a new
And more beautiful edition,
Corrected and amended
By its Author!

III

John Randolph of Roanoke and Some Contemporaries

Plagued with an itching leprosy of wit.
   Ben Jonson, *Every Man Out of His Humour*

Although there was comparatively little wit, excepting Franklin's displayed by American politicians during the eighteenth century, in the first half of the nineteenth there appeared an abundance of witty political orators—Henry Clay, John Calhoun, Daniel Webster, John Randolph of Roanoke, Thomas Hart Benton, Davy Crockett, and Sam Houston. The form of wit in which all these men most excelled was political invective. John F. Kennedy, when he was still in the United States Senate, said in a speech that he delivered at various colleges urging young men to go into politics, "Of course, the great talents of these political leaders did not restrain them from engaging in the same kind of political abuse that concerns us today. Our Senate Committee last year, for example, readily agreed that Clay, Calhoun and Webster were the three most obvious choices for the list of our greatest Senators. Yet listen, for example, to these words spoken about Henry Clay: 'He prefers the specious to the solid, and the plausible to the true. . . . He is a bad man, an impostor, a creator of wicked schemes.' Those words were spoken by John C. Calhoun. On the other hand, who said that John C. Calhoun was a rigid, fanatic, ambitious, selfishly partisan and sectional 'turncoat,' with 'too much genius and too little common sense,' who would either die a traitor or a madman? Henry Clay, of course. When Calhoun boasted in debate that he had been Clay's political master, Clay retorted: 'Sir, I would not own him as a slave.' Both Clay and Calhoun from time to time fought with Webster; and from the other House, the articulate John Quincy Adams viewed with alarm 'the gigantic intellect, the envious temper, the ravenous ambition and the rotten heart of Daniel Webster.' "

The one man who would probably appear on no one's list of the greatest Senators of the United States, but who would surely be the first choice of all as the greatest American master of political invective, is John Randolph of Roanoke, who said of Edward Livingston: "He is a man of splendid abilities, but utterly corrupt. Like rotten mackerel by moonlight, he shines and stinks." On the selection of Richard Rush as Secretary of the Treasury, Randolph said, "Never were abilities so much below mediocrity so well rewarded; no, not when Caligula's horse was made Consul."

No historian and no biographer of this extraordinary man, born to the Virginia aristocracy in 1773, has ever fully explained his complicated character. Although he served his country in politics for over a third of a century, as a member of the House of Representatives, as United States Senator, as American Ambassador to Russia, and in many other capacities, he never rose to the political prominence that his birth, brilliance, education, and energy deserved and that was accorded to men of much lesser abilities than his. He is remembered today only as the possessor of the most biting tongue ever heard in American public life.

It was rumored throughout his life, and confirmed medically after his death, that he was impotent. Perhaps this was the major cause of his bitterness; Randolph's answer to Tristam Burges of Rhode Island in the Congress reflected the depth of that bitterness: MR. BURGES: "Sir, Divine Providence takes care of his own universe. Moral monsters cannot propagate. Impotent of everything but malevolence of purpose, they can no otherwise multiply miseries than by blaspheming all that is pure and prosperous and happy. Could demon propagate demon, the universe might become a pandemonium; but I rejoice that the Father of Lies can never become the Father of Liars. One adversary of God and man is enough for one universe." MR. RANDOLPH: "You pride yourself upon an animal faculty, in respect to which the slave is your equal and the jackass infinitely your superior."

Or perhaps it was his bad health, or, perhaps, the scandal of adultery and infanticide connected with the name of his older brother, Richard, whom he had idolized. Whatever the causes of his bitterness, they produced the greatest conservative and the most brilliant Cassandra of American political history. His own words, "I am an aristocrat. I love justice and hate equality," constitute the best description of himself, and "Change is not reform," the best definition of his conservative political philosophy. He wrote, "When I speak of my country, I mean the Commonwealth of Virginia," and he has had heirs in this point of view as worthy as John C. Calhoun and Robert E. Lee and as unworthy as the present governors of Arkansas, Alabama, and Mississippi. He was acutely aware of "my unprosperous life . . . the fruit of an ungovernable temper," and knew that he was, as Tristam Burges had said, "hated of men and scorned by women." Yet despite his problems, physical and psychological, he fought courageously against all the giants of his age, Jefferson, Madison, John Marshall, John Quincy Adams, Clay, Webster, Calhoun, and Jackson, when they threatened the principles in which he believed.

Randolph added *Fari quae sentiat* (Say what you think) to his family motto, and indeed he did. When his cousin,

Thomas Jefferson, was elected the first Republican President of the United States, Randolph became Republican Chairman of the powerful Ways and Means Committee and Jefferson's Floor Leader in the House of Representatives. He was effective in both posts, and was well on his way to a successful political career until the Yazoo land scandals. Then, instead of defending and supporting his own party, he was so outraged by this gigantic fraud, in which he had had no part, that he attacked his own Postmaster General, Gideon Granger. "His gigantic grasp embraces with one hand the shores of Lake Erie and stretches with the other to the Bay of Mobile. Millions of acres are easily digested by such stomachs. . . . The retail trade of fraud and imposture yields too small and slow a profit to gratify their cupidity. They buy and sell corruption in the gross, and a few millions more or less is hardly felt in the account. The deeper the play the greater their zest for the game; and the stake which is set upon their throw is nothing less than the patrimony of the people."

Not satisfied with this, he went on to attack the House Committee on Claims, not excluding those who were members of his own party. "Sir, when the war-worn soldier of the Revolution, or the desolate widow and famished offspring of him who sealed your independence with his blood, ask at the door of that committee for bread, they receive the Statute of Limitations. On such occasions you hear of no equity in the case. Their claims have not the stamp and seal of iniquity upon them. *Summum jus* is the measure dealt out to them. The equity of the committee is reserved for those claims which are branded with iniquity and stamped with infamy."

And finally, by 1832, he would comment on Thomas Jefferson himself "I cannot live in this miserable, undone country, where, as the Turks follow their sacred standard, which is a pair of Mahomet's green breeches, we are governed by the old red breeches of that prince of projectors, St. Thomas of Cantingbury; and surely, Becket himself never had more pilgrims at his shrine than the saint of Monticello."

He was equally bitter in his attacks on the Adams family of Massachusetts: "I bore some humble part in putting down the dynasty of John the First, and by the grace of God, I hope to aid in putting down the dynasty of John the Second." That John Quincy Adams (whose own "instinct for the jugular" was noted by Rufus Choate) felt the sting of Randolph's lash may be seen when the gentleman from Massachusetts applied Ovid's words to the Virginian:

> "His face is ashen; gaunt his whole body,
> His breath is green with gall; his tongue drips poison."

That no man was more effective in the destruction of John Quincy Adams and the success of Jackson is the general verdict of history; and that fifty years later the Adams family still despised Randolph may be seen by reading Henry Adams's biography of the Virginian.

Randolph was opposed to all measures that increased governmental power; therefore, of course, he opposed government debt. He once said on the floor of the House: "Mr. Speaker, I have discovered the philosopher's stone! It is this, Sir: pay as you go! Pay as you go!" And he spoke of "That most delicious of all privileges . . . spending other people's money." Even though he was a states'-rights man, he was opposed to any increase of power for the states, not only of state legislators but also of state judges, saying at the Constitutional Convention of the State of Virginia: "The principles of free government in this country . . . have more to fear from over-legislation than from any other cause. Yes, Sir . . . they have more to fear from armies of legislators and armies of judges than from any other, or from all other, causes. Besides the great manufactory at Washington, we have twenty-four laboratories more at work; all making laws. . . . Among all these lawyers, judges and legislators, there is a great oppression on the people, who are neither lawyers, judges, nor legislators, nor ever expect to be . . . an oppression barely more tolerable than any which is felt under the European governments. Sir, I can never forget that, in the great and good book, for which I look for all truth and all wisdom, the book of Kings succeeds the book of Judges."

Randolph's wit ranged from the pun to the most brilliant repartee. He once said, regarding two congressmen, Robert Wright and John Rea (pronounced *ray*), that the House possessed two anomalies: "A Wright always wrong; and a Rea without light." He described the first great American political boss, the devious Martin Van Buren of New York, as one who "rowed to his object with muffled oars." He could even be witty on the subject dearest to his heart, as when he said, "Asking one of the States to surrender a part of her sovereignty is like asking a lady to surrender a part of her chastity." No better example of his insight into human nature and politics exists than his comment: "Denouncing me? That is strange. I never did him a favor." When he was attacked by a new member of Congress who had been elected to fill a vacancy caused by death, Randolph did not rise to answer; but some days later, discussing a bill with which the departed member had been much concerned, the Virginian observed that the bill had lost much in the death of his dear friend "whose seat remains vacant."

He said of Madison's pamphlet on neutral rights, "Against eight hundred ships in commission we enter the lists with a three-shilling pamphlet," and he remarked of Ben Hardin of Kentucky, "He is like a carving knife whetted on a brickbat." Speaking almost daily in 1820 about Clay's Missouri Compromise, he was regularly interrupted in his filibusters by Philomen Beecher of Ohio, who would jump up, whenever Randolph paused, and move the "Previous question," only to be reminded by the Speaker that the gentleman from Virginia had the floor. Randolph paid no attention to the first few such interruptions, but finally said: "Mr. Speaker, in the Netherlands, a man of small capacity, with bits of wood and leather, will, in a few moments, construct a toy that, with the pressure of the finger and thumb, will cry 'Cuckoo! Cuckoo!' With less ingenuity, and with inferior materials, the people of Ohio have made a toy that will, without much pressure, cry 'Previous Question, Mr. Speaker!' " The House roared with laughter, and Beecher never again crossed swords with Randolph.

Although the Virginian enjoyed insulting people he knew, he was equally capable of gratuitously insulting strangers, particularly if they made overtures to him. When a man forced himself on Randolph in a hotel lobby, saying, "I have had the pleasure of passing your house recently," Randolph replied: "I am glad of it. I hope you will always do it, sir." Such bad temper, along with Randolph's comparative lack of success in politics, reminds one of the words of Francis Bacon, no mean man with words himself, and an experienced political animal: "Anger makes dull men witty, but it keeps them poor."

As has happened to the first wit of every age, many quips not his were ascribed to Randolph, to the point that he once complained, "All the bastard wit of the country has been fathered on me."

The instances of his sarcasm in the Congress are too many to list, but none were more bitter or, as it turned out, more correct than his attacks on the "War Hawks" who led the United States into the disastrous War of 1812: "It seems this is to be a holiday campaign; there is to be no expense of blood or treasure on our part; Canada is to conquer herself; she is to be subdued by the principles of fraternity. The people of that country are first to be seduced from their allegiance, then converted into traitors, as preparatory to making them good citizens. Although I must acknowledge that some of our flaming patriots were thus manufactured, I do not think the process would hold good with a whole community."

Randolph never forgave or trusted Calhoun after the latter's "War Hawk" days and it is, therefore, possible to understand his attacks on the man whom history considers his political heir. Randolph once addressed the South Carolinian: "Mr. Speaker! I mean Mr. President of the Senate and would-be President of the United States, which God in His infinite mercy avert."

Randolph could say to the House, "Like true political quacks, you deal only in handbills and nostrums," and when himself attacked by a series of fellow members, could, like King Lear, answer with contempt,

> "The little dogs and all,
> Tray, Blanch and Sweet-heart, see, they bark at me!"

There was a meeting of the Pennsylvania delegation at Gadsby's Hotel on Pennsylvania Avenue at which Randolph managed to infuriate the entire group. He said, "I want to offer a toast to the two greatest Pennsylvanians who ever lived; Albert Gallatin, a native of Switzerland, and Benjamin Franklin, a native of Massachusetts." Nor was this the most outrageous toast he ever offered. If proof is needed that he feared no one and would attack anyone, there is the story that when the feeling over the Jay Treaty with England was at its height, Randolph offered the toast "George Washington . . . may he be damned," and only when no one drank, did he add ". . . if he signs Jay's treaty."

Randolph received as well as delivered insults, and perhaps none was better deserved by this self-confessed snob, who proudly traced his Virginia ancestry back through the Indian Princess Pocahontas and the Chief Powhatan, than the one dealt him by Congressman Fawcett of Pawtucket. Fawcett had been a cobbler in Rhode Island. When he was asked scornfully by Randolph what he had done with his leather apron when he came to the Congress, he replied, "I cut it into mocassins for the barefoot descendants of Pocahontas."

Randolph was the greatest but not the only master of invective in the Congresses of his time. Another was Sam Houston of Tennessee and Texas, of whom Andrew Jackson remarked, "There goes a man made by the Lord Almighty and not by his tailor." Houston had been a drunk, kept a common-law wife, and thoroughly enjoyed all the delights of the flesh. Then, after his second marriage, he became a teetotaler, gave up swearing, and proceeded to enjoy all the delights of repentance. It was Houston who said of Thomas Jefferson Green, "He has all the characteristics of a dog—except loyalty," and who, when asked if he knew Jefferson Davis, who had been Senator from Mississippi when Houston was Senator from Texas, replied, "Yes, I know Mr. Davis, he is as ambitious as Lucifer, cold as a snake and what he touches will not prosper."

There was also Thomas Hart Benton, of whom John F. Kennedy said in the same speech quoted from above, "Missouri's first Senator, Thomas Hart Benton, the man whose tavern brawl with Jackson in Tennessee caused him to leave the state, was described in these words in his obituary: 'With a readiness that was often surprising, he could quote from a Roman Law or a Greek philosopher, from Virgil's Georgics, The Arabian Nights, Herodotus or Sancho Panza, from the Sacred Carpets, the German reformers or Adam Smith, from Fenelon or Hudibras, from the financial reports of Necca or the doings of the Council

of Trent, from the debates on the adoption of the Constitution or the intrigues of the kitchen cabinet or from some
forgotten speech of a deceased Member of Congress.'"
This could equally well have been written of Randolph,
Webster, or Calhoun at that time in the history of America
when the education of Members of Congress more nearly
approximated that of Members of Parliament. Benton's
opinion of the power of his own invective was shown one
day when he had planned to excoriate Calhoun, but
heard that Calhoun was ill. He said, "Benton will not speak
today, for when God Almighty lays His Hands on a man,
Benton takes his off." At another time, he said in the Congress: "Mr. President, I never quarrel, sir. But sometimes I
fight, sir, and whenever I fight, sir, a funeral follows."

Being opposed to almost all legislation, Randolph could,
and often did, speak for hours with no object other than to
delay a vote, but there is no comparison between the brilliance and wit of his filibusters and the later variety of
Huey Long with its recipes for fried oysters and potlikker.
Only Benton, however, could speak for four days, a speech
that, Randolph observed, lasted a day longer than the
French Revolution of 1830, and it was Benton who was
permitted by both participants to witness the famous duel
between Randolph and Clay and who wrote an admiring
account of it.

No man more clearly symbolized what Randolph opposed than Henry Clay of Kentucky, of whom Randolph
once remarked, "Clay's eye is on the Presidency; and my
eye is on him." As Randolph symbolized the eighteenth
century Virginia gentleman and the maintenance of the
status quo, Clay stood for unlimited growth to the West
and for change. Of course, history, geography, and eco-
nomics were all on the side of Clay. The Kentuckian had
a fine wit, which could be charming, as when he said to a
lady who remarked that he did not remember her name,

"No, for when we last met long ago I was sure your beauty and accomplishments would very soon compel you to change it." He could also be brutal, as when, during a dull and lengthy speech, the speaker, General Alexander Smyth, turned to Clay to remark, "You, Sir, speak for the present generation; but I speak for posterity," and Clay interrupted, "Yes, and you seem resolved to speak until the arrival of your audience."

One day when Daniel Webster and Henry Clay were sitting in front of the old National Hotel in Washington, a man came by, driving a bunch of mules. Webster observed, "Clay, there goes a number of your Kentucky constituents." To this, Clay replied, "They must be going up to Massachusetts to teach school."

Clay's lash was also felt by Senator James Buchanan of Pennsylvania, whom Clay taunted with cowardice in the War of 1812. Once Buchanan claimed to have marched to the defense of Baltimore.

MR. BUCHANAN: "True, I was not in any engagement, as the British had retreated before I got there."

MR. CLAY: "You marched to Baltimore, though?"

MR. BUCHANAN: "Yes, sir."

MR. CLAY: "Armed and equipped?"

MR. BUCHANAN: "Yes, armed and equipped."

MR. CLAY: "But the British had retreated before you arrived?"

MR. BUCHANAN: "Yes."

MR. CLAY: "Will the Senator from Pennsylvania be good enough to inform us whether the British retreated in consequence of his valiantly marching to the relief of Baltimore, or whether he marched to the relief of Baltimore in consequence of the British having already retreated?"

It is not surprising, then, that there were often vitriolic words between Clay and Randolph. It is alleged that once, meeting on a narrow sidewalk, Clay proudly said, "I, Sir, do not step aside for a scoundrel," wherewith Randolph, stepping into the muddy Washington street, replied, "On the other hand, I always do." There are some versions that reverse the story, giving Clay the last word.

But the most famous episode between the two came as the result of a speech of Randolph's accusing the high-living Clay of conspiring with the dour and pious John Quincy Adams. "I was defeated horse, foot and dragoons . . . cut up and clean broke down by the coalition of Blifil and Black George . . . by the combination, unheard of till then, of the Puritan with the blackleg." Such words, of course, required Clay to challenge Randolph, and the duel took place on April 8, 1826. When Randolph's pistol misfired, Clay gallantly granted him another pistol, and on the first exchange both missed. On the second exchange, Clay's bullet went through Randolph's coat, whereupon Randolph deliberately fired above Clay's head. Then, when Clay ran to shake Randolph's hand, the Virginian remarked, "You owe me a new coat, Mr. Clay."

Even though Randolph had supported and materially helped elect Andrew Jackson, it was evident that the President's point of view on states' rights was so diametrically opposed to Randolph's that a break between them was inevitable. During the nullification in South Carolina, after Jackson's proclamation, the then governor of Virginia sent a letter to the President, asking that if it became necessary to send United States troops into the South, they not be sent through his state. He said that if Jackson did send them through Virginia, they would have to pass over the governor's dead body. In view of the challenges today of certain southern governors to the authority of the national government, Jackson's reply is of particular interest. "If it becomes necessary for the United States troops to go to South Carolina, I, as Commander-in-chief of the army, will be at their head. I will march them by the shortest route. They may pass through Virginia; but if the governor makes it necessary to pass over his dead body, it will be found that I have previously taken off both ears." The wily Van Buren, aware of the differences that separated Jackson and Randolph, arranged that the President appoint the Virginian as Ambassador to Russia. It was in this post that Randolph's health finally gave way, and he was forced to return to America.

In 1833, as Randolph lay dying of tuberculosis in Philadelphia, he may have wondered, as others have since, why a man of his brilliant capabilities had spent his whole life fighting always "against" rather than "for." The doctor who attended him stated that Randolph's main concern was that on his death all his slaves be freed. Perhaps he was also thinking of his own words: "Life is not as important as the duties of life."

JOHN RANDOLPH OF ROANOKE

DRESSING FOR AN OXFORD BAL MASQUÉ.

"*The question is, is Man an Ape or an Angel?* (A Laugh.) *Now, I am on the side
of the Angels.* (Cheers.)"—Mr. Disraeli's Oxford Speech, Friday, November 25.

IV

Benjamin Disraeli

True wit is nature to advantage dress'd,
What oft was thought, but ne'er so well express'd.
                              Pope, *Essay on Criticism*

The first half of the nineteenth century saw the art of political invective reach a peak in American politics that has not been sustained. In Great Britain, on the other hand, both invective and wit have been constants of the English parliamentary system from the seventeenth century through today. English honorable gentlemen have excoriated one another wittily, classically, and continually. But for violence of invective, none have ever exceeded the Irish. Consider, for example, the end of a speech of Daniel O'Connell against Benjamin Disraeli, delivered in Dublin in 1835 at a trades-union meeting: " . . . . It will not be supposed therefore that when I speak of D'Israeli as a descendant of a Jew, that I mean to tarnish him on that account. They were once the chosen people of God. There were miscreants amongst them however, also, and it must certainly be from one of these that D'Israeli descended (Roars of laughter). He possesses just the qualities of the impenitent thief who died on the Cross, whose name, I verily believe, must have been D'Israeli (Roars of laughter). For aught I know, the present D'Israeli is descended from him, and, with the impression that he is, I now forgive the heir-at-law of the blasphemous thief who died upon the Cross (Loud cheers and roars of laughter)."

Brutal as this attack was, it was not unprovoked. Disraeli had three times unsuccessfully sought election to Parliament as a Radical, and in doing so had solicited and received a letter of recommendation from O'Connell. Although, like Sheridan, he found it difficult to be a party man, Disraeli had finally come to see that he must be one if he was to achieve the political prominence he craved and that it could not be as a Radical, but within one of the two major parties, the Tories or the Whigs. He therefore deserted the Radicals and joined the Tories and sought election as their candidate for Taunton. There he had called O'Connell a traitor and so had called down upon himself the wrath of the man of whom Sidney Smith had said, "The only way to deal with such a man as O'Connell is to hang him up and erect a statue to him under the gallows."

The Tories (Conservatives) were traditionally the party of the landed aristocrats and the party most loyal to the King and the Church. The Whigs (who later came to be called Liberals) were traditionally the aristocrats of business and the City. Why Disraeli felt more at home as a Tory is one of the contradictions in this extraordinary man that make his life as fit a study for psychiatrists as for historians. It was but one of many contradictions, no more odd than that this skeptic Jew turned Christian should be an ardent defender of the Church of England, which he himself once described as "a defunct mythology." It is equally puzzling that this cynical novelist and ruthless politician, whose books and speeches are full of the most skeptical aphorisms, could be the most sentimental, tender, and loyal husband, blissfully married to a woman fifteen years older than himself.

In answer to the Dublin speech, Disraeli challenged both O'Connell (who had already killed a man in a duel) and his son, but was refused by both. He therefore answered the Irishman in speeches and in letters addressed both to

O'Connell and *The Times*, saying, "He has committed every crime that does not require courage," and, "Yes, I am a Jew, and when the ancestors of the right hon. gentleman were brutal savages in an unknown island, mine were priests in the Temple of Solomon."

Born in 1804 to a well-to-do Jewish family, Disraeli was baptized into the Church of England at the age of twelve, only because his father, an agnostic, had been fined forty pounds by his synagogue for declining to serve as a warden and had thereupon resigned and a friend had luckily pointed out to him how helpful to the future of his children conversion to Christianity would be. Again like Sheridan, Disraeli hated school: "I was a most miserable child; and school I detested more than ever I abhorred the world in the darkest moments of my experienced manhood." There is no doubt that he was mocked at school because of his origins, and he secretly took boxing lessons, and subsequently answered and ended insults with his fists.

After primary school Disraeli did not go to either public school or university, but educated himself and subsequently studied for the law. But, at twenty, "I determined descending those magical waters [the Rhine] that I would not be a lawyer," a profession he once described as "ever illustrating the obvious, explaining the evident, and expatiating the commonplace." He also tried, and failed, as a speculator and a publisher and then embarked, burdened with debt, on a career of dandy and author, writing "Let me die eating ortolans to the sound of soft music," "A want of tact is worse than a want of virtue," and " 'I rather like bad wine,' said Mr. Mountchesney; 'one gets so bored with good wine.' " But his own dress and actions as a young man exceeded the most affected manners of his fictional characters. On a visit to Gibraltar he wrote, "I have the fame of being the first who has passed the Straits with two canes, a morning and an evening cane. . . . It is wonderful the effect that these magic wands produce. . . . I also have my fan, which makes my cane extremely jealous." And later, in Malta: "To govern men, you must either excel them in their accomplishments, or despise them. . . . Affectation tells here even better than wit. Yesterday, at the racket court, sitting in the gallery among strangers, the ball entered, and lightly struck me, and fell at my feet. I picked it up, and observing a young rifleman excessively stiff, I humbly requested him to forward its passage into the court, as I had really never thrown a ball in my life. The incident has been the general subject of conversation at all the messes today!"

This role of affected fop did, as its author intended, serve as what would be called today a public-relations device, and caused him to be much discussed. It caused, however, more unfavorable comment than favorable, and "that damned bumptious Jew-boy" was no longer invited to those officers' messes where he was being discussed.

Disraeli wrote "every man has a right to be conceited until he is successful," and though his conceits of dress and hair style, as well as his wit, caused him to be much known and talked of in society in London, they also created a reputation that was to plague him for years, and hurt the advancement of his career in politics.

In his early efforts to enter Parliament, when Disraeli had refused to join either the Tories or the Whigs and had as a so-called Radical really disdained party, he had said: "I care not for party. I stand here without party. . . . Englishmen, rid yourself of all that political jargon and factious slang of Whig and Tory—two names with one meaning, used only to delude you—and unite in forming a great national party which alone can save the country from impending destruction." Accused of being a Tory in disguise, he replied that "the closest thing to a Tory in disguise is a Whig in power." In his novel *Coningsby*, a typical politician makes the following observations:

" 'I am all for a religious cry,' said Taper. 'It means nothing, and, if successful, does not interfere with business when we are in.' "

" 'A sound Conservative government,' said Taper musingly. 'I understand: Tory men and Whig measures.' "

This man, who was completely to remake the Tory Party, to serve it humbly and loyally, and to set up its first real party machinery, which still exists today, had begun with the same disdain for party as Sheridan, and had, as Winston Churchill would later, actually changed his party affiliation during his career. He wrote in his early novel, *Vivian Grey*, "There is no act of treachery or meanness of which a political party is not capable; for in politics there is no honor"; and, "No one is petted so much as a political apostate, except, perhaps, a religious one." But, whereas Sheridan had refused to be disciplined in his party, and therefore was never a real leader in it, Disraeli, from the same starting place, learned to discipline himself, once he had made up his mind and joined the Tories.

He who was to become one of the consummate political speakers of his age wrote in *Vivian Grey*, "Nothing is more undignified than to make a speech. It is from the first an acknowledgement that you are under the necessity of explaining, or conciliating, or convincing or confuting; in short that you are not omnipotent, but opposed." This speech was put in the mouth of a character whom the author called Lord Beaconsfield.

Much more honest and typical of his real feeling about politics are these frank words spoken to his constituents at Shrewsbury: "There is no doubt, gentlemen, that all men who offer themselves as candidates for public favour have motives of some sort. I candidly acknowledge that I have, and I will tell you what they are; I love fame; I love public reputation; I love to live in the eyes of the country; and it

is a glorious thing for a man to do who has had my difficulties to contend against."

Disraeli's maiden speech in the House at first appeared
to be a disaster. There was such shouting and hooting by
the Radicals, and particularly by the Irish friends of O'Connell, that virtually none of the speech was heard or recorded, except the last prophetic words, "Ay, sir, and
though I sit down now, the time will come when you *will*
hear me." But although he was not heard in this speech, it
was in one sense a success. Most maiden speeches are
short, dull, politely received, and immediately forgotten.
But the English sense of fair play was such that Disraeli's
reception brought him both sympathy and admiration for
his courage. Even Sheil, O'Connell's lieutenant, said after
it, "If ever the spirit of oratory was in a man, it is in that
man; nothing can prevent him from being one of the first
speakers in the House of Commons."

Progressively his stature as a speaker in the House did
grow, and his feelings about the importance of political
parties changed. The great Tory landowners wanted strict
Corn Laws that gave them high tariff protection against
imported foreign grain, and as a consequence high prices
for their own farm produce. The Whigs wanted free trade
or, at least, low or minimal tariffs so that the cost of food to
the laborers in Whig factories would be cheap (as would
be the raw materials they needed to import); as a result
the workers could be paid less and the goods they made
exported from England at attractively low prices. (This
problem of protection versus free trade was a major one
prior to Disraeli's day, and continued into our own century,
when the Tory policy of protection under Joseph Chamberlain so outraged the young Winston Churchill that he left
the Conservative benches and crossed the floor of the
House of Commons to join the Liberals.) Peel, as the leader
of the Tories when they were the Opposition and the

Whigs were in power, had been a staunch and vocal protectionist. When the Tories came to power and his control
of the House seemed absolute and permanent, he had a
genuine change of heart and came to believe in free trade.
He was an autocratic leader, and expected his Tory fol-
lowers also to change their views on protection to what
had traditionally been the Whiggish view. But Disraeli
would not, saying, "while we are admiring the principles
of relaxed commerce, there is extreme danger of our ad-
mitting the principles of relaxed politics. I advise, therefore, that we all—whatever may be our opinions about free
trade—oppose the introduction of free politics. Let men
stand by the principle by which they rise, right or
wrong. . . . Do not, then, because you see a great personage
giving up his opinions—do not cheer him on, do not give
him so ready a reward to political tergiversation. Above all,
maintain the line of demarcation between parties, for it is
only by maintaining the independence of party that you
can maintain the integrity of public men, and the power
and influence of Parliament itself."

It was over this very issue of a party's loyalty to its
avowed principles that Disraeli, an unimportant and disdained Tory Member, destroyed the most powerful man in
England, his Tory Prime Minister, Peel. Never in his
career were his wit and brilliance more evident. Peel was
at the height of his power, and treated harshly not only the
Opposition but also recalcitrant members of his own party,
so that when Disraeli observed of him in the House, "The
right honourable baronet, with all the courtesy which he
reserves only for his supporters . . . ," the Tories smiled.
When Peel showed bad temper in a debate, Disraeli remarked, ". . . in a popular assembly it is sometimes expedient
to enact the part of the choleric gentleman," but went on to
tell his fellow Tories not to be alarmed by their leader's
simulated emotion, and asked Peel not to view his own op-

position as hostile, but rather as friendly. Thereupon, Peel rose and spoke in a manner that clearly revealed his desire to destroy this gadfly once for all:

"He undertakes to assure the House that my vehemence was all pretended. . . . I on the contrary will do him entire justice; I do believe that his bitterness was . . . entirely sincere. The hon. gentleman has a perfect right to support a hostile motion . . . but let him not say that he does it in a friendly spirit:

'Give me the avowed, the erect, the manly foe,
Bold I can meet—perhaps may turn his blow!
But of all plagues, good Heaven, thy wrath can send,
Save me, oh, save me from the candid friend!' "

This quotation of Peel's was ill-chosen, for it was from George Canning. Canning had been Peel's friend, but Peel had fought him bitterly on the issue of Catholic emancipation, only to reverse himself and embrace that cause after Canning's death. Disraeli refused to answer immediately, and took several days to prepare his attack. Then, when he rose, he first chastened Peel for asking Tories to adopt Whig principles, saying, "The right honourable gentleman caught the Whigs bathing, and walked away with their clothes. He has left them in the full enjoyment of their liberal position, and he is himself a strict conservative of their garments." The entire House, excepting only its leader, laughed and cheered. And Disraeli continued:

"If the right hon. gentleman may find it sometimes convenient to reprove a supporter on his right flank, perhaps we deserve it. I for one am quite prepared to bow to the rod; but really, if the right hon. gentleman, instead of having recourse to obloquy, would only stick to quotation, he may rely on it it would be a safer weapon. It is one he always wields with the hand of a master; and when he does appeal to any authority, in prose or verse, he is sure to be successful, partly because he never quotes a passage that has not previously received the meed of Parliamentary approbation, and partly and principally because his quotations are so happy.

"The right hon. gentleman knows what the introduction of a great name does in debate—how important is its effects, and occasionally how electrical. He never refers to any author who is not great, and sometimes who is not loved [here he paused, while the House waited for the blow to fall]—Canning for example. That is a name never to be mentioned, I am sure, in the House of Commons without emotion. We all admire his genius. We all, at least most of us, deplore his untimely end; and we all sympathise with him in his fierce struggle with supreme prejudice and sublime mediocrity—with inveterate foes and with candid friends. The right hon. gentleman may be sure that a quotation from such an authority will always tell. Some lines, for example, upon friendship, written by Mr. Canning, and quoted by the right hon. gentleman! The theme, the poet, the speaker—what a felicitous combination! Its effect in debate must be overwhelming; and I am sure, if it were addressed to me, all that would remain would be for me thus publicly to congratulate the right hon. gentleman, not only on his ready memory, but on his courageous conscience."

The ovation which ensued was tremendous; indeed, the effect of Disraeli's speech on the House was so great, the cheering so prolonged, that when Peel rose to answer as best he could, he had to stand a long time in silence, waiting for the cheers to subside.

It is difficult to determine how much, in his fight with Peel, Disraeli was motivated by honest conviction and how much by personal animosity. He had written asking Peel for a place in his Cabinet and had been rather curtly refused. The effect on Disraeli had been so great that his wife had secretly written Peel asking that her husband be given some office. "Do not destroy all his hopes and make him feel his life has been a mistake." Peel refused again, and at the same time gave office to young Gladstone, then a Tory, whose inferior capabilities but superior social and educational background must have been all too clear to Disraeli.

Having found an issue on which he could destroy Peel, Disraeli returned to it again and again, and his attacks on Peel continued. He would sometimes pretend to defend Peel and scold his fellow protectionists for complaining of their leader's betrayal, saying: "There is no doubt a difference in the right hon. gentleman's demeanor as leader of the Opposition and as Minister of the Crown. But that's the old story; you must not contrast too strongly the hours of courtship with the hours of possession. 'Tis very true that the right hon. gentleman's conduct is different. I remember him making his protection speeches. They were the best speeches I ever heard. It was a great thing to hear the right hon. gentleman say: 'I would rather be the leader of the gentlemen of England than possess the confidence of Sovereigns.' That was a grand thing. We don't hear much of 'the gentlemen of England' now. (Great cheering.) But what of that? They have the pleasures of memory—the charms of reminiscence. They were his first love, and, though he may not kneel to them now as in the hour of passion, still they can recall the past; and nothing is more useless or unwise than these scenes of crimination and reproach, for we know that in all these cases, when the beloved object has ceased to charm, it is in vain to appeal to the feelings. (Great laughter.) . . . And that, sir, is exactly the case of the great agricultural interest—that beauty which everybody wooed and one deluded. There is a fatality in such charms, and we now seem to approach the catastrophe of her career. . . . For my part, if we are to have free trade, I, who honor genius, prefer that such measures should be proposed by the hon. member for Stockport

[Cobden] than by one who through skillful parliamentary manoeuvres has tampered with the generous confidence of a great people and a great party. For myself, I care not what may be the result. Dissolve, if you please, the Parliament you have betrayed, and appeal to the people, who, I believe, mistrust you. For me there remains this at least— the opportunity of expressing thus publicly my belief that a Conservative Government is an organised hypocrisy."

From that day forward, the Members of the House of Commons waited impatiently for each new attack of Disraeli upon his chief. The man who had once said he did not believe in parties now constantly cried for a real opposition, saying that the Whigs' policy was the same as Peel's and that the Tories were in truth following a Whiggish leader who "bamboozles one party and plunders the other, till, having obtained a position to which he is not entitled, he cries out 'Let us have no more party questions, but fixity of tenure.'" Disraeli demanded that there be a return to the Commons of "the legitimate influence and salutary check of a constitutional Opposition. . . . Let us do it at once in the only way in which it can be done, by dethroning this dynasty of deception, by putting an end to this intolerable yoke of official despotism and parliamentary imposture." And so the session of 1845 ended, with Peel still in power but no longer able to feel, as he must have before Disraeli's attacks, that if all power is delightful, absolute power is absolutely delightful.

During the recess came word of a failure of the potato crop in Ireland, which seemed to prove Peel's free-trade policy correct. But the "famine" was a false alarm. The Duke of Wellington said, "Rotten potatoes have done it all; they put Peel in his damned fright." And even the great Whig himself, Melbourne, said to the Queen concerning Peel's action, "Ma'am, it's a damned dishonest act." The Ministry fell and was offered to Stanley, who had once remarked, during the Reform troubles with the House of Lords in 1832, "If the Lords resist, His Majesty can put coronets on the heads of a whole company of his Guards." But now, thirteen years later, Stanley was tired, and preferred to hand the problem back to Peel.

When the Parliament met again in January of 1846, Disraeli continued his attack on Peel's desertion of his protectionist principles and conversion to free trade. "Sir, there is difficulty in finding a parallel of history. The only parallel . . . is an incident in the late war in the Levant, which was terminated by the policy of the noble lord opposite. I remember when that great struggle was taking place, when the existence of the Turkish Empire was at stake, the late Sultan, a man of great energy and fertile in resources, was determined to fit out an immense fleet to maintain his empire. Accordingly a vast armament was collected. The crews were picked men, the officers were the ablest that could be found, and both officers and men were rewarded before they fought. There was never an armament which left the Dardanelles similarly appointed since the days of Solyman the Great. The Sultan personally witnessed the departure of the fleet; all the muftis prayed for the expedition, as all the muftis here prayed for the success of the last general election. Away went the fleet, but what was the Sultan's consternation when the Lord High Admiral steered at once into the enemy's port. Now, sir, the Lord High Admiral on that occasion was very much misrepresented. He, too, was called a traitor, and he, too, vindicated himself. 'true it is,' said he, 'I did place myself at the head of this great armada; true it is that my sovereign embraced me; true it is that all the muftis in the Empire offered up prayers for the expedition; but I have an objection to war. I see no use in prolonging the struggle, and the only reason I had for accepting the command was that I might terminate the contest by betraying my master.' (Tremendous Tory cheering.)"

When Peel claimed that he had ended agitation, when he was obviously acting as a result of agitation by the Anti-Corn-Law League, Disraeli said: "But, really, when he told us that his Conservative administration had put down agitation, when he said this in the face of the hon. member for Durham [Bright]—then, sir, I confess that the right hon. baronet did manage to achieve the first great quality of oratory, that he did succeed in making an impression on his audience! Put down agitation! Will he rise and deny that he is legislating or about to legislate with direct reference to agitation? (Loud cheers.) What other excuse has he, for even his mouldy potatoes have failed him . . ."

And still he went on, "We accepted him [Peel] for a leader to accomplish the triumph of protection, and now we are to attend the catastrophe of protection. (Loud laughter.) Of course the Whigs will be the chief mourners. (Loud laughter.) They cannot but weep for their innocent, although it was an abortion (loud cheers and laughter); but ours was a fine child. Who can forget how its nurse dandled it, fondled it? (Loud laughter.) What a charming babe! Delicious little thing! so thriving! (Loud laughter.) Did you ever see such a beauty for its years? This was the tone, the innocent prattle; and then the nurse, in a fit of patriotic frenzy, dashes its brains out (loud laughter), and comes down to give the master and mistress an account of this terrible murder. The nurse, too, a person of a very orderly demeanor, not given to drink, and never showing any emotion, except of late, when kicking against protection."

The outcome of this battle was to have more significance than merely the temporary resolution of protection versus free trade. The more lasting result was the remaking of the Tory Party, with Disraeli as its leader in fact, though he was not to be its titular head for many more years. During all the readings of the Corn bill, the invective continued. Disraeli called Peel "a burglar of other's intellect," and said that ". . . there is no statesman who has committed political larceny on so grand a scale." He said further of Peel, "The right hon. gentleman is reminiscent of a poker. The only difference is that a poker gives off occasional signs of warmth"; and, "The right hon. gentleman's smile is like the silver fittings on a coffin." Of the hundred and twelve Tories who voted with Peel against protection, which they had been elected to uphold, Disraeli said: "Why, what a compliment to a Minister—not only to vote for him, but to vote for him against your opinions (much cheering), and in favour of opinions which he had always drilled you to distrust. (Loud cheers.) That was a scene, I believe, unprecedented in the House of Commons. Indeed, I recollect nothing equal to it, unless it be the conversion of the Saxons by Charlemagne, which is the only historical incident which bears any parallel to that illustrious occasion. (Great cheers and laughter.) Ranged on the banks of the Rhine, the Saxons determined to resist any further movement on the part of great Caesar; but when the Emperor appeared, instead of conquering he converted them. How were they converted? In battalions—the old chronicler informs us they were converted in battalions and baptised in platoons. (Roars of laughter.) It was utterly impossible to bring these individuals from a state of reprobation to a state of grace with a celerity sufficiently quick. When I saw the hundred and twelve fall into rank and file, I was irresistibly reminded of that memorable incident on the banks of the Rhine. (Loud cheers.)"

And he ended his speech with these prophetic words: "I know that the public mind is polluted with economic fancies—a depraved desire that the rich may become richer without interference of industry and toil. I know, sir, that all confidence in public men is lost. (Great cheering.) But, sir, I have faith in the primitive and enduring elements of the English character. It may be vain now, in the midnight of their intoxication, to tell them that there will be an awakening of bitterness; it may be idle now, in the spring-tide of their economic frenzy, to warn them that there may be an ebb of trouble. But the dark and inevitable hour will arrive. Then, when their spirits are softened by misfortune, they will recur to those principles that made England great, and which, in our belief, will only keep England great. (Prolonged cheers.) Then too, sir, perchance they may remember, not with unkindness, those who, betrayed and deserted, were neither ashamed nor afraid to struggle for the 'good old cause'—the cause with which are associated principles the most popular, sentiments the most entirely national, the cause of labour, the cause of the people, the cause of England."

Sir Robert Peel's Corn bill passed, but the same night he was thrown out of office by the desertion of the party he had betrayed, and he is remembered today, when he is remembered at all, as the man who established the London Police, who are still called "Bobbies," and as the first great politician destroyed by Disraeli's wit.

But Disraeli's destruction of one enemy had earned him another, the Queen. An ardent free trader, as was her adored Consort, Albert, she had admired Peel for his change of policy, and even as late as 1851 she was to say to Stanley, when the latter proposed Disraeli as his leader in the Commons: "I do not approve of Mr. Disraeli. I do not approve of his conduct to Sir Robert Peel." There is perhaps no greater tribute to Disraeli's persuasiveness than his transformation of Victoria from a distrustful enemy to an adoring sovereign. It took years of wit and charm and flattery. The Queen was an amateur author, and Disraeli, the best-known novelist of his day, would sometimes address her as, "We authors, Ma'am," or say, "Your Majesty is the head of the literary profession." He said to Matthew Arnold, "Every-one likes flattery; and when you come to Royalty, you should lay it on with a trowel." His own definition of his method for pleasing the Queen was, "I never deny; I never contradict; I sometimes forget"; and he said also, "Gladstone speaks to the Queen as if she were a public department. I treat her with the knowledge that she is a woman."

But if he was flattering with the Queen, his tongue did not lose its sharpness when he was dealing with lesser contemporaries. He described J. W. Henley as having "the countenance of an ill-conditioned Poor Law Guardian censured for some act of harshness." Or he could say in the Commons in 1852, concerning Charles Barry, the architect of the new Houses of Parliament, which had just opened, that the low standard of architecture in England was due to the fact that no architect had ever been shot, like Admiral Byng, *"pour encourager les autres."* He said of Charles Greville, "He was the most conceited person with whom I have ever been brought in contact, although I have read Cicero and known Bulwer Lytton." And of one Member of whom it had been suggested he was out of his depth, "Out of his depth! He's three miles from the shore." When it was said that his attacks on John Bright were too harsh and that Bright was, after all, a self-made man, Disraeli replied, "I know he is and he adores his maker."

Although he enjoyed the use of wit, he was aware of its dangers. He knew when to hold back, having written, "Next to knowing when to seize an opportunity, the most important thing in life is to know when to forego an advantage," and he pointed out, in *Henrietta Temple,* "Nature has given us two ears, but only one mouth." Although Disraeli often made light of his own wit and its worth, and once said, "A majority is always the best repartee," his humor and invective continued nevertheless.

Disraeli wrote of Palmerston that he was "really an impostor, utterly exhausted, and at the best only ginger-beer and not champagne, and now an old painted pantaloon, very deaf, very blind, and with false teeth, which would fall out of his mouth when speaking if he did not hesitate and halt so in his talk." However, when an associate gave Disraeli evidence of an illicit love affair of Palmerston's, suggesting he use it in an election to discredit the old man, Disraeli said, "Palmerston is now seventy. If he could provide evidence of his potency in his electoral address, he'd sweep the country." This provides an interesting contrast between the English voters of that day and those of today, whose reaction to the Profumo affair has been so markedly different. In *Endymion* Disraeli had portrayed Palmerston as the aging Don Juan, Lord Roehampton, and had had him reply to the remark, "I cannot imagine a position more unfortunate than that of an exiled prince," with: "I can. To have the feelings of youth and the frame of age."

In the main Disraeli really lived by his own aphorism, "Life is too short to be little," but he was still at his best in attack. He had said of Stanley that he was "the Prince Rupert of parliamentary discussion; his charge is resistless; but when he returns from the pursuit he always finds his camp in the possession of the enemy," and thereafter Stanley was cursed with the title of "the Rupert of debate." Criticized for his invective against Peel, he replied, "Revolutions are not made with rose-water." Disraeli was quick to admire panache in others, and when Lord Robert Cecil paused to yawn while delivering his own maiden speech, Disraeli said admiringly, "He'll do." The characters in Disraeli's novels, naturally enough, often have the same acid wit as their author: "'I believe that nothing in the newspapers is ever true,' said Madame Phoebus. 'And that is why they are so popular,' added Euphrosyne, 'the taste of the age being so decidedly for fiction.'" Or the author could write of his own creation, "Mr. Kremlin himself was distinguished for ignorance, for he had only one idea, and that was wrong." He had various of his characters express various of his own opinions, such as, "If every man were straightforward in his opinions, there would be no conversation. The fun of talk is to find what a man really thinks, and then contrast it with the enormous lies he has been telling all dinner, and, perhaps, all his life"; and, "Depend upon it, when a man or a phrase is much abused, there is something in both." Many of the best aphorisms in Disraeli's novels were not funny at all, but acute observations that have been so much quoted that they have become clichés, such as "Adventures are to the adventurous," and "The English nation is never so great as in adversity."

In studying how well Disraeli could abuse others, it is easy to lose track of how well he could take abuse and how often he did so, especially when he embraced causes that could only hurt him politically but that he felt morally bound to uphold. One of these was his long fight to remove the civil and political disabilities of Jews, in which he supported Russell and the Whigs and alienated his fellow Tories, including his own Tory leader, Lord Stanley. In 1847 Baron Lionel de Rothschild was elected to represent the City of London but would not take the oath "on the true faith of a Christian." Disraeli always felt and said that Christians, among whom he numbered himself, were the heirs of the Jews. "Where," he asked in the Commons, "is your Christianity if you do not believe in their Judaism?" He told his fellow Tories that they were "influenced by the darkest superstitions of the darkest ages that ever existed in this country" and that Conservatives make a mistake in persecuting Jews, who are essentially a conservative race, and in driving them into the camps of revolution and up-heaval, bringing to them formidable intellectual powers: Has not the Church of Christ made the history of the Jews the most celebrated history in the world? On every sacred day you read to the people the exploits of Jewish heroes, the proofs of Jewish devotion, the brilliant annals of past Jewish magnificence. Every Sunday—every Lord's Day—if you wish to express feelings of praise and thanksgiving to the Most High, or if you wish to find expression of solace in grief, you find both in the works of the Jewish poets. [He ended his speech:] I cannot sit in this House with any misconception of my opinion on this subject. Whatever may be the consequences on the seat I hold, I cannot, for one, give a vote which is not in deference to what I believe to be the true principles of religion. Yes, it is as a Christian that I will not take upon me the awful responsibility of excluding from the legislature those who are of the religion in the bosom of which my Lord and Savior was born." The Rothschilds and other wealthy Jews were Whigs, and Disraeli's championing of their cause year after year against the overwhelming feeling of his own party was an act of courage, and not politically motivated.

From his childhood and throughout his life, Disraeli suffered from anti-Semitism. Macready, the actor, had referred to him as "this miserable, circumcised, *soi-disant* Christian," and on the hustings he often suffered from hecklers who called out "Shylock!" and "Old clothes!" Disraeli took pride in his Jewish ancestry; and although he was during the whole of his adult life the outspoken defender of both the Church of England and the English peerage, he could leave a session in which he had defended the Church and say to Walpole, "You and I have just been voting for a defunct mythology," and he could say to Lord John Manners that there was indeed no real English nobility, "We owe the English peerage to three sources: the spoliation of the Church; the open and flagrant sale of its honors by the early Stuarts; and the borough-mongering of our own times. When Henry IV called his first Parliament, there were only twenty-nine temporal peers to be found. Of these twenty-nine only five remain." He said that the only pedigree of long civilization was that of the House of Israel and his family, far older than any in England. As he did on every subject he felt strongly about, Disraeli wrote a novel on his feelings about Judaism, *Tancred*. This inspired Carlyle to comment on the "Jewish jack-asseries" of this "Hebrew conjurer," and to ask, "How long will John Bull allow this absurd monkey to dance on his chest?" Disraeli was regularly caricatured in *Punch* as a Jewish dealer in cast-off notions and a ringletted viper by John Leech, and yet in 1868, when Leech's widow died, Disraeli arranged that a pension that was to have ceased with her be continued in order to help her children.

And it was not only as a defender of the Jewish religion that Disraeli called down scorn on himself, but also as the upholder and defender of the Church of England. He had no illusions about the Church, commenting when he became Prime Minister, "The sense of power is delightful. It is amusing to receive the letters I do, especially since Deaneries were in the market." Disraeli himself preferred the High Church and all its symbols and ceremonies, saying it was "part of our history, part of our life, part of England itself," and calling it "the only Jewish institution that remains." He said, "the characteristic of the present age is a craving credulity." When Dean Stanley stated that the Athanasian Creed should be deleted from the Book of Common Prayer, Disraeli said, "Mr. Dean: no dogmas, no deans." He said that "every religion of the Beautiful ends in orgy"; but he could joke about his preference, saying of his own parish priest at Hughenden, "My friend the vicar will take what I call a collection and he calls an offertory, and it will be placed on what he calls an altar or on what his parishioners call a table." As with most politicians, he hated to push for any religious legislation, but when his Queen expressed "Her *earnest* wish . . . that Mr. Disraeli should go *as far as he can without embarrassment* to the Government, in *satisfying* the *Protestant* feeling of the country . . . ," he did his best to influence the Churchmen, whom he sometimes referred to as "Rits and Rats" (ritualists and rationalists), to put off Romanist practices and splendors. He wrote, "As for Pantheism, it is Atheism in domino," and, "A Protestant, if he wants aid or advice on any matter, can only go to his solicitor." But what Disraeli really felt about all religion is best expressed in a bit of dialogue from his *Endymion,* "Sensible men are all of the same religion." "And pray what is that?" "Sensible men never tell."

Among the best known of Disraeli's epigrams are these three: "I have always thought that every woman should marry, and no man"; "No man is regular in his attendance at the House of Commons until he is married"; and "You should treat a cigar like a mistress; put it away before you are sick of it." As a young man he had affected a cynical attitude toward women while at the same time being always flattering and solicitous in their society. He frankly admitted to his wife, who was fifteen years older than he, that his interest in her when he first considered marriage was her money; and after their marriage he often made jokes at her expense. "She is an excellent creature, but she can never remember which came first, the Greeks or the Romans." And yet their whole married life was one of extraordinary happiness and continuous love perhaps unparalleled by that of any other public figure. He often wrote two or three affectionate notes to his wife during the course of a single day, even though he had seen her the same morning and would see her again that same night. It was typical of Disraeli that what he really cared most about he often made the most fun of, perhaps hoping his affected cynicism might hide his real sentiment.

Early in Disraeli's career the Tory Lord Chancellor, Lyndhurst, had said to him, "Never defend yourself before a popular assembly, except by retorting the attack; the hearers, in the pleasure which the assault gives them, will forget the previous charge." And both in the Commons and on the hustings Disraeli usually followed this advice. Heckling on the hustings was quite usual, and, as was the case with all English politicians, Disraeli had to be ready to answer. When he was interrupted with "Speak up! I can't hear you," he answered, "Truth travels slowly, but it will reach even you in time." When someone shouted, "Speak quick," he replied: "It is very easy for you to speak quick, you only utter stupid monosyllables, but when I speak I must measure my words. I have to open your great thick head. What I say is to enlighten you. If I bawled like you, you would leave this place as great a fool as you entered it." Early in his career as a Tory, when a man twitted Disraeli about his earlier and different Radical views, Disraeli replied, "We all sow our wild oats, and no one knows the meaning of that phrase better than you." When an elector shouted that Disraeli's wife had picked him out of the gutter, Disraeli answered, "My good fellow, if you were in the gutter no one would pick you out."

His books as well as his speeches are full of Disraeli's remarkable aphoristic wit. Sometimes he spoke or wrote specifically of politics or politicians, as when he wrote, "He who anticipates his century is generally persecuted when living, and is always pilfered when dead"; "I have often observed that nothing ever perplexes an adversary so much as an appeal to his honor"; and "There are exceptions to all rules, but it seldom answers to follow the advice of an opponent." But even more often his wit was applicable not only to political men but to man in general. "Something unpleasant is coming when men are anxious to tell the truth," and "Nobody is forgotten when it is convenient to remember him"; or " 'My idea of an agreeable person,' said Hugo Bohun, 'is a person who agrees with me.' " As a very successful novelist he could write, "An author who speaks about his own books is almost as bad as a mother who talks about her own children," and "You know who the critics are? The men who have failed in literature and art."

Disraeli had crossed swords verbally with all the greatest of his contemporaries. He had said to Palmerston, "You owe the Whigs a great gratitude, my lord, and therefore, I think, you will betray them. Your lordship is like a favorite footman on easy terms with his mistress. Your dexterity seems a happy compound of the smartness of an attorney's clerk and the intrigue of a Greek of the lower empire." He had said of Lord John Russell, "You are now exhaling upon the constitution of your country all that long-hoarded venom and all those distempered humors that had for years accumulated in your petty heart and tainted the current of your mortified life," and, "If a traveller were informed that such a man was leader of the House of Commons he may begin to comprehend how the Egyptians worshipped an Insect." And yet all these earlier fights and feuds were merely preliminary skirmishes when compared with his final battles with Gladstone.

The two men could not have been more unlike. Gladstone was as handsome and heavy-handed as Disraeli was ugly and witty. He came from a fine Protestant background and had done extremely well at Eton and Oxford, going into politics only because his father had refused to allow him to become a clergyman. A note in the diary of Gladstone's wife reads, "Engaged a cook after a long conversation on religious matters, chiefly between her and William." Gladstone entered Parliament at twenty-one and was an Under-Secretary at twenty-five, but he did not remain a Tory. He became a Liberal, perhaps because he realized that there was not enough room in one party for both Disraeli and himself. He was so pious and prayerful that he could switch parties and principles easily and still feel righteous. He is perhaps best described by one of his friends, Labouchère, who said, "I don't object to Gladstone always having the ace of trumps up his sleeve, but merely to his belief that God Almighty put it there."

Disraeli's first great victory at the polls came when he did himself what he had accused Peel of doing, stealing the Whigs' clothes. The Whigs had for years talked of electoral reform and the Tories had fought against it, but under Disraeli's leadership the Tories passed a Reform bill, and Gladstone's rage in the House was so violent at having this plank stolen from his platform that Disraeli very quietly and sarcastically pointed it up, saying. "The right hon. gentleman gets up and addresses me in a tone which, I must say is very unusual in this House. Not that I at all care for the heat he displays, although really his manner is sometimes so very excited and so alarming that one might almost feel thankful that gentlemen in this House, who sit on opposite sides of this table, are divided by a good broad piece of furniture."

Gladstone chose as the issue on which to dislodge Disraeli the "dis-establishment of the Irish Church." He said it was unjust for a Catholic country to have to support a state church that was Protestant, and cried for "justice for Ireland." Disraeli, as always, took the side of the Church of England, poked fun at Gladstone's sudden interest in a subject he had avoided all the while he was in power, and commented, "Strange that a desire to make Bishops should lead a man to destroy Churches." But Gladstone's "pilgrimages of passion" affected the voters more than Disraeli's wit, and the latter's government fell.

"My mission is to pacify Ireland," said Gladstone, and Disraeli remarked, "Mr. Gladstone used to blacken the characters of the Irish Members and now he is blackening their boots." But although as Prime Minister Gladstone put an end to the Protestant Irish Church and passed a new

Land Act, the Irish were not pacified. Their violence increased. When Gladstone had to ask for a secret parliamentary committee, Disraeli remarked, "I remember one of Her Majesty's Ministers saying, I think last year; 'Anyone can govern Ireland with troops and artillery.' So it seems; even that right hon. gentleman."

Although Gladstone was a passionate, almost evangelistic, stump orator, Disraeli was not given to making public political speeches, and he commented on the difference in 1872, saying, "The ministers are so busy going about apologising for their failures; that I think it a pity to distract the public attention from the proceedings." But Disraeli did occasionally speak outside his own constituency and the House of Commons, as, for example, in Manchester, where he described Gladstone's Ministry as acting "like a body of men under the influence of some deleterious drug. Not satiated with the spoliation and anarchy of Ireland, they began to attack every institution and every interest, every class and calling in the country. . . . As time advanced it was not difficult to perceive that extravagance was being substituted for energy by the Government. The un-natural stimulus was subsiding. Their paroxysms ended in prostration. Some took refuge in melancholy, and their eminent chief alternated between a menace and a sigh. As I sat opposite the Treasury Bench the Ministers reminded me of one of those marine landscapes not very unusual on the coasts of South America. You behold a range of exhausted volcanoes. Not a flame flickers on a single pallid crest. But the situation is still dangerous. There are occasional earthquakes, and ever and anon the dark rumbling of the sea."

Disraeli could and did bedevil Gladstone in a great variety of ways, many of them lighthearted. When he was asked by one of Gladstone's daughters at a dinner party about a certain diplomat, Disraeli replied, "He is the most dangerous man in Europe, myself excepted—as your father would say; your father excepted—I should prefer to say." Or when he was asked the difference between a misfortune and a calamity, he answered, "Well, if Gladstone fell into the Thames, that would be a misfortune; and if anybody pulled him out, that, I suppose, would be a calamity."

Disraeli was soon Prime Minister again, having led the Conservatives to a great victory at the polls, and his career now reached its peak. The Queen was made Empress of India, the Egyptian shares of the Suez Canal were bought with the help of the Rothschilds, and England's interests in Europe upheld without war. When Russia attacked Turkey, Gladstone professed to view it as a fight between Christians and the Infidel, but Disraeli more accurately said of the Czar, "he and all his court would don the turban tomorrow, if he could only build a Kremlin on the Bosphorus." He made light (incorrectly) of the alleged torture of Christians by the Turks. "I doubt whether there is prison accommodation for so many, or that torture has been practiced on a great scale among an Oriental people who seldom, I believe, resort to torture, but generally terminate their connection with culprits in a more expeditious manner." But Gladstone saw the issue as one that would appeal to the emotions of the voters and not only made a great series of speeches but also wrote a pamphlet, "The Bulgarian Horrors," which Disraeli described as "of all the Bulgarian atrocities, the worst." By now Disraeli was old. He had accepted an earldom in order to sit in the Lords and be excused constant attendance in the House of Commons. "When I meet a man whose name I can't remember," he had said, "I give myself two minutes, then if it is a hopeless case, I always say, 'And how is the old complaint?'" And perhaps at this point in his life he often remembered his words, "Youth is a blunder; Manhood a struggle; Old Age a regret." Disraeli was resolved to prevent the Russians acquiring access to the Mediterranean, but he did not want to

go to war on the side of the Turks in order to prevent it.
Gladstone's fervid attacks must also have reminded Disraeli
of his own words, "How much easier it is to be critical than
to be correct"; and "Little things affect little minds."

The matter was finally settled at the Berlin Congress in
June, 1878, which Bismarck had hoped to control but which
even he came to recognize was dominated by "the old Jew."
The treaty Disraeli brought back was hailed in England as
the victory it certainly was, but since it brought Disraeli's
popularity to a new peak, it was described by Gladstone as
"an insane covenant." This remark called forth what is probably Disraeli's best-known comment. "Which do you believe most likely to enter an insane convention, a body of
English gentlemen honored by the favor of their Sovereign
and the confidence of their fellow-subjects, managing your
affairs for five years, I hope with prudence, and not alto-
gether without success, or a sophistical rhetorician, in-
ebriated with the exuberance of his own verbosity, and
gifted with an egotistical imagination that can at all times
command an interminable and inconsistent series of arguments to malign an opponent and glorify himself?"

Even as he was dying, Disraeli's sense of humor did not
leave him, and he said, as he corrected the proofs of his last
speech, "I will not go down to posterity talking bad grammar."

In spite of the cynicism he affected in many of his mots,
Disraeli believed in the great possibilities for achievement
by the individual through his own efforts and his own wit.
Disraeli's life was proof of this belief, having begun without family or great fortune and reached "the top of the
greasy pole" by the force of his own individual genius. He
had little use for "the people" in general. In his novel *Coningsby* the hero asks, "But what is the individual against a
vast public opinion?" "Divine," answers the stranger. "God
made man in His own image, but the Public is made by

Newspapers, Members of Parliament, Excise Officers, Poor Law Guardians." Nor did Disraeli have any use for the then new theories of abstract economic determinism, what he called the "Manchester School": "Competition is always at the head of the list; then follow, you may be sure, energy and enterprise. These remedies are not facts—they are only phrases. What is this competition, of whose divine influence we hear so much? Define it, tell us its sex and character. Is it a demigod or a nymph? It inspires all their solutions of economical difficulties. Is the shipping interest in decay? Competition will renovate it. Are the Colonies in despair? Energy will save them. Is the agricultural interest in danger? Enterprise is the panacea." He was aghast that the commercial principle ruled the country, and said prophetically, "but you may rest assured that, if you convert the senate into a counting house, it will not be long before the nation degenerates into a factory." Though he was of the opinion, "Increased means and increased leisure are the two civilizers of man," he had little faith in man's salvation by science. In his novels he had written, "The pursuit of science leads only to the insoluble"; and, "I think that, ere long, science will again become imaginative, and that, as we become more profound, we may also become more credulous."

At the Sheldonian Theatre, Oxford, in 1864, he spoke of his belief in the individual and divine nature of man as opposed to the belief (which has increased in the world since his time) that man is merely an animal (or machine) subject to immutable economic and psychological forces. His words were laughed at then and have been laughed at since, but this great wit believed them with all seriousness. Referring to Darwin's *The Origin of Species*, published five years earlier, he said, "Why, my Lord, man is a being born to believe. And if no Church comes forward with its title-deeds of truth, sustained by the tradition of

sacred ages and by the conviction of countless genera-
rations, to guide him, he will find altars and idols in his
own heart and his own imagination. . . . The discoveries
of science, we are told, are not consistent with the teach-
ings of the Church. . . . What is the question now placed
before society with a glib assurance the most astounding?
The question is this—Is man an ape or an angel? My
Lord, I am on the side of the angels. It is between these
two contending interpretations of the nature of man,
and their consequences, that society will have to decide.
Their rivalry is at the bottom of all human affairs. . . ."

V

Abraham Lincoln

Melancholy men are of all others the most witty.
Aristotle

It has been a standard joke among European art dealers for many years that in his lifetime Corot painted no more than two thousand canvases, of which three thousand are in the United States. It is, however, a good deal easier to tell a fake Corot from a real Corot than to tell a fake Lincoln story from a real one. Throughout his life Lincoln was a constant storyteller, and when he achieved fame many stories not his were attributed to him by the teller in order to give them cachet. Books alleged to be Lincoln joke books were brought out, such as *Old Abe's Jokes—Fresh from Abraham's Bosom* and *Old Abe's Joker, or Wit at the White House.* In his *Anecdotes of Abraham Lincoln,* Isaac N. Arnold admitted that perhaps half were stories Lincoln had actually told. Nicolay said that, in all, Lincoln's stories might total one hundred. Lincoln said to Noah Brooks that perhaps one-sixth of the stories credited to him were his; "I remember a good story when I hear it, but I never invented anything original. I am only a retail dealer."

This is precisely what he was. Born in Kentucky, and well acquainted with the Bible, Lincoln all his life told stories in the biblical-parable tradition and in the southern tradition that still exists today. His anecdotes were to illustrate, amplify, or explain a point, not the brilliant epigram or witty repartee of a Sheridan or a Randolph. Sumner pointed out how Lincoln often used a story to support a point, saying, "His ideas moved as beasts entered Noah's ark, in pairs." He told so many stories that, by November 21, 1863, he was characterized in the New York *Herald* as "the American Aesop."

Among the earliest Lincoln stories are those he told as a young lawyer traveling by horseback on the circuit from one county court to another. Once, when the opposing lawyer objected to a certain juror because he knew Lincoln, Judge Davis overruled the objection because it was a reflection on Lincoln's honor. When Lincoln examined several jurors to see if they knew the opposing lawyer, the judge reprimanded him, saying, "Now, Mr. Lincoln, you are wasting time. The mere fact that a juror knows your opponent does not disqualify him." "No, Your Honor," Lincoln replied, "but I am afraid some of the gentlemen may not know him, which would place me at a disadvantage." Speaking of another lawyer, Lincoln once said, "He can compress the most words into the smallest ideas better than any man I ever met." Lincoln loved to tell stories of the log-cabin frontier, such as the one of the housewife who refused to buy a Bible from a traveling Methodist minister because she had one. Asked to produce it, she and her children searched high and low and finally found only a few worn pages of the Good Book. She stuck to her story that she had a Bible, adding, however, "But I had no idea we were so nearly out!"

First in the Legislature in Illinois, and later in the United States Congress, Lincoln continued to display his wit and also to simplify his style, ridding it of what he called "fizzle-gigs and fireworks." Lincoln began his political career as a Whig, and he crossed swords with George Forquer, who had left the Whigs to accept a Democratic appointment at $3,000 a year, which enabled him to build a fancy house with a lightning rod, still a novelty in Illinois. When For-

quer attacked Lincoln after the latter had spoken in Springfield, Lincoln said in reply, "I desire to live, and I desire
place and distinction; but I would rather die now than,
like the gentleman, live to see the day that I could change
my politics for an office worth three thousand dollars a
year, and then feel compelled to erect a lightning rod to
protect a guilty conscience from an offended God."

When Lincoln ran for Congress in 1846 against Peter
Cartwright, the Methodist hellfire-and-damnation evangel-
ist spread the word that Lincoln was godless. Lincoln went
to a revival in Springfield where Cartwright said, "All who
desire to give their hearts to God, and go to heaven, will
stand," and many stood. Then Cartwright cried, "All who
do not wish to go to hell will stand," and everyone except
Lincoln stood. "I observe," Cartwright then said, "that
many responded to the first invitation to give their hearts
to God and go to Heaven. And I further observe that all of
you save one indicated that you did not desire to go to hell.
The sole exception is Mr. Lincoln, who did not respond to
either invitation. May I inquire of you, Mr. Lincoln, where
you are going?"

"I came here as a respectful listener," Lincoln replied.
"I did not know that I was to be singled out by Brother
Cartwright. I believe in treating religious matters with due
solemnity. I admit that the questions propounded by
Brother Cartwright are of great importance. I did not feel
called upon to answer as the rest did. Brother Cartwright
asks me directly where I am going. I desire to reply with
equal directness. I am going to Congress."

And he did. It was while he was in Congress that his
national reputation as a storyteller began to grow. He spoke
out against the Mexican War, calling it a war of aggression
and saying it reminded him of the Illinois farmer who said
about land, "I ain't greedy; I only want what jines mine."
In a speech in the House in 1848 on the candidacy of

Well known as a joke-teller and much criticized for it, Lincoln is shown here with General McClellan, the Democrat who ran against him in 1864. The shovel reflects the charge that McClellan's army dug more than it fought

Lincoln's re-election in 1864 prompted *Harper's Weekly* to note that the country would have "Long Abe" a little longer

General Zachary Taylor, Lincoln taunted the Democrats of New York on divisions in their ranks, saying, ". . . as a drunken fellow once said when he heard the reading of an indictment for hog stealing. The clerk read on till he got to, and through the words, 'did steal, take and carry away, ten boars, ten sows, ten shoats, and ten pigs,' at which he exclaimed: 'Well, by golly, that is the most evenly divided gang of hogs I ever did hear of.' If there is any gang of hogs more evenly divided than the Democrats of New York are about this time, I have not heard of it."

Lincoln also made a famous attack in Congress on General Lewis Cass of Michigan, the Democratic candidate for the Presidency in 1848, addressing himself to the General's accounts with the government in 1831: "Mr. Speaker, I adopt the suggestion of a friend, that General Cass is a general of splendidly successful charges—charges, to be sure, not upon the public enemy, but upon the public treasury. I have introduced General Cass's accounts here chiefly to show the wonderful physical capacities of the man. They show that he not only did the labor of several men at the same time, but that he often did it at several places many hundred miles apart, at the same time. And at eating, too, his capacities are shown to be quite as wonderful. From October, 1821, to May, 1822, he ate ten rations a day in Michigan, ten rations a day here in Washington, and near five dollars' worth a day besides, partly on the road between the two places. And then there is an important discovery in his example—the art of being paid for what one eats, instead of having to pay for it. Hereafter if any nice young man shall owe a bill which he cannot pay in any other way, he can just board it out. Mr. Speaker, we have all heard of the animal standing in doubt between two stacks of hay and starving to death; the like of that would never happen to General Cass. Place the stacks a thousand miles apart, he would stand stock still midway between them, and eat them both at once; and the green grass along the line would be apt to suffer some too, at the same time. By all means, make him President, gentlemen. He will feed you bounteously—if—if there is any left after he shall have helped himself."

What changed Lincoln from just another western congressman to a presidential candidate was his fame acquired debating Senator Stephen A. Douglas. Douglas described Lincoln's first speech in the Illinois Legislature: "When Lincoln first made his appearance in the Illinois House of Representatives, and was desirous of delivering his sentiments on a certain measure, he rose and began: 'Mr. Speaker, I conceive—' but could go no further. Thrice he repeated unsuccessfully the same attempt; when Douglas, who had more confidence, and had been a year longer in the House, completely dumbfounded Abe by saying: 'Mr. Speaker, the honorable gentleman has conceived three times, and brought forth nothing.'"

By 1858, however, Douglas found that Lincoln had improved as a speaker, when he was nominated by the Illinois Republicans to try to unseat Douglas in the United States Senate. Their debates were followed not only in Illinois but throughout the country. During one of them Douglas said that his first meeting with Lincoln was across a store counter where Lincoln sold whiskey. In reply, Lincoln said, "What Mr. Douglas has said, gentlemen, is true enough; I did keep a grocery, and I did sell cotton, candles and cigars, and sometimes whiskey; but I remember in those days that Mr. Douglas was one of my best customers. Many a time have I stood on one side of the counter and sold whiskey to Mr. Douglas on the other side, but the difference between us now is this: I have left my side of the counter, but Mr. Douglas still sticks to his as tenaciously as ever." Lincoln continued to refer to Douglas's love of drink during the debates: "Douglas has said that his father was a cooper by trade and had apprenticed him to learn the cabinet-making trade, which is all well enough, though I was not aware until now that his father was a cooper. I have no doubt, however, that he was one, and am certain that he was a very good one for—[here Lincoln bowed toward Douglas] he has made one of the best whiskey casks I have ever seen!" At another point Lincoln said that Douglas's argument was "as thin as the homeopathic soup that was made by boiling the shadow of a pigeon that had been starved to death."

Though Lincoln enjoyed joking at the expense of others, he also joked frequently at his own expense, often about his ugliness. "One day," Lincoln said, "when I first came here, I got into a fit of musing in my room and stood resting my elbows on the bureau. Looking into the glass, it struck me what an ugly man I was. The fact grew on me and I made up my mind that I must be the ugliest man in the world. It so maddened me that I resolved, should I ever see an uglier, I would shoot him on sight. Not long after this, Andy [naming a lawyer present] came to town and the first time I saw him I said to myself: 'There's the man.' I went home, took down my gun, and prowled around the streets waiting for him. He soon came along. 'Halt, Andy,' said I, pointing the gun at him; 'say your prayers, for I am going to shoot you.' 'Why, Mr. Lincoln, what's the matter? What have I done?' 'Well, I made an oath that if I ever saw an uglier man than I am, I'd shoot him on the spot. You are uglier, surely; so make ready to die.' 'Mr. Lincoln, do you really think that I am uglier than you?' 'Yes.' 'Well, Mr. Lincoln,' said Andy deliberately and looking me squarely in the face, 'if I am any uglier, fire away.'"

On those occasions when he spoke of his ancestry or of himself, Lincoln was always modest or even self-deprecating. He remarked, "I don't know who my grandfather was, and I am much more concerned to know what his grandson will be." To a man gathering information for a campaign biography, he said, "There is no romance nor is there anything heroic in my early life. The story of my life can be condensed into one line, and that line you can find in Gray's 'Elegy': 'The short and simple annals of the poor.'"

It was after he became President of the United States and the Civil War began that Lincoln's persistent use of humor became widely known. He was constantly criticized both for his penchant for telling stories and for his desire to hear and read them. When only a day after the horrors of Fredericksburg, Lincoln insisted on reading examples of the humor of Artemus Ward to Isaac N. Arnold, the congressman expressed shock that the President could indulge in levity when the whole land was bowed in sorrow. Arnold said that Lincoln threw down Ward's book and cried out, with tears streaming down his face and his great body quivering, "Mr. Arnold, if I could not get momentary respite from the crushing burden I am constantly carrying, my heart would break!"

Secretary of War Stanton was furious that on the evening of Election Day, November 8, 1864, Lincoln was not anxious to see the returns as they came in, but instead read Petroleum V. Nasby, one of his favorite sources of humor. On another occasion he had said, "We may have to treat Stanton as they are sometimes obliged to treat a Methodist minister I know out West. He gets wrought up to so high a pitch of excitement in his prayers and exhortations that they put bricks in his pockets to keep him down. But I guess we'll let him jump awhile first."

Secretary of the Treasury Chase was also frequently upset by Lincoln's jokes, but most especially before his renomination. The New York *Evening Post* had reported that talk about whether he would be renominated reminded Lincoln of a state official in Illinois who asked a traveling preacher wanting a permit to preach in the state house, "On what subject?" "On the second coming of our Savior." "Oh, bosh, if our Savior had ever been to Springfield and got away with his life, he'd be too smart to think of coming back again." Chase's view of Lincoln's frivolity must not have been changed when the Treasury Secretary described the nation's black financial condition, and Lincoln said, "Well, Mr. Secretary, I don't know [what can be done about it] unless you give your paper mill another turn." Lincoln had another story on paper currency concerning a dialogue he had overheard while going down the Mississippi on a steamboat. The captain, bargaining to buy wood for fuel, said to the seller on the bank, "Is that your wood?" "Certainly." "You want to sell it?" "Yes." "For cash?" "Yes." "Will you take wildcat currency?" "Certainly." "Well, how will you take it?" "Cord for cord."

Lincoln was aware that one reason Chase was critical of him was that he wanted the Presidency himself. Lincoln said to Henry Jarvis Raymond, owner of the *New York Times*, ". . . you were brought up on a farm, were you not? Then you know what a *chin fly* is. My brother and I . . . were once plowing corn on a Kentucky farm, I was driving the horse, and he holding the plough. The horse was lazy; but on one occasion rushed across the field so that I, with my long legs, could scarcely keep pace with him. On reaching the end of the furrow, I found an enormous *chin fly* fastened upon him, and knocked him off. My brother asked me what I did that for. I told him I didn't want the old horse bitten in that way. 'Why,' said my brother, 'that's all that made him go!' Now if Mr. C[hase] has a presidential *chin fly* biting him, I'm not going to knock him off, if it will only make his department go."

Lincoln also joked with Hugh McCulloch, Secretary of the Treasury, during his second term, who was once announced with a delegation of New York bankers. As the party filed into the room he preceded them and said to the President, in a low voice, "These gentlemen from New York have come on to see you about our new loan. As bankers they are obliged to hold our national securities. I can vouch for their patriotism and loyalty, for, as the good Book says, 'Where the treasure is, there will the heart be also.'" To which Lincoln replied, "There is another text, Mr. McCulloch, I remember, that might equally apply, 'Where the carcass is, there will the eagles be gathered together.'"

But it was not only Lincoln's Cabinet members and intimates who complained of his constant joking. The whole country was aware of his habit, and the President knew it. He told the story about two Quaker women in a railway coach during the war, and one saying, "I think Jefferson Davis will succeed." "Why does thee think so?" asks the other. "Because Jefferson is a praying man." "But so is Abraham a praying man," the other says. "Yes," the first woman concluded, "but the Lord will think Abraham is joking." Lincoln was attacked before his renomination in Baltimore by the New York *Herald*, which characterized him as nothing but a clown, "a joke incarnated, his election a very sorry joke, and the idea that such a man as he should be President of such a country as this a very ridiculous joke." Richard Henry Dana asked in a letter, "Can this man Lincoln *ever* be serious?" Aware of all this criticism, Lincoln often explained and excused his love for humor. "Some of the stories are not so nice as they might be, but I tell you the truth when I say that a funny story, if it has the element of genuine wit, has the same effect on me that I suppose a good square drink of whiskey has on an old toper; it puts new life into me."

Lincoln told all kinds of stories, a few were of that variety known today as shaggy dog stories. One was about a man visiting an insane asylum and meeting an inmate who demanded a salute, saying, "I am Julius Caesar." When he saw the inmate again later, the madman again demanded a salute, saying, "I am Napoleon Bonaparte." "Yes, Napoleon, but a while ago you told me you were Julius Caesar." "Yes, but that was by another mother." He told stories about himself and his family. Once when he was carrying two of his sons, Willie and Tad, and both were howling, he was asked what was the matter. "Just what's the matter with the whole world. I've got three walnuts and each wants two."

But in the main Lincoln's stories were about his problems in government and, in the early years, when the war was going badly, about his generals. He was particularly unhappy about the reluctance of General McClellan to allow his Army of the Potomac to fight. He said of McClellan, "He's got the slows," and once, after the Battle of Antietam when he was visiting the army, he waved his hand in despair and said, "Hatch—Hatch, what is all this?" "Why, Mr. Lincoln," Hatch replied, "this is the Army of the Potomac." "No, Hatch, no. This is General McClellan's bodyguard."

He once wrote the General, "My dear McClellan: If you don't want to use the army I should like to borrow it for a while. Yours respectfully, A. Lincoln." In another letter from Washington, D.C., on October 24, 1862, he wrote, "Major-General McClellan: I'm afraid I have just read your dispatch about sore-tongued and fatigued horses. Will you pardon me for asking what your horses have done since the Battle of Antietam that can fatigue anything. A. Lincoln."

He once visited McClellan's headquarters with an aide, and found it empty. He heard hammering in the woods nearby and went to see what it was. He found some soldiers building something, and asked what it was. "It's a new privy for the General," was the answer. "Is it a one-holer or a two-holer?" Lincoln asked. "A one-holer, sir," the soldier answered. When he was out of earshot of the soldiers, Lincoln said to his aide, "Thank God it's a one-holer, for if it were a two-holer, before McClellan could make up his mind which to use, he would beshit himself."

Asked the size of the Confederate Army, Lincoln replied, "About 1,200,000 men according to the best authority." When doubt was expressed as to this figure, the President went on, "1,200,000—no doubt of it. You see, all our generals, when they get whipped, say the enemy outnumbers them three to five to one, and I must believe them. We have 400,000 men in the field. . . ."

Worn out with McClellan's waiting, Lincoln replaced him with General Hooker. In order to give an impression of activity, Hooker sent a dispatch headed, "Headquarters in the Saddle." "The trouble with Hooker," said Lincoln, "is he's got his headquarters where his hindquarters ought to be."

But when he got a general who fought, Lincoln backed him up. After the victory at Shiloh, Lincoln was urged by A. K. McClure to dismiss Grant because it was widely believed he had been drunk at Shiloh. Lincoln said, "I can't spare this man—he fights!" Senator Benjamin Wade of Ohio came to the White House to urge Grant's dismissal, and Lincoln said, "Senator, that reminds me of a story. . . ." "Yes, yes," Wade interrupted, "it is with you, sir, all story, story. You are the father of every military blunder that has been made during this war. You are on the road to hell, sir, . . . and you are not a mile off this minute!" Lincoln replied, "Senator, that is just about the distance from here to the Capitol, is it not?" Lincoln once said to General Butler, "When General Grant once gets possessed of a place, he seems to hang on to it as if he had inherited it." There are, of course, many versions of a story that Lincoln said he would like to send a barrel of the brand of whiskey Grant drank to each of his generals, but Major Thomas T. Eckert said that Lincoln told him he had heard this story, that it was a good one, and that he wished he had told it—but he did not. Lincoln supposed it was "charged to him to give it currency," but went on, "the original is back in King George's time. Bitter complaints were made against General Wolfe that he was mad. The King, who could be more justly accused of that, replied: 'I wish he would bite some of my other generals.'"

Grant himself was capable of strong invective. When he expressed his contempt for a certain officer, and another general protested that the man in question had been through ten campaigns, Grant said, "General, so has that mule, yonder, but he's still a jackass." Well known as a master of invective in Lincoln's time was the club-footed and cold Thaddeus Stevens, who once said to a Lancaster lawyer who had double-crossed him, "You must be a bastard, for I knew your mother's husband and he was a gentleman and an honest man!" Stevens warned Lincoln that Simon Cameron was not a suitable man to be Secretary of War, and Lincoln asked, "You don't mean to say you think Cameron would steal?" "No," Stevens replied, "I don't think he would steal a red-hot stove." When Lincoln repeated the story to Cameron, the latter became outraged and insisted that Stevens retract. Stevens then said to Lincoln, ". . . I believe I told you he would *not* steal a red-hot stove. I now take that back."

Lincoln himself could, on occasion, be sharp-tongued, as when it was said to him of a certain man, "It may be doubted whether any man of our generation has plunged more deeply into the sacred fount of learning," and Lincoln replied, "Yes, or come up drier." According to a political circular sent out by Shields, Democratic State Auditor of Illinois, Lincoln declared, "What they say is a lie, and not a well-told one at that. It grins out like a copper dollar.

Shields is a fool as well as a liar. With him truth is out of the question and to get a good passable lie out of him, you might as well strike a fire from a cake of tallow." There are several versions of a story that a visitor came upon Lincoln in the White House blacking his own boots and expressed surprise, whereupon Lincoln snapped, "Why, whose boots do *you* black?" But such anecdotes on Lincoln are rare. He was a forgiving man and one who hated to refuse any reasonable request. Speaking of his willingness to forgive an old opponent, he said, "I choose always to make my 'statute of limitations' a short one."

He refused to answer all the attacks, lies, and rumors about himself, saying it would involve "a perpetual flea hunt." "If I were trying to read, much less answer all the attacks made on me, this shop might well be closed for any other purpose. I do the very best I know how: the very best I can: and I mean to keep on doing it to the end. If the end brings me out all right, what is said against me will not amount to anything. If the end brings me out all wrong, then a legion of angels swearing I was right will make no difference."

When a woman criticized Lincoln, saying that rather than speaking kindly of the Confederates he should destroy them, Lincoln answered, "What, Madam, do I not destroy them when I make them my friends?"

When his whole Cabinet with the exception of one member was against him, Lincoln mildly told the story of the drunk at the Illinois revival who slept when the preacher asked, "Who are on the Lord's side?" and the whole audience excepting himself rose, and who, after the preacher had then asked, "Who are on the side of the Devil?" awoke, rose, and standing there alone said, "I don't exactly understand the question but I'll stand by you, parson, to the last. But it seems to me that we're in a hopeless minority."

Lincoln was constantly trying to help office seekers who

badgered him, and granting pardons to soldiers whose mothers came to see him in their behalf. Lincoln said to General Egbert L. Viele, "I have one vice, and I can call it nothing else, it is not to be able to say 'No.' Thank God for not making me a woman, but if He had, I suppose He would have made me just as ugly as He did, and no one would ever have tempted me." Tad and Willie Lincoln made a doll they called Jack and dressed him as a Zouave. They sentenced him to be shot for sleeping on picket duty, and then asked their father for a pardon. Lincoln stopped his work and wrote out on Executive Mansion stationery: "The doll Jack is pardoned. By order of the President. A. Lincoln."

After the conduct of the war, Lincoln's main concern was if and when to declare the Negro slaves free. He was under tremendous pressure from elements in his own Republican Party, as well as from his own personal feelings on the issue. Yet even on this issue he could and did joke. Ambassador Adlai Stevenson tells the following story, as told to him by his grandfather, Adlai Stevenson: "Several months before Lincoln issued the great Proclamation of Emancipation which gave freedom to the whole race of Negro slaves in America, my friend Senator Henderson of Missouri came to the White House one day and found Mr. Lincoln in a mood of deepest depression. Finally, the great President said to his caller that the most constant and acute pressure was being brought upon him by the leaders of the most radical elements of the party to free the slaves. 'Sumner and Stevens and Wilson simply haunt me,' declared Mr. Lincoln 'with their importunities for a proclamation of emancipation. Wherever I go and every way I turn, they're on my trail. And still in my heart I have the deep conviction that the hour is not yet come.' Just as he said this, he walked to the window looking out upon Pennsylvania Avenue and stood there in silence. His tall figure silhouetted against the light of the window pane, every line of it and of his gracious face expressive of unutterable sadness. Suddenly his lips began to twitch into a smile and his eyes lighted with a twinkle something like mirth. 'The only schooling I ever had, Henderson,' he remarked, 'was in a log schoolhouse when reading-books and grammars were unknown. All our reading was done from the Scriptures, and we stood up in a long line and read in turn from the Bible. Our lesson one day was the story of the faithful Israelites who were thrown into the fiery furnace and delivered by the hand of the Lord without so much as the smell of fire upon their garments. It fell to one little fellow to read the verse in which occurred for the first time in the chapter the names of Shadrach, Meshach, and Abednego. Little Bud stumbled on Shadrach, floundered on Meshach, and went all to pieces on Abednego. Instantly the master dealt him a cuff on the side of the head and left him wailing and blubbering as the next boy in line took up the reading. But before the boy at the end of the line had done reading, he subsided into sniffles and finally became quiet. His blunder and disgrace were forgotten by the others in his class until his turn was approaching to read again. Then, like a thunderclap out of the sky, he sent up a wail which even alarmed the master, who, with rather unusual gentleness inquired, 'What's the matter now?' Pointing with a shaking finger at the verse which a few moments later would fall to him to read, Bud managed to quaver out the answer, 'Look there, master. There comes them same damn three fellers again.' Then his whole face lighted with such a smile as only Lincoln could give, and he beckoned Senator Henderson to his side, silently pointing his long bony finger to three men who were at that moment crossing Pennsylvania Avenue toward the door of the White House. They were Sumner, Wilson and Stevens."

One of Lincoln's most famous stories was told when he

was asked how he liked being President of the United States, and he replied: "You have heard the story, haven't you, about the man who was tarred and feathered and carried out of town on a rail? A man in the crowd asked him how he liked it. His reply was that if it was not for the honor of the thing, he would much rather walk." One of Lincoln's most annoying problems was the steady flow of office seekers who pestered him. He once said he had read of a certain King who wanted to go hunting, and asked the Court Minister if it would rain. The Minister told him the weather would be fair. Setting out, the royal party met a farmer riding a jackass. He warned the King it was going to rain. The King laughed, and went on; but no sooner had he begun hunting than a heavy downpour drenched him and his party. He went back, threw out the Minister, and called for the farmer. "Tell me how you knew it would rain." "I did not know, Your Majesty. It's not me, it's my jackass. He puts his ear forward when it's going to be wet." The King sent the farmer away, and had the jackass brought and put in place of the Minister. "It was here," said Lincoln, "that the King made a great mistake." "How so?" he was asked. "Why, ever since that time, every jackass wants an office." Lincoln was acquainted with political wit that had preceded his own. When friends of Governor Curtin sought to obtain for him a foreign mission, Lincoln wanted to help; unfortunately, the missions were all full. "I am in the position of young Sheridan when his father told him he must cease his rakish life and take a wife. To which he answered, 'All right, Father, but whose wife shall I take?'"

A New Jersey congressman once brought two citizens of that state to visit the President. Seeking to impress Lincoln, he introduced them as being "among the weightiest men in southern New Jersey." Upon their departure, Lincoln said to one of his aides who was standing by, "I wonder that

end of the state didn't tip up when they got off it." Right
up to the end he had no respite from people who wanted
to see him and to bring their friends. During the last week
of Lincoln's life, Attorney General Speed was about to
ask the President to do him the honor of meeting a friend
of his in the reception room. But when he saw how terribly
weary Lincoln looked, the Attorney General began to
apologize for disturbing him. "Speed," Lincoln said, "you
remind me of a story of Henry Ward Beecher. One day as
he was going to preach, he saw some boys playing marbles
in the street. He stopped and looked at them very hard.
'Boys,' he said presently, 'boys, I am scared at what I see.'
'Then,' replied one of the boys, 'why the hell don't you
run away?' "

According to W. J. Lampton, Lincoln's last joke was
made on the last day of his life. The President did not want
to go to Ford's Theatre because he had already seen the
comedy playing there, *Our American Cousin.* He tried to
avoid going, but Mrs. Lincoln's plans for a theater party
had already been upset by General and Mrs. Grant's last-
minute inability to attend, and she insisted that Lincoln
go to the theater. "All right," the President said. "All right,
Mary, I'll go, but if I don't go down in history as the
martyr President I miss my guess."

VI

David Lloyd George

There is no possibility of being witty without a little ill-
nature; the malice of a good thing is the barb that makes
it stick.

Sheridan, *The School for Scandal*

After his first dinner as Prime Minister, David Lloyd
George wrote, "Never had there been a 'ranker' raised to
the Premiership—certainly not excepting Disraeli, who had
not passed through the staff college of the old universities."
This judgment was correct, for in every respect his dis-
advantages had exceeded even Disraeli's. His Welsh origin
and religious nonconformity made him as much an outsider
as Disraeli, and he had none of the latter's advantages of
wealth and easy, if not formal, education.

He was born on January 17, 1863, at Manchester, and if
he was, as he sometimes claimed, descended from the
great Welsh king, Owen Glendower, his family had now
fallen far from its former eminence. His father, William
George, was a chronically unsuccessful schoolmaster, who
died when Lloyd George was less than eighteen months
old. His mother then turned to her bachelor brother, Richard Lloyd, a shoemaker and lay minister of Llanystumdwy,
who took on the care of the family and the education of
David. Lloyd George, who later took full political advantage of being a "cottage-bred boy," described his uncle's
home as "comfortable but thrifty and pinched. Our bread
was homemade; we scarcely ate fresh meat, and I remember that our greatest luxury was half an egg for each child

on Sunday mornings." Richard Lloyd belonged to an offshoot of the Baptist Church called the Church of Christ, whose members believed it blasphemous for a man to be paid for preaching the Holy Gospel. Therefore, members of the congregation did the preaching, and Lloyd was foremost among these lay preachers. It was from this uncle that young David got his independent religious and political views.

Two early influences on Lloyd George more important than the poverty that he tended somewhat to exaggerate in his later years were the Established Church and the local squire. Lloyd George, although he was a nonconformist, was required, as were all citizens, to tithe to the Church of England. Perhaps even more rankling than this religious injustice was a political one. All voters were expected to vote in parliamentary elections, not as they pleased, but for the candidate chosen by the local squire. Otherwise they faced the threat of eviction. Even as a schoolboy David was so incensed by injustice that he fomented and led a strike in the parish school against the saying of the Anglican creed and catechism. It was successful, and this odious requirement was thereafter eliminated.

But other youthful forms of rebellion were not always so successful. In later years Lloyd George also admitted to poaching. "The land round our village was strictly preserved, but that did not prevent our having our full share of nature's bounty in the form of apples and nuts." However, "A boy once killed a hare, and as a result he had to be sent away by his widowed mother from the farm she occupied; failing that, she was told she would be turned out of her home." All this helps explain Lloyd George's violent invective against the Church of England and his favorite target, "the dukes."

He decided to study for the law, which required a knowledge of French, so he and his uncle both taught themselves

the language with only the help of an old French dictionary and a book on French grammar. During this period
from the age of seventeen to nineteen he spoke, both in
Welsh and in English, on every opportunity that presented
itself, at local meetinghouses and with the local debating
society. He also wrote regularly to the newspapers under
the name "Brutus," and the style of his invective against
the Tories and the Church of England was already that
which was later to make him so famous. He denounced
"supercilious and exacting landlords," the "sores inflicted
by satanic landlordism," and attacked the House of Lords
as a "lumber room of musty prejudice" and an "asylum of
hereditary delusions." One should "alleviate the misery of
the poor before pandering to the vanity of the rich," and
not "send a punt to save a boat's crew because the lifeboat
is wanted for a pleasure trip."

Young Lloyd George's law studies were successful, and
he qualified in 1884. Refusing to be a managing clerk, he
struck out on his own and quickly made a reputation as a
conscientious fighter for the underdog. He was at the same
time both a practicing lawyer and a Radical politician, and
made his reputation in a case that he carried successfully
to the High Court. In it he defended the right of noncon-
formists to be buried in the local parish churchyard. In
1888 he married the loyal and understanding lady who
was to give him four children, the youngest son and daughter eventually joining their father as Members of Parliament. Lloyd George became an alderman, and then in
1890, in a by-election, was elected to Parliament for the
first of many times as the Member for Carnarvon Boroughs.
He was elected as a Radical, and defeated his Conservative
opponent by only eighteen votes.

In his maiden speech on June 13, 1890, during a debate
on provisions for compensating owners of suppressed
public-house licenses, Lloyd George, who was still at this

point a violently vocal temperance man, said that there had never been so puny an attempt to fight the great evil of drink "since the Lilliputian king drew his hanger to attack Gulliver." He chided Lord Randolph Churchill, saying, "as with many another temperance advocate the holidays seem to have affected his principles," and went on to include Mr. Joseph Chamberlain in his attack, "the right honorable gentleman and the noble lord seem to be a kind of political contortionist, after the manner of the American performers who can set their feet in one direction and their faces in another, and no one knows which way they intend to travel." In his first session in the House he voted against the orders of his own Liberal Party whip and stated he would never "make mere party the god of his idolatry." He even had the courage to oppose a bill to which his leader, Mr. Gladstone, was particularly partial. According to Lloyd George, the old man then got up: "He proceeded to demolish me, to take every feather from me, and as I sat fascinated by the skill and gravity and weight of this extraordinary Parliamentary performance, I couldn't help enjoying it although I was myself the victim."

It was as the champion of Welsh nationalism and Welsh nonconformity and as an extreme Radical that Lloyd George made his first reputation in the House of Commons and in Wales, but his national reputation was made on an issue that could easily have ruined him forever politically. It was his "pro-Boer," or antiwar, position, which he took solely as a matter of conscience. His was an emotional judgment. He hated to see what he considered the persecution of a small people, the Dutch, by the English, as much as he hated the English oppression of the Welsh. Both Welsh and English public opinion favored the Boer War, and he risked his whole career on this issue and even risked his life, for he was nearly lynched in Birmingham for his "pro-Boer" views.

His repartee and invective in the House of Commons against Joseph Chamberlain and the Conservatives also enhanced his reputation. On the issue of protectionist high tariffs versus free trade, which at this moment caused young Winston Churchill to leave the Conservatives and join the Liberals, Lloyd George was particularly acid. When Joseph Chamberlain seemed to find it extraordinary that Lloyd George defended free trade because it had worked so well in the last century, the Welshman said, "Really, is it an objection to a thing that it is old—a thing which has been tried for sixty years and has brought prosperity? Is that not all the more reason for sticking to it? Besides, there are a good many old things that we should not like to see thrown over. The Sermon on the Mount is pretty old—the first great deliverance against the policy of retaliation (Cheers). Mr. Chamberlain says that we must not believe in its principles. He says that they don't work. He says that the jewelers of Birmingham cannot thrive on New Testament lines."

Lloyd George also coupled with an attack on Chamberlain an attack on what was for many years his favorite enemy, "the dukes," saying of Chamberlain's meeting in Glasgow, "It was attended by three dukes, two marquises, three or four earls and as many lords as there were ministerial resignations. Mr. Chamberlain spoke of the day when every working man should have a pig. A few years ago the policy was a few acres and a cow, now it is three dukes and a pig." Both Lloyd George and his audiences enjoyed this kind of attack, and he used it in various forms. In the fall of 1903 he said at Oldham, "Mr. Chamberlain has appealed to the workmen, and there were very fine specimens of the British workmen on his platform. There were three dukes, two marquises, three or four earls. They had gone to help the workman to tax his own bread. The Corn Laws meant high rents for them, and when a statesman of Mr. Chamberlain's position comes forward and proposes a return to the old Corn Law days, lords and dukes and earls and squires all come clucking towards him like a flock of fowls when they hear the corn shaken in the bin."

But Lloyd George's greatest attack on the peers was to come some years after he became a Cabinet Member. In 1905 when Sir Henry Campbell-Bannerman became Liberal Prime Minister, he appointed the Welshman to his Cabinet as President of the Board of Trade. In this first Cabinet appointment, Lloyd George was resolved to do a good job, and he did. Temporarily abandoning his position as chief parliamentary gadfly, he worked seriously and effectively and was most successful, particularly in the settlement of the railway dispute of 1906 and also in the Merchant Shipping Act of that same year. As a result, when Herbert Henry Asquith became Liberal Prime Minister in 1908 he appointed Lloyd George Chancellor of the Exchequer. It was in the post of Chancellor that Lloyd George made his first great effort to change radically the social conditions in England.

In introducing his 1909–1910 Budget, which proposed substantially to increase the income tax and which proposed an unheard-of tax of 20 per cent on the unearned increment in land values, Lloyd George described it as a "war budget" against poverty, which state he hoped might soon become "as remote to the people of this country as the wolves which once infested its forests." Then, as though the Budget itself were not shocking enough to the landed aristocracy and the City, Lloyd George made matters worse by delivering a series of inflammatory speeches, including the famous one in Limehouse. He pointed up the differences between the rich and the poor more clearly than had ever been done before by an English politician. In the slums of East London, on July 30, 1909, he spoke to four thousand of the very poorest citizens of Limehouse about the rapacity of the parasitic landowners living on unearned increases in land value: "Who created these? Who made that golden swan? Was it the landlord? Was it his energy, his brains? . . . It is rather hard that an old workman should have to find his way to the gates of the tomb bleeding and footsore, through the brambles and thorns of poverty. We cut a new path for him—an easier one, a pleasanter one, through fields of waving corn. We are raising money to pay for the new road—aye, and to widen it, so that two hundred thousand paupers shall be able to join in the march."

In addition to this demagogic invective that angered and frightened the peers, Lloyd George could also deliver himself of lighthearted wit about his new tax. In the House he was attacked by a Conservative Member, Mr. Joynson-Hicks, who had been an impecunious lawyer named Mr. Hicks until he married an heiress named Joynson and joined her name to his. When Joynson-Hicks made fun of Lloyd George's phrase "unearned increment," and challenged the Chancellor to explain and define it, Lloyd George at once interrupted to say, "On the spur of the moment I can think of no better example of unearned increment than the hyphen in the right honourable gentleman's name."

The recollection of his unwilling obeisances to his local squire could be felt in Lloyd George's attacks on the aristocrats: "How these dukes harass us. They're as expensive to keep up as a dreadnought and not half so useful." But both the substance of his Budget and his intemperate invective in its behalf were to rouse the peers to a suicidal rebellion. Although virtually all the lords and bankers were equally opposed to his Budget, in his fight for it Lloyd George's most violent personal attack was in a luncheon speech against Lord Rothschild, who had criticized the Budget in a speech in the City. "We are not to have temperance reform in this country. Why? Because Lord Rothschild has sent a circular to the Peers to say so. We must have more Dreadnoughts. Why? Because Lord Rothschild has told us so at a meeting in the City. We must not pay for them when we have got them. Why? Because Lord Rothschild says no. You must not have an estate duty and a super-tax. Why? Because Lord Rothschild has sent a protest on behalf of the bankers to say he won't stand it. You must not have a tax on reversions. Why? Because Lord Rothschild as chairman of an insurance company said he wouldn't stand it. You must not have a tax on undeveloped land. Why? Because Lord Rothschild is chairman of an industrial housing company. You must not have Old Age Pensions. Why? Because Lord Rothschild was a member of a committee that said it should not be done. Are we really to have all the ways of reform, financial and social, blocked by a notice board: 'No thoroughfare: By order of Nathaniel Rothschild'?"

Lloyd George had had a difficult enough time getting his Budget through the House of Commons, where it was the subject of debate for seventy-three days and caused a number of all-night sittings and some five hundred and fifty divisions, but when it reached the House of Lords the attacks on the Budget increased as did Lloyd George's attacks on its attackers. "Who is really on the other side? Lord Curzon unmistakably. . . . Lord Curzon is not a very wise or tactful person. All I would say about him is this—I think he is less dangerous as a ruler of the House of Lords than as a ruler of India. For further particulars apply to Lord Kitchener. . . . Then there is Lord Milner. There is one thing in common between Lords Milner and Curzon; they are both very clever men but they both belong to that class of clever men which has every gift except the gift of common sense. . . . He has a peculiar genius for running institutions and countries into destructive courses."

(A demonstration of how the political sands shift and how little permanent damage is sometimes done by the most bitter invective came when, only a few years later, as Prime Minister, Lloyd George appointed the "not very wise or tactful" Lord Curzon to a number of posts in his Cabinet; and Lloyd George's chief aide at the Peace Conferences in 1918 was the possessor of the "peculiar genius for . . . destructive courses," Lord Milner.)

How good a Budget it really was is seriously open to question today. Left to the ordinary course of events, had it been sent back with some reasonable changes by the Lords to the Commons and then passed by both Houses, it would not likely have changed the course of English history and made Lloyd George's reputation. However, when Joseph Chamberlain from his retirement expressed the hope that the House of Lords would force a General Election on the issue of this Budget, under the leadership of Lord Lansdowne it followed his advice, and in doing so not only made Lloyd George's reputation but also signed its own death warrant. Whether or not the English voter understood the novelties and intricacies of the Budget, one thing he clearly understood was that he did not want the hereditary House of Lords to have the power to veto legislation passed by the elective House of Commons. The election was, therefore, a great defeat for the House of Lords, and the new Parliament introduced immediately legislation to preclude the blocking of the will of the Commons again. Although the death of the King, the desertion of the Irish Members, and the advent of the First World War delayed the legislation and agreements that now limit the power of the House of Lords, their real beginnings were in this struggle over the Lloyd George Budget.

In the years between his first Budget and the outbreak of the First World War, Lloyd George continued, as Chancellor of the Exchequer, to address himself to the improvement of social conditions by means of legislation; and he obtained passage of the first National Health Insurance bill and the first unemployment Insurance bill. His invective in the House was rarer for a time, though when the Duke of Devonshire characterized the policy of the Government's "Disestablishment Bill" as "robbery of God," Lloyd George noted that the foundations of the Duke's fortune were "desecrated shrines and pillaged altars." "Look at the story of the pillage of the Reformation. They robbed the Church, they robbed the monasteries, they robbed the almshouses, they robbed the poor, and they robbed the dead. Then they come here, when we are trying to recover some part of his pillaged property for the poor, to whom it was originally given, and they venture, with hands dripping from the fat of sacrilege, to accuse us of the robbery of God."

But during these years Lloyd George's speeches were limited somewhat by what was known as "the Marconi Affair." He had invested a thousand pounds in shares of the American Marconi Company at the same time as British postal authorities were discussing a contract with British Marconi; and although it is clear that he was ill advised rather than venal, and he received a vote of confidence from the House of Commons after the entire matter was fully investigated, Lloyd George was censured· by many, and for a time his public image was hurt.

As do all great men, Lloyd George had his blind spots. One of these was his failure correctly to appraise the threat of Imperial Germany in the years before the First World War. Though Winston Churchill had earlier had the same mistaken point of view, he had changed it, and now that he was at the Admiralty, he was strong for preparedness. Lloyd George in introducing the Budget of 1913 noted the "very startling . . . total of one hundred and ninety-five million pounds," and said much of it was caused by "panics and nightmares." He compared these to the wasteful preparations fifty years earlier against a feared attack by France at a time when in truth Napoleon III wanted nothing from England but her friendship. As late as New Year's Day of 1914 he was quoted in the *Daily Chronicle* as saying that British relations with Germany were infinitely more friendly than they had been for years.

But once war came, Lloyd George threw himself into the war effort with all his characteristic energy and eloquence, and some of his public appeals to the people of England have an inspirational quality similar in spirit, if not in style, to those that Winston Churchill would deliver a quarter of a century later. At Queen's Hall, on September 19th, Lloyd George said: "It is a great opportunity, an opportunity which comes only once in many centuries to the children of men. For most generations sacrifice comes in drab guise and weariness of spirit. It comes to you to-day as to all of us, in the form of the glow and thrill of a great movement for liberty, that impels millions throughout Europe to the same noble end. We have been living in a sheltered valley for generations. We have been too comfortable and too indulgent,—many, perhaps, too selfish,— and the stern hand of fate has scourged us to an elevation where we can see the everlasting things that matter for a nation—the great peaks we had forgotten of Honour, Duty, Patriotism, and clad in glittering white, the towering pinnacle of Sacrifice pointing like a rugged finger to Heaven. We shall descend into the valleys again, but as long as the men and women of this generation last they will carry in their hearts the image of those mighty peaks whose foundations are not shaken, though Europe rock and sway in the convulsions of a great war."

As Chancellor of the Exchequer for the first ten months of the war, it was Lloyd George's job to put England's war finances on a sound basis, and he did it well. Then the increasing scandal of lack of preparedness and equipment for the British Army caused the break-up of the Liberal Government on May 19, 1915, and the formation of the first Coalition Government of Asquith and Bonar Law. A Ministry of Munitions, separate from the War Office of Lord Kitchener, was created and given to Lloyd George. Here was a Herculean task that suited the Welshman. England's production of arms was suitable only for a peace-time army, and Lord Kitchener wanted a two-million-man army and sufficient weapons for it. Lloyd George rapidly increased the production of both weapons and high-explosive shells. Indeed, he was accused of overpreparing when he budgeted not for fifty or seventy but for a hundred divisions. Continued charges of overbuilding and over-production led to the appointment by the Cabinet of a committee to investigate the accusations. At the end of the committee's meeting, Lloyd George's secretary observed, "I suppose, sir, that means the end of your program." "No," snapped Lloyd George, "it means the end of the committee." Indeed large as Lloyd George's orders for munitions were, they were invariably for less than the professional soldiers finally called for.

Once his program for the Ministry of Munitions was established, Lloyd George increasingly tried to influence the conduct of the war in areas that were the responsibility of Lord Kitchener at the War Office. The Welshman's efforts, however, were not successful. It was Asquith's view that military decisions must be left to professional soldiers.

Kitchener's policies were also attacked in the newspapers of Lord Northcliffe, of whom Lloyd George once said, "I would as soon rely on a grasshopper . . ." But even Lord Northcliffe's attacks could not dislodge the obsessively secretive hero-general. Kitchener complained that the reason he hated to tell anything to politicians was that they all repeated what they heard to their wives, except for Asquith, who repeated it to other people's wives.

Lloyd George fought for compulsory military conscription and forced it through the Asquith Cabinet. Then, in June of 1916, Lord Kitchener died, and Lloyd George became Secretary for War. He was faced that autumn with the collapse of Imperial Russia. Lloyd George became increasingly disillusioned with Asquith as a war leader, and increasingly convinced that he and he alone could win the war. He therefore proposed a three- or four-member War Committee with extraordinary powers. Lloyd George further proposed that he should be a member of the Committee but that the Prime Minister should not. Asquith refused, and in December of 1916 Lloyd George broke with him. In the resultant change of government, Lloyd George became Prime Minister.

Although he appointed a Cabinet, he ran his own show completely. His treatment of his Foreign Secretary, Lord Curzon, was so peremptory and curt that Lord Swinton once said to Lloyd George, "If you treated me even half as badly as you treat Curzon, I'd resign tomorrow morning." Lloyd George replied: "Oh, but he does resign, but there are two messengers at the Foreign Office. One has a limp; he comes with the resignation. The other was a champion runner; he always catches him up."

It was as wartime Prime Minister that Lloyd George reached the highest point of his career and popularity, and was able to bring about many of the changes he had urged unsuccessfully as a member of Asquith's Cabinet. In 1918 he finally realized his desire for a unified Allied Command, and this, against all British military tradition, under a foreigner, Marshal Foch of France. His powers of persuasion were also brought to bear on his American allies. He convinced Woodrow Wilson to send over American troops before they were fully trained, to meet the German reinforcements flooding the Western Front after the fall of Russia.

As the head of the British delegation to the Peace Conference in 1919, his success was more open to question. Consideration of elective politics at home affected his policies abroad. As the head of a wartime Coalition Government with no opposition, Lloyd George had possessed more absolute power than any ruler in England since Cromwell. There is no doubt that this non-opposed government under his leadership was effective when the only objective of every citizen, regardless of party, was winning the war. Although he wanted a General Election, there having been none since 1910, Lloyd George hoped to continue the Coalition to work out not only conditions for peace but also the rebuilding of England into "a country fit for heroes to live in," where "inhuman conditions and wretchedness must surrender like the German Fleet." Argument can be made against a government with no opposition even in time of war, when the only objectives are survival and victory, but in peacetime certainly the manner in which a country is to be governed must be argued freely by those seeking to govern.

Lloyd George sought to continue his Coalition Government by promising to each group what it wanted, ignoring the conflicts created by such promises. Nowhere was this clearer than in his attitude on how defeated Germany should be treated. He began with a point of view not far removed from that of President Wilson: "no annexations, no contributions, no punitive damages." But to remain as head of a Coalition Government he was increasingly forced to adopt the "hang the Kaiser" and "make Germany pay" point of view of many British voters as expressed by Sir Eric Geddes: "We will get everything out of her [Germany] that you can squeeze out of a lemon and a bit more. . . . I will squeeze her until you can hear the pips squeak."

Although in the beginning the Peace Conference was attended by representatives of all thirty countries that had helped defeat the Central Powers, there was a gradual reduction to ten, then five, then four, and finally only three. These were Lloyd George of Great Britain, who wanted a peace of conciliation; Georges Clemenceau of France, who wanted a peace of victory and revenge; and Woodrow Wilson of the United States, who wanted the New Jerusalem.

An interesting insight into the other two architects of the Peace Treaty which followed "the war to end all wars" may be had by reading a few examples of their wit. "The Tiger" Clemenceau was once approached by a friend, Dubost, who was seeking the Presidency of the French Republic and of whom it was being widely said he was too stupid. He complained to his old friend Clemenceau, "They are saying everywhere that I am only an imbecile—but I am no more stupid than another. . . ." Whereupon Clemenceau asked, "Which other?" He was also merciless toward members of his own Cabinet, and once remarked, "Why should it be my fate to have as my Minister of Finance the only Jew in France who knows nothing about finance?" When he was asked why he didn't get Ministers of greater quality to serve in his Cabinet, he replied, "Geese, not eagles, saved the Capitol." Clemenceau once interrupted a speech of Jean Jaurès in the Chamber of Deputies, saying, "All the same, you are not God." "And you," replied Jaurès, "are not the Devil." Clemenceau then asked, "How do you know?"

Clemenceau has been called the villain of Versailles. J. M. Keynes said that Clemenceau saw European history as "a perpetual prize fight, of which France had won this round, but of which this round is certainly not the last." At least he was clear on what he wanted: the best, toughest trade he could make for France with what he thought was the best possible insurance against future German aggression. He was, after all, a skeptical realist who said, "War is too important to leave to the Generals."

Clemenceau expressed his skeptical view of the French and their politics when he said, "How beautiful the Republic was under the Empire." Of the Versailles negotiations, he remarked that although God Almighty had been satisfied with Ten Commandments, Wilson required Fourteen Points. His view of Wilson and Lloyd George is best reflected in his comment to a friend who criticized the Treaty, "Well, it was the best I could do, seated as I was between Jesus Christ and Napoleon Bonaparte."

Woodrow Wilson, too, had an extraordinary and, at times, biting wit, concerning his fellow politicians, himself, and even the difficulties he had both abroad and at home with the Versailles Treaty and the League of Nations. His fellow Princetonian, Adlai Stevenson, tells a story of when Wilson was Governor of New Jersey, he received a phone call from Washington advising him that his good friend, a United States senator from New Jersey, had just died. Wilson was so shocked that he canceled all appointments and sat at his desk, stunned. Within a few minutes of receiving the bad news, he had a phone call from a New Jersey politician who said bluntly, "Governor, I would like to take the Senator's place." Wilson said nothing for a moment, and then replied, "Well, you may quote me as saying that's perfectly agreeable to me if it's agreeable to the undertaker."

Serious as Wilson was about his theories that governments should represent the ethnic makeup of the governed, he could say to Prime Minister Orlando of Italy, who was urging that inasmuch as the population, the language, and the institutions of Fiume were overwhelmingly Italian, Italy's claim to Fiume was indisputable, "Mr. Prime Minister, do you know that if you advanced that same argument with respect to New York City you could claim a sizable piece of Manhattan Island?" Concerning Wilson's decision to oppose the cession of Fiume to Italy, Colonel House asked him, "But, Mr. President, aren't you afraid the Senate will be indignant when it learns of your decision?" Wilson replied, "I suppose it will, as soon as it finds out where Fiume is located."

Wilson's dream of the millennium was brought to nothing by his inability to convince either the Congress or the American people that the United States should join the League of Nations. An excellent piece of congressional invective occurred after Henry Cabot Lodge had made his last great speech in the Senate against the League and it was evident that Wilson and the Democrats were defeated. It remained to the Democratic Whip, Senator Thaddeus Caraway of Arkansas, to say something in reply. Caraway rose and said, "I have long heard of the reputation for wisdom and wit of the Senator from Massachusetts, but his speech today has convinced me that his mind is like the land of his native state, barren by nature and impoverished by cultivation."

Lloyd George, too, had some acid opinions of the leaders of his former allies. He described Wilson as "this extraordinary mixture of real greatness thwarted by much bitterness," and said of Poincaré and Briand, "Poincaré knows everything and understands nothing—Briand understands everything and knows nothing." In his book *My Political Life*, L. S. Amery recalls, "At the first discussion with Lloyd George, Clemenceau complained that our Admiral, Calthorpe, had accepted the Turkish surrender when, by pre-war agreement, the French Navy was supposed to be in command in the Mediterranean. This was too much for Lloyd George who flared up: 'What have you French ever done in the war against the Turks, whom we have beaten single-handed, except to attach half a battalion of niggers to Allenby to see that he didn't steal the Holy Sepulchre?'"

But Lloyd George's best wit and ridicule were reserved for English politicians. His gift for characterizing his opponents was at once a source of admiration and of fear. He described Lord Gladstone, the son of the former Prime Minister, as "a pygmy posturing before the footlights in the robes of a giant," and Reginald McKenna as "a ready reckoner, a competent arithmetician, a banker in blinkers" (whereas it was said of Lloyd George, with considerable truth, "he uses figures as adjectives").

Lloyd George's most bitter abuse was directed at Liberals who defected from the party, for, although he could be tolerant of political apostasy when it brought Winston Churchill from the Tory to the Liberal benches, when Liberals defected, whether they actually joined the Tories or merely called themselves by another name, such as National Liberal, and voted with the Tories, they brought down upon themselves the full fury of Lloyd George's oratorical wrath. When Sir John Simon crossed the floor of the House of Commons and sat with the Tories, although he called himself a National Liberal, Lloyd George delivered himself of one of the most devastating attacks that had been heard in the House for many years: "My orthodoxy to Liberalism has been questioned but the right honourable gentleman has been the milk of the Gospel to Liberalism and it is as if there are two types of men in this world, those who drink and those who do not, and it is as if the right honourable gentleman has been a total abstainer all his life and has suddenly taken to drink and there he is; he swayed from side to side and landed amidst the Tory drunkards. The right honourable gentleman has sat for so long on the fence that the iron has entered into his soul. Now, Mr. Speaker, there have been many honourable and right honourable gentlemen greater than the right

"THE CHEF."
Too many Broths don't spoil this Cook.

DAVID LLOYD GEORGE
(Copyright, *Punch*, London)

FRANKLIN DELANO ROOSEVELT
(Culver Pictures, Inc.)

honourable gentleman who have crossed the floor of this House and have done so out of conviction, but never has an honourable or right honourable gentleman crossed it before and left behind him such a slimy trail."

Lloyd George said of Sir Herbert Samuel, who had been a Minister in the Liberal Government of 1906 and whom he appointed High Commissioner in Palestine (and who then came back and attacked Lloyd George at the time of the split in the Liberal Party), "The right honourable gentleman has suggested I have some peculiar animus against him. Nothing could be further from the truth. I gave him his first, his greatest, his most distinguished, his most appropriate promotion. I made him the first Procurator of Judea since Pontius Pilate."

When Alfred de Mond had annoyed Lloyd George by becoming a semi-Tory, the Welshman said, "I seized him by the tail, but it came off in my hand." When a former Tory decided to call himself an Independent, and came to Wales to stand for Parliament against a friend of Lloyd George, the latter made a speech at a political meeting in Wales in which he started off very quietly: "There was a man called Jack Jones and his wife, whose name was Mary. They kept a flock of sheep and they had a very difficult time as they hadn't much money. One day they bought a sheep dog. It was a beautiful dog, but to their horror it turned out to be a killer. So they said to each other, 'What can we do?' At last Mary said, 'The only thing to do is to change his name and sell him.' So they changed his name. *But he was a killer just the same!*" The so-called Independent, needless to say, was soundly defeated.

Perhaps the greatest possible tribute to Lloyd George's wit, and at the same time a tribute to his first wife, to whom he had so often been unfaithful, was her laughing at the breakfast table over her husband's stories and saying to his friends, with tears running down her face, "You wouldn't think I should laugh so at his jokes after all these years, would you? But I can't help it."

Lloyd George was called everything from a "little Welsh solicitor" and the "cad of the Cabinet" to "half pantaloon and half highwayman" and "a modern Jack Cade." Asquith said of both Lloyd George and Winston Churchill that they thought with their mouths, and Margot Asquith said of Lloyd George, "He could not see a belt without hitting below it." Stanley Baldwin applied to him Carlyle's description of a contemporary: "He spent his whole life in plastering together the true and the false and therefrom manufacturing the plausible" and in his *Essays in Biography*, Keynes wrote, "How can I convey to the reader, who does not know him, any just impression of this extraordinary figure of our time, this syren, this goat-footed bard, this half-human visitor to our age from the hag-ridden magic and enchanted words of Celtic antiquity? One catches in his company that flavour of final purposelessness, inner irresponsibility, existence outside or away from our Saxon good and evil, mixed with cunning, remorselessness, love of power, that lends fascination, enthralment and terror to the fair-seeming magicians of North European folklore."

Lord Attlee recalls that in the House Lloyd George was being constantly interrupted by a Labor Member, named Davy Kirkwood, sitting across the gangway, who sometimes encouraged and sometimes abused him, and that once Lloyd George stopped to say, "I'll make a bargain with my honourable Friend. I'll do without his applause and I'll do without his criticism." Whereupon another Member, Mr. Campbell-Stephen, interrupted, "But you never keep your bargains."

The only time anyone remembers Lloyd George really bested in the House was in an exchange with Wedgwood Benn, the father of the present Member who has had such difficulty renouncing his title in order to serve in the House of Commons. Lloyd George had never forgiven the short, lively Benn for deserting him to join the Socialist Government. To understand the savor of Benn's remark, it must be remembered that Lloyd George sold peerages to a much greater extent than any other Prime Minister and that he kept the fortune so amassed, the so-called "Lloyd George Chest," for his own political use, sitting on it rather than turning it over to the Liberal Party. Also, Lloyd George was thought by some to enjoy most particularly the company of the very rich. One day in the House of Commons, pointing his finger at the tiny Benn, Lloyd George spoke derisively of "This little pocket Moses who is going to lead the peoples to the New Jerusalem." Benn, quick as lightning, jumped up and said, "Anyhow, I have never bowed down to the Golden Calf."

As also holds true for most politicians today, Lloyd George was frequently required to attend public banquets, then as now not the most entertaining way to spend an evening, and sometimes these got on his nerves. Always somewhat vain, Lloyd George was once introduced by a chairman who said, "I had expected to find Mr. Lloyd George a big man in every sense, but you see for yourselves he is quite small in stature." Lloyd George answered: "In North Wales we measure a man from his chin up. You evidently measure from his chin down."

Lloyd George lost popularity by supporting the Greeks in their fight against Turkish rule, and England nearly became involved in the war. Driven by the Sinn Feiners to use force in Ireland, as had his most illustrious predecessors, Lloyd George lost the Labor Members of his Coalition Government. When with the help of his Colonial Secretary, Winston Churchill, he made the Irish settlement giving southern Ireland Dominion Home Rule, the Tories left, and his Coalition Government broke up in October of 1922.

His own Liberal Party fell apart, with so many Liberals going over to the Labor Party during the twenties that the Labor Party (Socialists) replaced the Liberals as the official Opposition Party. The number of Liberal Members of Parliament has continued to fall, until today there are only six.

Lloyd George continued to serve in the House of Commons, and his personal prestige was great in spite of his vanished power. His last great attack was on Neville Chamberlain after the outbreak of the Second World War. In the past he had said of Chamberlain that he "saw foreign policy through the wrong end of a municipal drainpipe" and that he might make "an adequate Mayor of Birmingham in a lean year." In May of 1940, in the House of Commons, Leopold Amery had hurled at Chamberlain, Cromwell's brutal words to the Long Parliament, "You have sat too long here for any good you have been doing. Depart I say, and let us have done with you. In the name of God, go!" Chamberlain appealed to his friends to stand by him, and Lloyd George said, "It is not a question of who are the Prim Minister's friends. It is a far bigger issue. He has appealed for sacrifice. The nation is prepared for every sacrifice so long as it has leadership, so long as the government show clearly what they are aiming at, and so long as the nation is confident that those who are leading it are doing their best. . . . I say solemnly that the Prime Minister should give an example of sacrifice, because there is nothing that can contribute more to victory in this war than that he should sacrifice the seals of office." The effect of this attack was so great that many Tory Members stayed in their seats at the division and refused to vote in the Government Lobby. Even though Chamberlain still had a majority, he resigned, making it possible for Winston Churchill to form his wartime Coalition Government.

It was the cause of considerable surprise and comment

when on December 31, 1944, the "cottag-bred boy" who had hurled so much abuse at "the dukes" and who had so curtailed the power of the peers in the House of Lords accepted a peerage and became Earl Lloyd George of Dwyfor. Less than three months later, on March 26, 1945, he died at Llanystumdwy where his uncle had raised him.

He has been described by Field Marshal Smuts as "the supreme architect of victory in the First World War." The leader of Great Britain in the Second World War, Winston Churchill, said of Lloyd George, "When the English history of the first quarter of the twentieth century is written, it will be seen that the greater part of our fortunes in peace and in war were shaped by this one man." But perhaps the best that can be quoted about the Welshman are other words of Winston Churchill, spoken in the House of Commons they both loved and served so well. Churchill always enjoyed provoking the House by speaking in such a way that his opening remarks would excite the Members to shouts of disapproval, whereupon he would make it clear that his point of view was one with which most of them agreed. Two days after Lloyd George's death, Churchill was speaking of him in the House, and said, "Presently Lloyd George had seized the main power in the state and the leadership of the government." Many honorable Members shouted "Seized?" and Churchill continued, "Seized. I think it was Carlyle who said of Oliver Cromwell, 'He coveted the place, perhaps the place was his.'" And the honorable Members cheered.

VII

Franklin Roosevelt's Dog

Joking and humor are pleasant, and often of extreme utility.

Cicero, *De Oratore*

There are many examples of wit that influenced the election of candidates or the enactment or rejection of specific legislation both in Great Britain and in the United States. But no other example so clearly affected the history of the world as the "Fala" portion of the speech Franklin Delano Roosevelt made on September 23, 1944, to open his campaign for a fourth term as President of the United States.

Any evaluation of Roosevelt as a political wit is difficult for two reasons. First, because, according to his friends, associates, and biographers, including both Professor Arthur Schlesinger, Jr., and Professor Frank Freidel, Roosevelt was not in any sense a creative wit in the tradition of Randolph, Disraeli, and Churchill. He enjoyed the wit of others, but he created little humor himself, except for the practical jokes he loved and a certain rather heavy-handed sarcasm that, except in a President, would not even be remembered. He had, however, both a very keen appreciation of the wit of others and of the effect of wit on the electorate, and as the consummate politician of this century in America, he made superb use of the opportunities for ridicule offered by the errors of his opponents. Second, Roosevelt was the first great leader who consistently used words, ideas, and entire speeches written by other men. Therefore, what was his wit and what was written for him is sometimes difficult to determine.

In his extraordinary book, *Working with Roosevelt,* Judge Samuel I. Rosenman, who was Roosevelt's chief speech writer from 1928 until the President died in 1945, discussed fully the need for and methods used by a speech writer. When the President must deliver literally thousands of messages, both oral and written, from major speeches to the opening of the annual Red Cross campaign, no one man can do this and still attend to the other business of the Presidency. Roosevelt, therefore, used a large number of speech writers, including, besides Rosenman, Harry Hopkins, Robert E. Sherwood, Raymond Moley, Rexford G. Tugwell, Hugh Johnson, Thomas G. Corcoran, Ben Cohen, Adolphe A. Berle, Jr., William Bullitt, Donald Richberg, Stanley High, Archibald MacLeish, Dorothy Thompson, and Louis Howe. In addition, hundreds of ideas, drafts, and parts of speeches came both by request and unsolicited from a wide variety of people both in and out of government, some not even American citizens.

Judge Rosenman points out again and again that Roosevelt, at least in the major speeches, so corrected, amended, and changed what was written for him that it became "his own." Rosenman also says that the regular speech writers came to know what the President liked, and automatically wrote in his style.

Many of the same people whom Roosevelt used to write his speeches also contributed their ideas on how the government in 1932 could cope with the problems of the depression. Roosevelt made use of such Columbia professors as Moley, Tugwell, Rogers, Berle, McGoldrick, and McBain, and when Louis Howe referred with contempt to this "brains trust," a new term in American politics was born. A number of such phrases that came to be thought of as Roosevelt's creations were, in fact, not. Rosenman, for example, states that he wrote the sentence in the acceptance speech that Roosevelt delivered at the Democratic Convention in Chicago on July 2, 1932, "I pledge you, I pledge myself, to a new deal for the American people." The two words came to symbolize an entire epoch in American history. According to Rosenman: "I had not the slightest idea that it would take hold the way it did, nor did the Governor when he read and revised what I had written. In fact, he attached no importance to the two monosyllables." Two other expressions used by Roosevelt, and much quoted as typically his, were "economic royalists" and "a rendezvous with destiny." The first was suggested by Stanley High, the second by Tommy Corcoran. The expression "I hate war," so often quoted by mimics of Roosevelt, who also attempted to imitate his Dutchess County accent, was suggested to Roosevelt by William Bullitt, who had heard it from Woodrow Wilson in 1917.

"Arsenal of democracy" was a phrase first used by Jean Monnet of France in conversation with Justice Felix Frankfurter, who was so taken with it that he convinced Monnet not to use it any more, but rather to let the President use it, which Roosevelt did in 1940.

Roosevelt clearly saw himself as the savior of the democratic system and private enterprise in America at a time when they were being replaced in many parts of the world by dictatorship and absolute state control of the economy, as in Italy and Germany. He therefore tremendously enjoyed ridiculing the American Liberty League types who attacked him as the destroyer of the American constitutional system and the American economy. "In the summer of 1933, a nice old gentleman wearing a silk hat fell off the end of a pier. He was unable to swim. A friend ran down the pier, dived overboard and pulled him out; but the silk hat floated off with the tide. After the old gentleman had been revived, he was effusive in his thanks. He praised his friend for saving his life. Today, three years later, the old gentleman is berating his friend because the silk hat was lost." (This "silk hat" story was Roosevelt's own, and an example of his method of injecting his own wit into a speech prepared for him by others.)

Quoting Macaulay, Roosevelt said, "The voice of great events is proclaiming to us: 'Reform if you would preserve.' Wise and prudent men—intelligent conservatives—have long known that in a changing world worthy institutions can be conserved only by adjusting them to the changing time. . . . I am that kind of conservative because I am that kind of liberal."

Roosevelt throughout his Presidency continued to ridicule his opponents who said he was destroying the American system, when in fact he had saved it. He particularly enjoyed making fun of the big businessmen who had been the most frightened in the early 1930's. In a campaign speech in Chicago on October 14, 1936, he said: "Some of these people really forget how sick they were. But I know how sick they were. I have their fever charts. I know how the knees of all of our rugged individualists were trembling four years ago and how their hearts fluttered. They came to Washington in great numbers. Washington did not look like a dangerous bureaucracy to them then. Oh, no! It looked like an emergency hospital. All of the distinguished patients wanted two things—a quick hypodermic to end the pain and a course of treatment to cure the disease. They wanted them in a hurry; we gave them both. And now most of the patients seem to be doing very nicely. *Some of them are even well enough to throw their crutches at the doctor.*"

Roosevelt was particularly attentive to criticism and to rumors and jokes about himself and his family; he enjoyed making use of them for his own ends. The most effective example of his doing so was the "Fala" speech, but he did it often both in speeches and in press conferences. He loved to joke with the newspapermen. Sometimes he combined his banter with the press with his tendency to poke fun at his associates. In 1932, when he was Governor of New York and had been nominated the presidential candidate of the Democratic Party at their Chicago Convention, he decided it would make excellent publicity to accept the nomination at the Convention instead of waiting, as candidates traditionally did, for representatives of the Convention to bring him word of his nomination. In addition, he decided to go to the Convention by airplane, which had never been done before. When a trimotored plane arrived at the airport in Albany, the reporters suspected it was for Roosevelt. According to the Associated Press story of June 29, 1932, he was asked if the plane was to take him to Chicago. "He only laughed. 'Now, I'll tell you what I'm going to do,' he said with pretended seriousness. 'I'm going to bicycle out to Chicago.

" 'I'm going to get one of those quintets—you know, five bicycles in a row.

" 'Father will ride in the first seat and manage the handlebars. Jim will ride second, then Elliott, then Franklin Jr., and then John.

" 'Sam [referring to Supreme Court Justice Samuel I. Rosenman] will follow —on a tricycle.' "

In 1937 there were already rumors of his planning to run for a third term in 1940. At a Democratic dinner on March 4, 1937, at the Mayflower Hotel in Washington, he humorously took advantage of these third-term rumors to make the point that, despite opposition from certain members of the Congress and the Supreme Court, he wanted to move ahead with his program. "A few days ago, a distinguished member of the Congress came to see me to talk about national problems in general and about the problem of the Judiciary in particular.

"I said to him: 'John, I want to tell you something that is very personal to me—something that you have a right to hear from my own lips. I have a great ambition in life.'

"My friend pricked up his ears.

"I went on: 'I am by no means satisfied with having twice been elected President of the United States by very large majorities. I have an even greater ambition.'

"By this time, my friend was sitting on the edge of his chair.

"I continued: 'John, my ambition relates to January 20, 1941.' I could feel what horrid thoughts my friend was thinking. So in order to relieve his anxiety, I went on to say: 'My great ambition on January 20, 1941, is to turn over this desk and chair in the White House to my successor, whoever he may be, with the assurance that I am at the same time turning over to him as President, a nation intact, a nation at peace, a nation prosperous, a nation clear in its knowledge of what powers it has to serve its own citizens, a nation that is in a position to use those powers to the full in order to move forward steadily to meet the modern needs of humanity—a nation which has thus proved that the democratic form and methods of a national government can and will succeed. . . .'"

According to Judge Rosenman, "The President had a lot of fun dictating that passage. We who heard him dictate it to Grace [Grace Tully, Roosevelt's secretary] were a little nonplussed ourselves as he began talking about not being satisfied with having been elected twice. He had even more fun delivering it to a hushed audience. The Congressman 'John' was about the same kind of character as the garage mechanic and the other assorted characters who, according to his speeches and press conferences 'visited' the President from time to time to discuss problems—and give him a chance to explain in a homely, conversational way some point he wanted to bring home."

Roosevelt took full advantage of both radio and the newspaper wire services to appeal directly to the people, and, like Churchill, despite his aristocratic accent, he established an extraordinary rapport with them, especially through his so-called Fireside Chats. Like Lincoln, Roosevelt often illustrated his point with a homely story that was also amusing. According to Robert E. Sherwood, one of Roosevelt's speech writers and one of the most successful playwrights of the day, "That man would be one of the best actors on our stage with his fine sense of timing and the way he can modulate his voice and change his expression." Roosevelt loved making his audiences laugh, and was well aware of the happy effect on the electorate of his own famous smile.

Roosevelt knew that his audiences expected attack and humor from him, and when he found a good example of either that went over well with an audience he was inclined to repeat it. In Madison Square Garden, in the 1940 campaign, he pointed out that the Republicans, rather than foreseeing the world crisis, had opposed him at every turn, and he singled out for mention three Republicans who had opposed his repeal of the embargo and whose names he had arranged in a particularly rhythmic cadence, "Martin, Barton and Fish." The audience so enjoyed it that the President continued in other speeches to list the three culprits, and soon the moment he said, "Martin," his audience joined in and shouted, "Barton and Fish"! At this time Bruce Barton was running for the United States Senate from New York, and the first time Roosevelt used the expression, Barton said, "I'm licked if he keeps it up." His prediction was correct, and even Willkie is said to have remarked that this phrase effectively hung around his neck the isolationist and reactionary voting record of the three Republican congressmen thus immortalized.

In this campaign Willkie was cursed with the endorsement of John L. Lewis, the head of the coal miners, and also the American Communists, who attacked Roosevelt because of his anti-Hitler position when the Hitler-Stalin Pact was still in effect. Roosevelt characterized this as an "unholy alliance" and attacked it both seriously and humorously. "There is something very ominous in this combination that has been forming within the Republican party between the extreme reactionary and the extreme radical elements of this country.

"There is no common ground upon which they can unite —we know that—unless it be their common will to power, and their impatience with the normal democratic processes to produce overnight the inconsistent dictatorial ends that they, each of them, seek. . . .

"We all know the story of the unfortunate chameleon which turned brown when placed on a brown rug, and turned red when placed on a red rug, but who died a tragic death when they put him on a Scotch plaid. We all know what would happen to Government if it tried to fulfill all the secret understandings and promises made between the conflicting groups which are now backing the Republican party."

In this same speech there is an example of Roosevelt's picking up an unfortunate statement by an obscure Republican and turning it to his own advantage (as he was to do four years later in his "Fala" speech). A Republican lawyer in Philadelphia had said in a speech, "The President's only supporters are paupers, those who earn less than $1200 a year and aren't worth *that*, and the Roosevelt family." The statement had been quoted by Arthur Krock in his column in the *New York Times*. Roosevelt quoted the sentence and then said, "I think we might just as well forget the Roosevelt family, but these Americans whom this man calls 'paupers,' these Americans who, in his view, are not worth the income they receive, small though it is—who are they?

They are only millions and millions of American families, constituting a very large part of the nation! They are only the common men and women who have helped build this country, who have made it great, and who would defend it with their lives if the need arose.

" 'Paupers' who are not worth their salt—there speaks the true sentiment of the Republican leadership in this year of grace."

Roosevelt had one man in his Cabinet, Harold Ickes, whose gift for invective is worth noting. Willkie, a prominent corporation lawyer, was being characterized by his supporters as the simple country-boy messiah come to save the Republic. Ickes called him "the rich man's Roosevelt; the simple, barefoot boy from Wall Street." It was also Ickes who announced, "Dewey has thrown his diaper in the ring," and who is supposed to have damaged Dewey's candidacy appreciably with his remark that Dewey looked "like the little man on top of the wedding cake." When there was disagreement between members of the government, Roosevelt tried to settle things humorously. When Henry Morgenthau, the Secretary of the Treasury, and Harold Smith, the Director of the Budget, were at each other's throats, Roosevelt sent a memorandum to Judge Rosenman, which the latter showed to both combatants, thereby ending hostilities.

> *Memorandum for S.I.R.*
> Get Harold Smith, usually known as "Battling Smith," into a room with the Secretary of the Treasury, usually known as "Sailor Morgenthau," lock them in and let the survivor out.
>
> F.D.R.

There was a good deal of humorous byplay between Roosevelt and his speech writers. For example, Roosevelt had been much plagued by his opponents who quoted from a speech he had made on October 19, 1932, in Pittsburgh.

In this speech, Roosevelt had promised to reduce government expenditures and, of course, he had done the opposite in his efforts to fight the depression. In the 1936 campaign the President asked Judge Rosenman to write a speech "explaining" the 1932 speech. After studying the earlier speech, Rosenman suggested, "Mr. President, the only thing you can say about that 1932 speech is to deny categorically that you ever made it."

On another occasion in 1936, his speech writers tried a joke on the President that backfired on them. In a certain section of a speech that urged the voters not to be intimidated by threats from their employers, after a sentence reading "In the polling booth we are all equals," they added the sentence "In the polling place, as in the men's room, all ιι en are peers." When Roosevelt came to Hyde Park he invited his aristocratic mother to have tea with him and began reading the speech to her. As he approached the page with the addition, his speech writers became more and more embarrassed and, finally, before he reachcd it, one silently rose and pointed to the sentence. The President smiled, more, one suspects, at the discomfort of the writers than at the joke itself, and skipping the offending sentence, continued to read the speech to his mother.

The President enjoyed disgressing from his prepared speeches and ad-libbing, which distressed his speech writers who, knowing that every word uttered by the President of the United States was studied and analyzed around the world, had carefully checked every word with the State Department, War, and Navy departments, and other appropriate agencies. The writers, therefore, formed a "Society for Prevention of Ad-Libbing" from which Roosevelt was regularly expelled when he spoke extemporaneously and regularly readmitted on his promise—never kept—not to do so in the future.

No American President has been more criticized in the

press on every score than was Roosevelt. The President
made reference to this humorously on various occasions,
including one reference to newspapermen who attacked
America's military strategy. "I can say one thing about
these plans of ours: They are not being decided by the
typewriter strategists who expound their views in the press
or on the radio.

"One of the greatest American soldiers, Robert E. Lee,
once remarked on the tragic fact that in the war of his day
all the best generals were apparently working on newspapers instead of in the Army. And that seems to be true in
all wars."

When he ran for a third term in 1940, Roosevelt and his
entire family were subjected to obscene personal abuse, and
his continuance in office was widely viewed with alarm. At
a Jackson Day Dinner on January 8, 1940, the President said
". . . There are, of course, some people—in addition to the
political viewers-with-alarm—who always look on the dark
side of life. There are some who complain that things are
not as they were once, and who firmly believe that everybody who disagrees with them is a moron or a crook. They
belong, it seems to me, to the type of unfortunate individual
—and almost every family has one of them—the unfortunate
individual of whom it is said 'he is enjoying bad health.'
(*Laughter*)

"Sometimes when I listen and listen to people like that I
can better understand old Uncle Jed."

[The President then proceeded to tell the following story
in an excellent New England accent that showed no trace
of his famous Dutchess County accent.]

" 'Uncle Jed,' said Ezra, one day, 'ben't you gittin' a leetle
hard of hearin'?'

" 'Yes,' said Uncle Jed, 'I'm afraid I'm gittin' a mite deef.'

"Whereupon Ezra made Uncle Jed go down to Boston, to
see an ear doctor.

"Uncle Jed came back. And Ezra asked what happened. 'Well,' said Uncle Jed, 'that doctor asked me if I had been drinkin' any. And I said, "Yes, I been drinkin' a mite."

"'And then that doctor said, "Well, Jed, I might just as well tell you now that if you don't want to lose your hearin' you've got to give up drinkin'."

"'Well,' said Uncle Jed, 'I thought it over; and then I said, "Doc, I like what I've been drinkin' so much better than what I've been a-hearin', that I reckon I'll jest keep on gittin' deef!"'" (*Laughter*)

The greatest political speech Roosevelt ever made was on September 23, 1944, at the Statler Hotel in Washington, D.C., where he opened his campaign for a fourth term before a dinner of the International Brotherhood of Teamsters. Months before, Roosevelt had confided to Paul Porter, the Publicity Chairman of the Democratic National Committee, that he intended to open the campaign there, saying, "Paul, you know I have a sentimental attachment for the teamsters, and besides [making gestures of applause] they have such *big* hands."

Roosevelt needed to make a great speech that night, one that would either address itself to the two great issues of that campaign or distract public attention from them. The two issues were, first, whether any man should be four times President of the United States and, second, the issue of his own health and strength. Throughout the country there was growing concern about Roosevelt's health, and his last public address at the Puget Sound Navy Yard in Bremerton had increased that concern, for it was halting and indecisive. Following the Bremerton speech there was much talk, and much was written in the press, to the effect that the old man was finished and that young Dewey, by the contrast of his strength and youth, would prove his charge that it was "time for a change" from the government of "tired old men."

Months before, some obscure Republican congressmen had spread the fictitious tale that on his way home from Alaska the President had discovered his Scottie dog, Fala, had been left behind, and sent a United States naval vessel back to retrieve his dog at a tremendous cost in public funds. The story had been repeated in a number of anti-administration newspapers, and Roosevelt, spotting this as a potential political jewel, had immediately forbidden anyone to answer, saying he wanted to save this for himself. Rosenman says that although he and Sherwood both worked on the "Fala" speech, the part on the dog was entirely Roosevelt's and is "the best example of invective in all history. It is not only derisive but funny at the same time and not an attack on an individual but against the whole Republican leadership."

In none of his other speeches were Roosevelt's sense of ridicule, his sarcasm, and his denunciation as effective. He began by indirectly making fun of Dewey's charge that he was "a tired old man." "Well, here we are together again—after four years—and what years they have been! You know, I am actually four years older—which is a fact that seems to annoy some people. In fact, there are millions of Americans who are more than eleven years older than when we started in to clear up the mess that was dumped in our laps in 1933."

As he always loved to do, the President then turned to the subject of labor. "We all know certain people who make it a practice to depreciate the accomplishments of labor—who even attack labor as unpatriotic—they keep this up usually for three years and six months in a row. But then, for some strange reason they change their tune—every four years—just before election day. When votes are at stake, they suddenly discover that they really love labor and that they are anxious to protect labor from its old friends.

"I got quite a laugh, for example—and I am sure you did

—when I read this plank in the Republican platform adopted at their National Convention in Chicago last July:

[He then read the following paragraph in the most pompous and solemn manner.] " 'The Republican Party accepts the purposes of the National Labor Relations Act, the Wage and Hour Act, the Social Security Act and all other Federal statutes designed to promote and protect the welfare of American working men and women, and we promise a fair and just administration of these laws.'

"You know, many of the Republican leaders and Congressmen and candidates, who shouted enthusiastic approval of that plank in that Convention Hall, would not even recognize these progressive laws if they met them in broad daylight. Indeed, they have personally spent years of effort and energy—and much money—in fighting every one of those laws. . . .

"The whole purpose of Republican oratory these days seems to be to switch labels. . . .

"Can the Old Guard pass itself off as the New Deal?

"I think not.

"We have all seen many marvelous stunts in the circus but no performing elephant could turn a handspring without falling flat on his back."

He went on to ridicule charges against him of not preparing for war. "There were some—in the Congress and out—who raised their voices against our preparations for defense—before and after 1939. . . . We now remember the voices. They would like to have us forget them now. But in 1940 and 1941—my, it seems like a long time ago—they were loud voices. . . .

"What the Republican leaders are now saying in effect is this: 'Oh, just forget what we used to say, we have changed our minds now—we have been reading the public opinion polls about these things and now we know what the American people want.' And they say: 'Don't leave the task of making the peace to those old men who first urged it and who have already laid the foundations for it, and who have had to fight all of us inch by inch during the last five years to do it. Why, just turn it over to us. We'll do it so skillfully—that we won't lose a single isolationist vote or a single isolationist campaign contribution.' "

The Republicans had been saying that the depression of the early thirties was a Democratic depression, so Roosevelt said, ". . . although I rubbed my eyes when I read it, we have been told that it was not a Republican depression but a Democratic depression from which this nation was saved in 1933—that this Administration . . . is responsible for all the suffering and misery that the history books and the American people have always thought had been brought about during the twelve ill-fated years when the Republican party was in power.

"Now, there is an old and somewhat lugubrious adage that says: 'Never speak of rope in the house of a man who has been hanged.' In the same way, if I were a Republican leader speaking to a mixed audience, the last word in the whole dictionary that I think I would use is that word 'depression.' "

He now came to defending his dog in the portion of his speech that he had written himself at the second Quebec Conference and sent down to Rosenman to be inserted. The President assumed a serious tone and mien that he maintained throughout the paragraph, despite the laughter and applause of his audience. "These Republican leaders have not been content with attacks on me, or my wife, or on my sons. No, not content with that, they now include my little dog, Fala. Well, of course, I don't resent attacks, and my family doesn't resent attacks, but Fala *does* resent them. You know, Fala is Scotch, and being a Scottie, as soon as he learned that the Republican fiction writers in Congress and out had concocted a story that I left him behind on the Aleutian Islands and had sent a destroyer back to find him —at a cost to the taxpayers of two or three, or eight or twenty million dollars—his Scotch soul was furious. He has not been the same dog since. I am accustomed to hearing malicious falsehoods about myself—such as that old, worm-eaten chestnut that I have represented myself as indispensable. But I think I have a right to resent, to object to libelous statements about my dog."

The effect, not only on the audience at the Statler but throughout the country, was extraordinary. The President's health as an issue in the minds of the voters disappeared, and thereafter, throughout the campaign, they believed Roosevelt to be the same witty, virile fighter he had always been. Even the issue of the fourth term was forgotten in the pleasure of seeing the old man "pour it on."

Instead of ignoring the "Fala" speech, Dewey made the mistake the next day of changing his prepared speech and attacking the President for being humorous about his dog while our boys were dying. Indeed, Dewey was so upset by the fantastic success of the "Fala" speech that Paul Porter wrote a memorandum that ended, "We have a new slogan in headquarters now—the race is between Roosevelt's dog and Dewey's goat." Aware of the impact the "Fala" joke had made on the public, Porter made a radio spot of just that part of the President's speech, introduced it with the tune "They Gotta Quit Kickin' My Dawg Aroun'," and spent an important percentage of the Democratic funds playing the spot on radio.

That the "Fala" speech distracted American voters from the Fourth-term issue is proved by the fact that although Roosevelt was reelected, the voters subsequently approved an amendment to the Constitution precluding any man from being more than twice elected President.

That the "Fala" speech distracted the voters from the state of the President's health is proved by the election returns. That the gods were not so distracted is proved by the fact that five months after the election returns were known, Franklin Delano Roosevelt was dead.

VIII

Winston Churchill

> Jesting often cuts hard knots more effectively than gravity.
>
> Horace, *Satires*

Although it is too early yet to be sure, the consensus seems to be that the greatest political figure of the twentieth century will have been Sir Winston Leonard Spencer Churchill. Almost weekly, events in the news confirm the prophetic vision in many but by no means all of his views, and any review of his life leads to the conclusion that he is the hero of the age. We cannot immediately address ourselves to his wit and invective, which, like everything else about him, were of heroic proportion, without first pointing out that he was primarily and instinctively a fighter and that all his other qualities, including his wit, served him in that role. He loved a good fight, and recognized this strong instinct in himself. "I have a tendency, against which I should, perhaps, be on my guard, to swim against the stream."

He came by it naturally enough, descended as he was from John Churchill, the First Duke of Marlborough. However, one need go no further back than his father, Lord Randolph Churchill, of whom Sir Winston wrote an excellent and worshipful biography, to find a fierce fighter. Lord Randolph's propensity to attack not only Gladstone and the Liberals but also "the old gang," as he called the Front Bench Members of his own Conservative Party whom he considered to have atrophied, earned for himself and three of his associates the satirical name of "The Fourth Party." The most famous of his virulent attacks on Gladstone made particular fun of the latter's well-known habit of chopping down trees on his estate at Hawarden. It was delivered in the House of Commons on January 24, 1884, and gives us a clear idea of the genesis of his famous son's ability to employ invective. "Vanity of vanities, says the preacher, all is vanity. Humbug of humbugs, says the Radical, all is humbug. Gentlemen, we live in an age of advertisement, the age of Holloway's pills, of Colman's mustard and of Horniman's pure tea, and the policy of lavish advertisement has been so successful in commerce that the Liberal Party with its usual enterprise has adapted it to politics. The Prime Minister [Gladstone] is the greatest living master of the art of personal political advertisement. Holloway, Colman and Horniman are nothing compared with him. Every act of his, whether it be for the purposes of health or recreation or of religious devotion is spread before the eyes of every man, woman and child in the United Kingdom on large and glaring placards. For the purposes of an autumn holiday, a large transatlantic steamer is specially engaged. The Poet Laureate adorns the suite and receives a peerage as his reward and the incidents of the voyage are luncheon with the Emperor of Russia and tea with the Queen of Denmark. For the purposes of recreation he has selected the felling of trees and we may usefully remark that his amusements like his politics are basically destructive. Every afternoon the whole world is invited to assist at the crashing fall of some beech or elm or oak. The forest laments in order that Mr. Gladstone may perspire and full accounts of these proceedings are forwarded by special correspondents to every daily newspaper every recurring morning. For the purposes of religious devotion, the advertisements grow larger. The parish church at Hawarden is insufficient to contain the thronging multitudes of fly catchers who flock to hear Mr. Gladstone read the lessons of the day and the humble parishioners are banished to hospitable Nonconformist tabernacles in order that mankind may be present at the Prime Minister's renderings of Isaiah or Jeremiah or the book of Job . . ." Lord Randolph went on to speak of Gladstone's well-publicized practice of giving chips from the trees he felled to his visitors. "Is not this, I thought to myself as I read the narrative, the perfect type and emblem of Mr. Gladstone's government of the Empire? The working classes of this country in 1880 sought Mr. Gladstone. He told them that he would give them and all the other subjects of the Queen much legislation, great prosperity and universal peace and he has given them nothing but chips. Chips to the faithful allies in Afghanistan, chips to the trusting native races of South Africa, chips to the Egyptian fellah, chips to the British farmer, chips to the manufacturer and the artisan, chips to the agricultural labourer, chips to the House of Commons itself. To all who lean upon Mr. Gladstone, who trusted in him and who hoped for something from him, chips, nothing but chips, hard, dry, unnourishing, indigestible chips."

Lord Randolph's sudden resignation from the Cabinet post he had waited so long to obtain turned out to be political suicide, and there seems to be no doubt that his son's driving ambition was in large measure to make up for the failure of his father to reach the success his talents deserved but from which his sometimes erratic behavior precluded him.

Winston Churchill was born on November 30, 1874, in the great palace of Blenheim built by his illustrious military ancestor in Oxfordshire. He did remarkably badly at Harrow and succeeded in gaining entry to Sandhurst, the British West Point, only on his third attempt. Here he was somewhat more successful, was graduated, received his commission, and saw active service in India with the Malakand Field Force in 1897 and the Tirah Expeditionary Force in 1898. He was also attached to the 21st Lancers, and took part in one of the most famous charges in English history at the Battle of Omdurman. Churchill wrote two excellent books on his soldiering and then took off to South Africa as a correspondent for the *Morning Post,* covering the Boer War. He was taken prisoner by the Boers after fighting them, contrary to the rules for correspondents, and later escaped from prison. Churchill always felt that a first-hand knowledge of active soldiering was necessary to men if they were to make useful military judgments at high levels. His also served him as a basis for his answer in Parliament some years later to Colonel Kenyon-Slaney. When Churchill, although a Tory, argued against Tory policy, the colonel called him a "traitor." Churchill answered, "I have noticed that when political controversy becomes excited, persons of choleric dispositions and limited intelligence are apt to become rude. If I was a traitor, at any rate I was fighting the Boers in South Africa when Colonel Kenyon-Slaney was slandering them at home. I had the honor of serving in the field for our country while this gallant fire-eating colonel was content to kill Kruger with his mouth in the comfortable security of England."

Having been successful as a soldier, a correspondent, and a writer, Churchill decided to enter Parliament, and was elected as a Conservative Member for Oldham in 1900. His maiden speech was introduced with borrowed wit. On his third day in Parliament, when he was waiting to make his first effort, the young Lloyd George rose before Churchill was due to speak and made a violent impromptu oration. Churchill did not know what reference to the Welshman to make when the latter should sit down. A fellow Tory, Mr. Thomas Gibson Bowles, suggested the mot that Churchill used and that is still quoted as typical of Churchill. Lloyd George gave way when Churchill rose, and the neophyte remarked of the honorable Member for Carnarvon Boroughs, "Instead of making his violent speech without moving his moderate amendment, he had better have moved his moderate amendment without making his violent speech." Although on this occasion Churchill did not credit Mr. Bowles, he did many years later in the Budget Debates of 1929 when Churchill again attacked Lloyd George, calling him "the Happy Warrior of Squandermania." He criticized Lloyd George's proposals for conquering unemployment through large-scale public works, saying, "The detailed method of spending the money has not yet been fully thought out, but we are assured on the highest authority that if only enough resource and energy is used there will be no difficulty in getting rid of the stuff. This is the policy which used to be stigmatised by the late Mr. Thomas Gibson Bowles as the policy of buying a biscuit early in the morning and walking about all day looking for a dog to give it to. At any rate, after this, no one will ever accuse the right hon. Gentleman of cheap electioneering."

As it seems to have been for many great men who go into politics, party loyalty was a problem for Churchill. Almost immediately after his first being elected to Parliament, he began to outrage his own Conservative Party by his independent views in favor of free trade, and once, in the session of 1903, all his fellow Conservatives left the Chamber in a body when he rose to speak. A fellow Conservative at this time expressed the feelings of the party by informing the House that beriberi had broken out in South Africa, and implied that Churchill had caught it: "I made that remark because I have heard that the most characteristic symptom of the disease is a terrific swelling of the head." In 1904, when his Conservative Leader, Joseph Chamberlain, tried to return to strong protectionist policies, Churchill, who had once remarked, "Mr. Chamberlain loves the working man, he loves to see him work," crossed the floor of the House

of Commons and joined the Liberals. This was only the
first of a number of changes of political party that Churchill
made. He was first a Tory, then a Liberal, then a Coalition
Liberal, then a Constitutionalist, and finally a Tory again.
Because of these shifts, which were always matters of conscience rather than ambition, he suffered much criticism
and endured periods of political ostracism. After his first
change from Tory to Liberal, he served as an Under-Secretary for the Colonies, and then, in 1908, at the age of thirty-
three, as President of the Board of Trade, and from 1909
to 1911 as Home Secretary. In 1911 he was made First Lord
of the Admiralty, and in 1914, when the First World War
broke out, the Navy was ready. Of Lord Charles Beresford,
one of his chief critics at this time, Churchill said, "He can
best be described as one of those orators who, before they
get up, do not know what they are going to say; when they
are speaking, do not know what they are saying; and, when
they have sat down, do not know what they have said."

In spite of his fine work as First Lord of the Admiralty,
Churchill was forced to resign when the Gallipoli campaign
failed in 1915. After serving briefly as Chancellor of the
Duchy of Lancaster, he went to France for more active
duty as a soldier, returned to the House of Commons in
1916, and in the following year was made Minister of
Munitions by Lloyd George. Secretly and on his own initia-
tive he developed and put into production the tank, a new
weapon, that according to the German General Luden-
dorff, helped appreciably in bringing victory to the Allies.
In 1919 Churchill was made Secretary for War, and Air
Minister. He was violently criticized for encouraging the
White Russians against the Bolsheviks. Always an outspoken enemy of Communism, he had early defined it as
"A ghoul descending from a pile of skulls," and his contempt for English Socialists was also shown early when he
said "They are not fit to manage a whelk stall."

He lost his seat in Parliament in 1922, and for two years concentrated on writing and painting. Then, changing parties again in 1924, he returned to the House as an independent Constitutionalist. In 1925 he rejoined the Tories after an absence of twenty years, and Stanley Baldwin made him Chancellor of the Exchequer. The government used the presses and staff of the *Morning Post* during the General Strike of 1926 to produce a newspaper they called the *British Gazette* so that the public would have at least some news, and Churchill was put in charge of it. When he was accused of partiality in reporting on the General Strike, he replied, "I cannot undertake to be impartial as between the Fire Brigade and the fire." An excellent example of Churchill's use of wit to relax the House of Commons occurred in 1927. The government had introduced a bill that allegedly crippled trade-union activities, and it was being bitterly opposed by the Labor Members. The debate had provoked such a state of tension, that an explosion appeared imminent. At the very height of the tension, Churchill, who was then Chancellor of the Exchequer, rose and looking quite his fiercest, said in his deepest voice, "I give you this warning; that if you unleash on us another General Strike . . ." and he paused and glowered, "we shall unleash on you . . ." and he paused, and there was general uproar at this unexpected ministerial threat, until he finished ". . . another *British Gazette*." Both sides roared with laughter, and the tension subsided.

Churchill fell out with Baldwin after the fall of the Conservative Government in 1929, and from then until 1940 he was only a private Member of the House, outspokenly critical of all governments, whether that of the Socialist Ramsay MacDonald or that of the Conservatives Stanley Baldwin and Neville Chamberlain. His was a lone voice crying out for rearmament and against appeasement. No better examples of Churchill's invective exist than those

directed against Ramsay MacDonald, whom Churchı̣
described on January 21, 1921, as "the greatest living maᴢ
of falling without hurting himself," when MacDonalᴅ
government lost vote after vote, but no one else had enough
votes to replace him. But Churchill's best attack was in the
House on January 28, 1933, when he said of MacDonald,
"I remember, when I was a child, being taken to the celebrated Barnum's Circus, which contained an exhibition of
freaks and monstrosities, but the exhibit on the programme
which I most desired to see was the one described as 'The
Boneless Wonder.' My parents judged that that spectacle
would be too revolting and demoralising for my youthful
eyes, and I have waited fifty years to see the Boneless Wonder sitting on the Treasury Bench."

Churchill said of the Baldwin-Chamberlain governments, "They are decided only to be undecided, resolved
to be irresolute, adamant for drift, solid for fluidity, all
powerful for impotence." Speaking in the House of Commons on March 14, 1934, against British pressure on the
French to reduce their army, he said, "The Romans had a
maxim, 'Shorten your weapons and lengthen your frontiers.'
But our maxim seems to be 'Diminish your weapons and
increase your obligations.' Aye and diminish the weapons
of your friends." In 1938 he wrote in an article, "We have
never been likely to get into trouble by having an extra
thousand or two of up-to-date aeroplanes at our disposal.
. . . As the man whose mother-in-law had died in Brazil
replied, when asked how the remains should be disposed of:
'Embalm, cremate, and bury. Take no risks.'" But he could
also make fun of himself, as when he remarked on being
invited by the Chamberlain Cabinet to meet von Ribbentrop, the German Ambassador, "I suppose they asked me
to show him that, if they couldn't bark themselves, they
kept a dog who could bark and might bite." When it was
learned that von Ribbentrop had actually attended a meet-

ing of the Chamberlain government in the Foreign Office on the same day that Hitler invaded Austria, Wedgwood Benn commented, "The only parallel I can think of for this would be if Napoleon had turned up at the Ball on the eve of Waterloo." Churchill wrote in *While England Slept,* "Dictators ride to and fro upon tigers which they dare not dismount. And the tigers are getting hungry."

After the declaration of war with Germany in September of 1939, Chamberlain appointed Churchill to his old post at the Admiralty. As the war continued to go badly, it became more and more obvious that public confidence rested only in Churchill. In May of 1940, after the attacks of Amery and Lloyd George, Chamberlain resigned, and Churchill took over, forming a Coalition Government.

It is hard now to remember how black things looked in those days and how much the courageous words and demeanor of Churchill inspired the people of Great Britain to fight. He told the House of Commons, on May 13, 1940, "I would say to the House, as I said to those who have joined this Government, 'I have nothing to offer but blood, toil, tears and sweat,' " and, "victory at all costs, victory in spite of all terror, victory however long and hard the road may be; for without victory there is no survival." On June 4, 1940, he said in the House, "We shall not flag or fail. We shall fight in France, we shall fight on the seas and oceans, we shall fight with growing confidence and growing strength in the air, we shall defend our island, whatever the cost may be, we shall fight on the beaches, we shall fight on the landing grounds, we shall fight in the fields and in the streets, we shall fight in the hills; we shall never surrender." In the House on June 18, 1940, he said, "Let us therefore brace ourselves to our duties, and so bear ourselves that, if the British Empire and its Commonwealth last for a thousand years, men will still say: 'This was their finest hour.'" Perhaps most moving of all were his words to the boys of Harrow on October 29, 1941. "Do not let us speak of darker days; let us rather speak of sterner days. These are not dark days: these are great days—the greatest days our country has ever lived; and we must all thank God that we have been allowed, each of us according to our stations, to play a part in making these days memorable in the history of our race."

But even in those "sterner days," Churchill also spoke words of humor and wit. In a radio broadcast to the French people on October 21, 1940, he said, "We are waiting for the long-promised invasion. So are the fishes."And in his speech to the Canadian Parliament on December 30, 1941, he said, "When I warned them [the French Government] that Britain would fight on alone whatever they did, their Generals told their Prime Minister and his divided Cabinet: 'In three weeks England will have her neck wrung like a chicken.' Some chicken! Some neck!"

The Prime Minister continued to joke on the serious subject of a possible German invasion of England. When he announced in 1943 that church bells would no longer be reserved for use as a warning in the event of invasion, and was asked at Question Time in the House of Commons what alternate plan had been devised, he said, "Replacement does not arise. I cannot help thinking that anything like a serious invasion would be bound to leak out."

It had been agreed that for the duration of the war there would be no General Elections. (Churchill in forming his Coalition Government had taken as his Deputy Prime Minister, Mr. Clement Attlee, the leader of the Socialist Party.) But there were a few Members of Parliament who felt that criticism of the government should continue. Perhaps some of these criticized because of personal dislike for members of the government, or envy, or because they lacked advancement, and some, because of party habit. But most felt a real conviction in their criticism, and hoped it would better the conduct of the war, as, for example, when Aneurin Bevan in 1943 characterized the Allied Command's approach to the conquest of Italy as being "like an old man approaching a young bride—fascinated, sluggish and apprehensive." Even Churchill's greatest admirers admit that, like all human beings, he made mistakes and that, like most human beings, he disliked critics who pointed them out. These inevitable mistakes, however, if they were to be corrected, not only had to be pointed out by these critics but also had to be made clear enough by them to the Members of Parliament, the British public, or to other Allied leaders so that Churchill should feel pressure, if not to admit error (which he never did), at least to correct his mistake. The problem of criticism of a government in time of mortal danger and of the use of wit and ridicule at such a time against the government has never before in the history of the world been so acute as it was in England during World War II. It is a problem of sufficient importance to be dealt with separately and is, therefore, discussed not here but in the next chapter, which concerns the invective and wit of Churchill's most violent wartime critic, Aneurin Bevan.

Both leaders of the Axis felt the sting of Churchill's contemptuous wit. He said of Mussolini, in April of 1941, "This whipped jackal, who to save his own skin, has made of Italy a vassal State of Hitler's Empire, is frisking up by the side of the German tiger with yelps not only of appetite—that could be understood—but even of triumph." And of Hitler, to whom he referred as "this bloodthirsty guttersnipe," he said in his speech to the American Congress in May of 1943, "In North Africa, we builded better than we knew. For this we have to thank the military intuition of Corporal Hitler. We may notice the touch of the master hand." In September of 1944, in the House of Commons, he remarked, "I always hate to compare Napoleon with Hitler, as it seems an insult to the great Emperor and warrior to compare him in any way with a squalid caucus boss and butcher." Referring again to Hitler as a military leader, he said, "When Herr Hitler escaped the bomb on July 21 he described his survival as providential. I think from a purely military point of view we can all agree with him. Certainly it would be most unfortunate if the Allies were to be deprived in the closing phases of the struggle of that form of warlike genius by which Corporal Schicklgruber has so notably contributed to our victory."

Churchill was asked how, with his long history of consistent opposition to the Bolsheviks, he could, in 1941, when Hitler attacked Russia, advocate support for the Russians. He replied, "If Hitler invaded Hell I would make at least a favorable reference to the Devil in the House of Commons."

Even in dealing with President Franklin D. Roosevelt, to whose judgment Churchill had more than once to defer, he kept his sense of humor. Roosevelt was never as aware of the danger from our Russian allies as was Churchill. He was already too ill to fight point by point with Stalin as Churchill wanted to do, and expressed a hope that the Yalta Conference should last at most only five or six days. In a Minute to President Roosevelt on January 10, 1945, Churchill wrote: "I do not see any other way of realizing our hopes about a World Organization in five or six days. Even the Almighty took seven."

His Minutes to various ministers of his own government all during the war reflect his irrepressible sense of humor. Churchill himself came from a noble family. Although no snob, he was a valiant defender of English traditions when they were meaningful and healthy, but when they threatened the war effort they could inspire such words as these, written on October 7, 1939, at the very beginning of the war, in a Minute to the Second Sea Lord and others: "Will you kindly explain to me the reasons which debar indi-

viduals in certain branches from rising by merit to com-
missioned rank? If a cook may rise, or a steward, why not
an electrical artificer or an ordnance rating or a shipwright?
If a telegraphist may rise, why not a painter? Apparently
there is no difficulty about painters rising in Germany!"
Or he could complain about the poor and slow repair and
servicing of tanks in the Tura Caves near Cairo in *The
Hinge of Fate*: "But I had my tables of facts and figures
and remained dissatisfied. The scale was far from small.
The original fault lay with the Pharaohs for not having
built more and larger Pyramids. Other responsibilities were
more difficult to assign." To the suggestion that the Minister of Defence and Secretary of State for War be renamed
because their titles were illogical, he replied on December
17, 1942, in the House of Commons, "We must beware of
needless innovations, especially when guided by logic."

Churchill had the touch that is rare even, or perhaps
especially, in giants (only Lincoln comes to mind as another example), the ability to make people feel that, with
all his brilliance and genius, he was still one of them, the
quality that made him "good old Winnie." Although his
humor could be subtle, and might contain a learned classical or biblical allusion, it could also be as simple and boyish
as the puns he adored or his reference to Hitler as "Corporal Schicklgruber." This it was that helped to shape the
image the English had of him as one of their own. Whenever he saw an opportunity for a play on a name, he took
it. When Alfred Bossom was making a speech in the House
of Commons, Churchill asked who he was and that the
name be spelled, and then remarked, "Bossom. Bossom.
It's really neither one thing nor the other." He said of the
Greek Prime Minister whose name was Plastiras, "Well,
I hope he doesn't have feet of clay too." Sir Winston is
one of the great creative artists who used the English
language as an artistic medium and many of his creations

have now become such an accepted part of the language
that their authorship is forgotten. But there was always
about him, lurking not far beneath the surface, a certain
boyishness. There was also a deep love for the English
people, which they felt and to which they responded. In
his *Memoirs*, General Lord Ismay, who was Churchill's
staff officer and personal representative on the Chiefs of
Staff Committee, wrote: "Two or three days after he became Prime Minister I walked with him from Downing
Street to the Admiralty. A number of people waiting outside the private entrance greeted him with cries of 'Good
luck, Winnie. God bless you.' He was visibly moved and as
soon as we were inside he dissolved into tears. 'Poor people,
poor people, they trust me and I can give them nothing but
disaster for quite a long time.'" This and the reports of
his fellow M.P.'s of the tears streaming down the face of
the Prime Minister as he inspected the bombed ruins of
his beloved House of Commons constitute as much a part
(though no greater a part) of the whole picture of
Churchill as do his words of wit and his words of courage.

In 1945, after having led his country and, to an important
degree, the entire Allied effort to victory in World War II,
Churchill was put out of office by the voters of Great Britain. From 1945 to 1951 he was leader of Her Majesty's
Loyal Opposition, in which post he more than fully lived
up to his father's injunction, "The duty of an Opposition is
to oppose." In 1951 the Socialists were defeated, the Tories
came back to power, and Churchill once again became
Prime Minister, serving until his resignation four years
later. This time he was for the first time not the Prime
Minister of a Coalition Government but a Conservative
Party Prime Minister, and free to attack the Socialist Opposition. In this postwar decade his wit and his invective
against the Socialists were more biting and more brilliant
than in any other period of his career, and he regularly

lived up to the definition of a gentleman as one who is never unintentionally rude. He still dearly loved to irritate and torment his opponents by his attacks; as he said in the House on May 12, 1952, "I can assure the right hon. Gentleman [Mr. Herbert Morrison] that the spectacle of a number of middle-aged gentlemen who are my political opponents being in a state of uproar and fury is really quite exhilarating to me." At another time Sir Winston dismissed an attack of Morrison's as a "weak, vague, wandering harangue which at no point touched the realities," and he once characterized Morrison, who had been Churchill's able Home Secretary in charge of Civil Defense during the war and was, in 1949, the Deputy Prime Minister and Socialist Leader of the House of Commons, as "a curious mixture of geniality and venom." On another occasion he described Morrison as "a man outpassed at the moment by his competitors, outdated even by his prejudices." As able as Morrison was, he was never a match for Churchill. In the House of Commons on November 11, 1947, the following exchange took place:

SIR WINSTON CHURCHILL: "Mr. Herbert Morrison is a 'master craftsman.'"

MR. MORRISON: "The Right Hon. Gentleman has promoted me."

SIR WINSTON CHURCHILL: "Craft is common both to skill and deceit."

Clement Attlee, who succeeded Churchill as Prime Minister in 1945 and who had been Churchill's Deputy Prime Minister in the Coalition Government throughout the war, often suffered more cruel attack from his own fellow Socialists than from Churchill. However, two of Sir Winston's comments on Attlee have been much repeated. He called Attlee "a sheep in sheep's clothing" and "a modest little man with much to be modest about." When Attlee was Prime Minister, Churchill's Olympian manner suggested that he felt Attlee was still responsible to him, which caused Herbert Morrison to remind Churchill that "another right hon. Gentleman now presides over the Cabinet." To this, Churchill replied, "I am quite willing to recognize the fact—such as it is."

Perhaps his real feeling about Attlee and the Socialists and their evangelistic tone was best expressed at Woodford on October 12, 1951. "Mr. Attlee, speaking of the achievements of his Government, said he was not satisfied with what had been done. Here are his words: 'How can we clear up in six years the mess of centuries?' 'The mess of centuries!' This is what the Prime Minister considers Britain and her Empire represented when in 1945 she emerged honoured and respected from one end of the world to the other by friend and foe alike after her most glorious victory for freedom. 'The mess of centuries'—that is all we were. The remark is instructive because it reveals with painful clarity the Socialist point of view and sense of proportion. Nothing happened that was any good until they came into office. We may leave out the great struggles and achievements of the past—Magna Carta, the Bill of Rights, Parliamentary institutions, Constitutional Monarchy, the building of our Empire—all these were part of 'the mess of centuries.' Coming to more modern times, Gladstone and Disraeli must have been pygmies. Adam Smith, John Stuart Mill, Bright and Shaftesbury, and in our lifetime, Balfour, Asquith and Morley, all these no doubt were 'small fry.' But at last a giant and a Titan appeared to clear up 'the mess of centuries.' Alas, he cries, he has had only six years to do it in. . . . Now the Titan wants another term of office."

Attlee, too, was capable of condensing a political attack into a single sentence readily understandable to any Englishman over the age of eight. Both Prime Minister Stanley Baldwin and his Foreign Secretary, Sir Samuel Hoare, had been educated at Harrow, and at the time of the Hoare-

Laval Pact, or, as Attlee saw it, the betrayal of Abyssinia, Attlee had said in the House of Commons, "It may be true or it may not that the Battle of Waterloo was won on the playing fields of Eton, but it is quite obvious that Abyssinia was lost on the playing fields of Harrow."

When he was asked recently which of all Sir Winston's witticisms was his favorite, the now Lord Attlee said it was Churchill's description of the action of a certain unsuccessful Tory candidate for Parliament who had then turned coat and stood as a Liberal for another House seat, as "the only recorded instance in history of a rat swimming *towards* a sinking ship."

Another favorite Socialist target of Sir Winston was Mr. Hugh Gaitskell, a graduate of Winchester and New College, Oxford, and a lecturer in political economy ·at the University of London. A pedagogue turned politician, a phenomenon not unknown in our own country, Gaitskell entered Parliament in 1945 and by 1947 was already Minister of Fuel and Power in the Socialist Government. He asked Britons as a measure for saving coal to take fewer baths. He told a meeting at Hastings, "I have never had a great many baths myself and I can assure those that have them as a habit that it does not make much difference to their health if they have fewer." Sir Winston's comment on this in the House on October 28, 1947, was, "When Ministers of the Crown speak like this on behalf of His Majesty's Government, the Prime Minister and his friends have no need to wonder why they are getting increasingly into bad odour. I had even asked myself whether you, Mr. Speaker, would admit the word 'lousy' as a Parliamentary expression in referring to the Administration, provided of course, it was not intended in a contemptuous sense but purely as one of factual narration."

Mr. Gaitskell moved on to the Treasury, where his attacks on the English language seemed to upset Sir Winston as much as his attacks on the English economy. Churchill wanted to know why he used "disinflation" for "deflation" and why not then "non-undisinflation"? He complained of the use of such jargon as "the infrastructure of a supranational authority," and explained that "infra" and "supra" were used "by the band of intellectual highbrows who are naturally anxious to impress British labour with the fact that they learned Latin at Winchester." His greatest attack in this vein was delivered at Cardiff on February 8, 1950: "I hope you have all mastered the official Socialist jargon which our masters, as they call themselves, wish us to learn. You must not use the word 'poor'; they are described as 'the lower income group.' When it comes to a question of freezing a workman's wages the Chancellor of the Exchequer speaks of 'arresting increases in personal income.' The idea is that formerly income taxpayers used to be the well-to-do, and that therefore it will be popular and safe to hit at them. Sir Stafford Cripps does not like to mention the word 'wages,' but that is what he means. There is a lovely one about houses and homes. They are in future to be called 'accommodation units.' I don't know how we are to sing our old song 'Home Sweet Home.' [Sir Winston then sang] 'Accommodation Unit, Sweet Accommodation Unit, there's no place like our Accommodation Unit.' I hope to live to see the British democracy spit all this rubbish from their lips."

One of the most remarkable things about Churchill (a Nobel Prize Winner for Literature in 1953, to name only one of his many high intellectual honors) was his ability to appear to his British audiences simply as one of their own and to attach any stigma of intellectualism to his Labor opponents. In a speech at Margate on October 10, 1953, Sir Winston called the Socialists "collective ideologists—those professional intellectuals who revel in decimals and polysyllables."

His efforts to discomfit Gaitskell took various forms.

Once, while Gaitskell was delivering a speech on economic
affairs in the House, Churchill suddenly sat up very straight
on the Opposition Front Bench instead of remaining in his
usual indifferent slouch, but his attention was not on the
speaker. He looked about distractedly, went through all
his pockets, apparently in vain, and then started looking
on the floor of the House. He seemed to be impervious to
the fact that he had by now stolen the interest of all Members on both sides of the House from Gaitskell's speech and
directed it toward himself. When Gaitskell was so
thoroughly rattled that he even lost the thread of his own
speech and hesitated, Sir Winston looked up in surprise and
explained in his famous mumble, "I was only looking for
my jujube." The story was carried in the press under the
headline "The Fall of the Pastille."

Churchill seemed to enjoy his attacks on Gaitskell more
than on any other Socialist, excepting only Aneurin Bevan,
and they were therefore frequent. The Prime Minister said
on July 30, 1952, in the House, in reply to an attack on the
government's economic policies by Gaitskell, "I was surprised to see the right hon. Gentleman the Member for
Leeds (Mr. Gaitskell), standing so smiling and carefree at
the Despatch Box as if he had no responsibility for the
shocking and shameful state to which our finances were
reduced during his tenure of the Exchequer. When a Minister has in a single year brought his country from the best
position it had held since the war to the verge of bank-
ruptcy, and when he has left to his successors heart-tearing
problems to face and solve, I wonder indeed that he should
find nothing to do but mock and jeer at the efforts that
others make to clear up the confusion and disorder that he
left behind him. I almost think it is a pity that he ever
escaped from Winchester."

When Churchill was speaking on the defense situation
on March 5, 1953, the following exchange took place:

THE PRIME MINISTER: "I must now warn the House that I am going to make an unusual departure. I am going to make a Latin quotation. It is one which I hope will not offend the detachment of the old school tie. . . . The quotation is, *Arma virumque cano,* which, for the benefit of our Winchester friends, I may translate as 'Arms and the men I sing.' That generally describes my theme."

MR. HUGH GAITSKELL (Labour): "Should it not be 'man,' the singular instead of the plural?"

THE PRIME MINISTER: "Little did I expect that I should receive assistance in a classical matter from such a quarter."

During the Budget Debates of 1953, Gaitskell had criticized the government's Budget. In Glasgow, Churchill had answered with a biting attack both on Gaitskell and his mentor, Dr. Dalton. As early as 1926 Churchill had said of Dalton, "The hon. Gentleman is trying to win distinction by rudeness," and Dalton, who had been Chancellor of the Exchequer for the Socialists from 1945 to 1947, chose to answer Churchill's Glasgow attack in the House of Commons on April 20, 1953.

MR. HUGH DALTON (Labour): "I am much obliged to the Prime Minister for listening to some of what I have to say. We now return to our public duty of debunking this Budget. This work was well begun by my right hon. Friend the Member for Leeds, South (Mr. Gaitskell), last Wednesday—so well begun that he obviously got under the Prime Minister's skin, as a speech made by the Prime Minister in Glasgow on Friday shows. The Prime Minister used these words of my right hon. Friend: 'This old-school-tie careerist—'"

THE PRIME MINISTER: "It was not correctly reported. I said, 'This old-school-tie-left-wing careerist.'"

MR. DALTON: "That amendment will be helpful to emphasize a comment I shall make in a moment. 'This old-school-tie-left-wing careerist may rightly claim to have

been the worst Chancellor since Mr. Dalton.' I could not let
these words slip past unnoticed today. . . . In these days we
tend to be too polite in political exchanges and I welcome
the robust and straightforward abuse from the Prime Minister, hoping he will not resent counter-attack. 'The worst
Chancellor since Mr. Dalton'—that may be a matter for
argument."

THE PRIME MINISTER: "May I assure the right hon. Gentleman that I did not attempt in any way to set myself up as a
judge of the competition between himself and the right
hon. Gentleman?"

But much of Churchill's best wit and invective was directed not against individual Socialists but rather against
Socialism and Socialist government itself, which he characterized as "government of the duds, by the duds, and for
the duds," and as a kind of government that would vanish
"unwept, unhonoured, unsung and unhung." Sir Winston
expressed his feelings clearly and briefly in Perth on May
28, 1948, when he said, "Socialism is the philosophy of
failure, the creed of ignorance and the gospel of envy." At
Woodford on January 28, 1950, he pointed out sarcastically
an aspect that voters could clearly understand when he
said: "Why should queues become a permanent, continuous feature of our life? Here you see clearly what is in
their minds. The Socialist dream is no longer Utopia but
Queuetopia. And if they have the power this part of their
dream will certainly come true."

His view of socializing industry was expressed in the
House of Commons on November 16, 1948, when he said
of the Labor Government's bill to nationalize steel, ". . . this
is not a Bill, it is a plot; not a plan to increase production,
but rather, in effect, at any rate, an operation in restraint of
trade. It is not a plan to help our patient struggling people,
but a burglar's jemmy to crack the capitalist crib."

But Churchill's deep resentment against the patronizing

aspect of the whole Socialist point of view was best expressed in Edinburgh on May 18, 1950. "In announcing one
of his minor concessions Dr. Dalton said, 'This is an experiment in freedom. I hope it will not be abused.' Could
you have anything more characteristic of the Socialist
rulers' outlook towards the public? Freedom is a favor; it is
an experiment which the governing class of Socialist politicians will immediately curtail if they are displeased with
our behavior. This is language which the head of a Borstal
Institution might suitably use to the inmates when announcing some modification of the disciplinary system. . . .
What a way to talk to the British people! As a race we have
been experimenting in freedom, not entirely without success, for several centuries, and have spread the ideas of
freedom, throughout the world. And yet, here is this Minister, who speaks to us as if it lay with him to dole out our
liberties like giving biscuits to a dog who will sit up and
beg prettily."

In the 1950's, at well over seventy, Churchill was as
formidable a foe as ever, and well aware that his opponents
hoped he would, if not die, at least resign. He delighted,
therefore, in referring to his own age and apparent inde-
structibility, as in this exchange in the House on May 28,
1952:

MR. HAROLD DAVIES (Labour): "Does the right hon.
Gentleman realize that the House is getting less information on the Korean situation than his equally great predecessor Mr. Gladstone was giving the House in the time of
the Crimean War?"

THE PRIME MINISTER: "I am afraid I have not at my
fingers' ends the exact part which Mr. Gladstone took in
the Crimean War; it was even before my time."

This greatest orator of his age even came to use his hearing aid as a weapon in debate. When a Member once tried
to induce him to speak of his retirement, Sir Winston turned

to his son-in-law, Captain Christopher Soames, and asked him to bring him his hearing aid, saying, "I don't want to miss any of this." When the hearing aid arrived, Sir Winston asked the Member, "Would you mind repeating what you've just said?" but of course Churchill gave not the slightest hint of any retirement plans.

Throughout his career Churchill made jokes at his own expense as well as at the expense of others. Aware of how poorly he spoke French, he said in a speech in Paris after the Liberation, "Be on your guard! I am going to speak in French—a formidable undertaking and one which will put great demands upon your friendship for Great Britain." He was at his best when he was criticized in 1948 for some of his past decisions and it was asked how they would look in the long light of history. He said, "For my part I consider that it will be found much better by all parties to leave the past to history, especially as I propose to write that history myself."

With smaller fry in the House, Sir Winston's answers or dismissals were usually more brief and sometimes more mild. They are reminiscent of Carter Glass's famous reply in a party caucus to one of his partisans who shouted, "Give 'em hell, Carter!" which was, "Hell? Why use dynamite when insect powder will do?"

As is so often the case, some of Churchill's best sayings have been his shortest, as when he said of Austen Chamberlain, "He always played the game and he always lost it," or to Wedgwood Benn, who had worked up such a rage that he could not speak, "The hon. Gentleman should not generate more indignation that he can conveniently contain." Lord Birkenhead said that Churchill spent the best years of his life preparing impromptu remarks. That many were prepared in advance there is no doubt. Churchill admitted waiting for months to make a remark to a Socialist Member named Silverman, who was so short that his feet barely touched the floor when he sat in the House. Silverman made a habit of interrupting Churchill, and finally did so several times in one day, whereupon Sir Winston said, "The hon. Member should not be so ready to hop down off his perch." Churchill could be complimentary with his wit, as when he said to A. P. Herbert, after his lively and controversial maiden speech, "That wasn't a maiden speech; it was a brazen hussy of a speech."

Perhaps the most famous of all Winston Churchill's exchanges was one he had with Nancy Astor, whose own reputation for acid wit and instant repartee was considerable. Lady Astor was at a dinner where for a considerable length of time she listened as Churchill expounded views on a great number of subjects, all of them at variance with her own strongly held views. Finally, unable any longer to hold her tongue, she burst forth: "Winston, if you were my husband, I should flavor your coffee with poison." Immediately Churchill answered with the greatest good humor, "Madam, if I were your husband, I should drink it."

Sir Winston's barbs, sometimes mischievous and impish, sometimes deadly, appear in his writing as well as in his spoken words, and some of the best of these are in his *Great Contemporaries* (Putnam's). In it he wrote of the ex-Kaiser, "The defense which can be made will not be flattering. . . . 'Look at him; he is only a blunderer.'" And of Trotsky, "He sits disconsolate—a skin of malice stranded for a time on the shores of the Black Sea and now washed up in the Gulf of Mexico. He possessed in his nature all the qualities requisite for the art of civic destruction—the organising command of a Carnot, the cold detached intelligence of a Machiavelli, the mob oratory of a Cleon, the ferocity of a Jack the Ripper, the toughness of Titus Oates." He wrote of Lenin in *The World Crisis* (Scribner's), "He alone could have found the way back to the causeway. The Russian people were left floundering in the bog. Their worst misfortune was his birth, their next worst—his death." And, "It was with a sense of awe that they [the Germans] turned upon Russia the most grisly of all weapons. They transported Lenin in a sealed truck like a plague bacillus from Switzerland into Russia."

Churchill's judgment of Woodrow Wilson is not far different from that of Lloyd George. Again in *The World Crisis*, he wrote, "The inscrutable and undecided judge upon whose lips the lives of millions hung. . . . He did not truly divine the instinct of the American people. First and foremost, all through the last, he was a party man. The spacious philanthropy which he exhaled upon Europe stopped quite sharply at the coasts of his own country."

One of Sir Winston's frequent targets was the ascetic Sir Stafford Cripps, of whom Churchill said in the House on December 12, 1946, "Neither of his colleagues can compare with him in that acuteness and energy of mind with which he devotes himself to so many topics injurious to the strength and welfare of the State." On another occasion Churchill said that Cripps "delivers his speech with an expression of injured guilt"; but it was Cripps's refusal to enjoy the delights of the table, so important to Churchill, that brought forth the latter's famous remark, "There but for the Grace of God, goes God," which almost equals, "He has all of the virtues I dislike and none of the vices I admire."

One of Churchill's most quoted replies, possibly apocryphal, was to a note from George Bernard Shaw. The playwright enclosed two seats to his new play and invited Churchill to attend the opening night "and bring a friend, if you have one." Churchill regretted that he was otherwise engaged on that evening but asked that Shaw send him two seats to the second performance, "if there is one."

Sir Winston has had a good deal to say about his well-known fondness for alcohol, including, "I have taken more out of alcohol than alcohol has taken out of me." When the end of Lend-Lease demonstrated that in spite of having won a great war, England was still largely dependent on the economic goodwill of the United States, many on both sides of the House resented this dependence. During the debate on the negotiation of further loans which, of course, pointed up this dependence, Churchill, who did not want to be quoted as having taken sides, urged as Leader of the Opposition that his supporters abstain from voting. The Socialist Foreign Minister, Ernest Bevin, commented, "I never thought I would live to see the day when Winston Churchill would be a total abstainer." Even with his King, Churchill was willing to joke about his drinking. One morning when the cold was particularly intense, King George suggested that in view of the inclement weather, a drink might be permissible. Churchill said that he had already taken precautions. "Already?" asked the King. "Yes, Your Majesty," replied the Prime Minister. "When I was younger, I made it a rule never to take strong drink before lunch and now it is my rule never to do so before breakfast."

In the case of all masters of oral invective and wit, we lose much in reading rather than hearing. Much is also lost when we do not see the gestures, the grimaces, and the effects on the audience. In no case is this more true than in Sir Winston's. The famous lisp, the perfect pause, the subtle or sudden change of tone or intonation or timbre, and, above all, the obvious energy must be imagined—the energy that made first-rate writing and consummate political practice insufficient, and demanded additional outlets of polo, piloting, painting, and even bricklaying (sufficiently skillful to earn him union membership). But even on the printed page the wit carries itself, and gives us some understanding of how it helped carry the man through his many trials. Throughout his life, Churchill has been under attack. His span has been so long that toward the end of it, when he was being attacked for being too conservative and reactionary, it was by people who had forgotten or never knew that early in his political career he had been attacked as too liberal and "a traitor to his class" for sponsoring the first English minimum wages in the sweated industries and the first limiting of hours of work. And throughout all the attacks, in the days of failure and ostracism, and during the terrible war years, the humor continued, as, one suspects, it will continue forever.

When Sir Winston was asked on his seventy-fifth birthday if he had any fear of death, he replied, "I am ready to meet my Maker. Whether my Maker is prepared for the great ordeal of meeting me is another matter."

IX

Aneurin Bevan

Wit will shine
Through the harsh cadence of a rugged line.
Dryden, *To the Memory of Mr. Oldham*

At the outset of the Second World War, the government of
Great Britain was given extraordinary powers, and a number of traditional political safeguards were, by agreement
between the two major parties, put aside for the duration
of the war. A Coalition Government was formed with Winston Churchill as Prime Minister. Though it contained a
large number of his former Conservative colleagues, it also
included Socialist members such as Clement Attlee in the
post of Deputy Prime Minister. It was agreed that there
should be no General Elections and that an effort should
be made to maintain the existing balance of power in the
House of Commons between Conservatives and Socialists
by not contesting in by-elections. In the early years of the
war, after the fall of France, there was a very real danger
of invasion, defeat, and occupation by the Germans, and
all these extraordinary measures, of course, were designed
to allow full concentration on the problems of winning the
war.

There was in England during this time a small but reso-
lute group of politicians who felt that even in time of national peril the government should have a real Opposition.
They felt that the democratic system should not be allowed
to atrophy and that the government should not be allowed

to go unquestioned and become dictatorial. They not only believed that such a course would be dangerous in principle but also that it would actually be dangerous to the most effective prosecution of the war. This group included, among others, Emanuel Shinwell and Earl Winterton (who thereby earned themselves the title of "Arsenic and Old Lace"), Leslie Hore-Belisha, Sydney Silverman, Aneurin Bevan, Dick Stokes, George Strauss, Tom Driberg, and Frank Bowles.

Churchill, in 1937 in his *Great Contemporaries,* had condemned George Bernard Shaw's criticism and wit during the First World War. "He was one of my earliest antipathies. . . . He is at once an acquisitive Capitalist and a sincere Communist. He makes his characters talk blithely about killing men for the sake of an idea; but would take great trouble not to hurt a fly. If the truth must be told, our British Island has not had much help in its troubles from Mr. Bernard Shaw. When nations are fighting for life, when the palace in which the jester dwells not uncomfortably is itself assailed, and everyone from prince to groom is fighting on the battlements, the jester's jokes echo only through deserted halls, and his witticisms and condemnations, distributed evenly between friend and foe, jar the ear of hurrying messengers, of mourning women and wounded men. The titter ill accords with the tocsin, or the motley with the bandages."

Even as staunch a Tory admirer of Churchill as Lord Beaverbrook (who served during the Second World War in Churchill's Cabinet) wrote, "Churchill on the top of the wave has in him the stuff of which tyrants are made." When during the Second World War, Sir Percy Harris said that criticism of the government was mandatory even in time of war and constituted the lifeblood of democracy, Churchill's attitude on the subject was again reflected in his answer in the House of Commons on November 12, 1941.

"There was a custom in ancient China that anyone who wished to criticize the government had the right to memorialize the Emperor and provided he followed that up by committing suicide, very great respect was paid to his words and no ulterior motive was assigned. That seems to me to have been from many points of view a wise custom, but I certainly would be the last to suggest that it should be made retrospective."

During the Second World War, Churchill was much more sensitive to criticism directed against himself and his government than before or after it. He could occasionally joke about it, as in 1942 when he said, "When I was called upon to be Prime Minister, now nearly two years ago, there were not many applicants for the job. Since then, perhaps, the market has improved." But in the main he answered his critics with angry invective, scorn, and all the political pressure he could muster.

The chief critic of Churchill during the war, and therefore the chief recipient of Churchill's wrath, was Aneurin Bevan. The wit and invective of Bevan are interesting in their own right as the products of the most brilliant political mind in England in the first half of the twentieth century, excepting only Churchill's. They are also interesting as a study of the place of wit and invective in politics in a time of mortal danger.

Bevan was born on November 15, 1897, in Tredegar, in the Welsh county of Monmouthshire. His father and grandfather were coal miners, and on both sides he came from Nonconformist stock. Like Lloyd George, Bevan had a fierce pride in his Welsh origin, to such a degree, indeed, that he forgot, when he decried "the bovine, phlegmatic Anglo-Saxons," that his mother was English. Unlike Lloyd George, however, Bevan in his youth and early manhood knew real poverty, which left him much more bitter than the older Welshman. His father encouraged Bevan's intellectual interests and his mother enforced economy and discipline in the household. Toward the end of his life Bevan said, "My Methodist parents used to say, 'Have the courage, my son, to say "No."' Well, it takes a good deal of courage, but we shall have to say 'No' more and more, because only by saying 'No' more and more to many things can you say 'Yes' to the most valuable things." Like John Randolph of Roanoke, Bevan was a brilliant nay-sayer, but whereas the Virginian offered no alternatives to what he opposed, Bevan did—Socialism.

One of ten children of whom seven lived, Bevan hated school and the tales of his rebellion against his headmaster include physical violence on both sides. He went to work at the age of eleven as a butcher boy, and the hardship of his youth compared to the luxury of Churchill's was pointed up by himself nearly half a century later in the House of Commons. Churchill mentioned in debate on November 18, 1952, that as Home Secretary in 1911 he had urged legislation fixing the closing hours of shops. Bevan said, "I didn't know until he mentioned it that the right honourable Gentleman, the Prime Minister, was pleading my case when he was making his speech in 1911, because at that time, and for two years previously, I had been a shop assistant working until twelve o'clock on Saturday night and one o'clock on Sunday morning, and I would have been very much more grateful if I had known that he had been so eloquent on my behalf at that time. . . . I went to work when eleven years old for two and six a week, though I may not have been worth more."

As Michael Foot points out in his brilliant biography, when Bevan was just fourteen he went to work in the mines, in the Tytryst colliery, a name that means in Welsh "the House of Sadness." During his seven years in the pits he earned the same reputation as a troublemaker with the Tredegar Iron and Coal Company as he had earned earlier in school. "That bloody nuisance, Bevan," was, by the time he was nineteen, chairman of the lodge of his union and as outspoken in his criticism of the union leadership as he was of the management. He was once told by Stephen Davis, the manager of the Tredegar Iron and Coal Company, "Look here, Bevan, there isn't room in this Company for you and me." Bevan replied, "I agree and I think you ought to go."

In addition to doing a full day's work, Bevan was educating himself by his omnivorous reading, and trying to eliminate his stutter both by reciting poetry and by learning from *Roget's Thesaurus* the synonyms for those words he found most difficult to pronounce. In 1919, on a union scholarship, he went to the Central Labour College in London, where he stayed two years. He considered the time spent at college to have been wasted.

In 1929 he was elected to Parliament from Ebbw Vale, which seat he continued to hold until his death. In his maiden speech he attacked two of the most prominent Members, Winston Churchill and Lloyd George. He characterized Churchill as "the bogey man of the country" and "the entertainer of the House of Commons," and said, "I arrived at the conclusion that his chameleon-like character in politics is founded upon a temperamental disability. He fills all the roles with such exceeding facility that his lack of political stability is at once explained." He was congratulated on the speech by Churchill, who said, "It is so seldom that we hear a real debating speech nowadays."

Bevan's favorite target for many years, however, was Neville Chamberlain, who "looked on the Labour Party as dirt" and who acted as though the unemployed were all idle by choice. Bevan said, "The worst thing I can say about democracy is that it has tolerated the right honourable gentleman for four and a half years." When Chamberlain became Prime Minister after the resignation of Stanley

Baldwin, Bevan said, "In the funeral service of capitalism the honeyed and soothing platitudes of the clergyman are finished, and the cortege is now under the sombre and impressive guidance of the undertaker." He went on, "He [Chamberlain] has the lucidity which is the by-product of a fundamentally sterile mind. . . . He does not have to struggle, like Churchill has, for example, with the crowded pulsations of a fecund imagination. On the contrary he is almost devoid of imagination. . . . Listening to a speech by Chamberlain is like paying a visit to Woolworth's; everything in its place and nothing above sixpence." Bevan did not cease his attacks on Chamberlain even after the latter had been replaced as Prime Minister in 1940 by Churchill, but only after the Man of Munich had left the government entirely.

A close friend of Bevan in his early days as a Member of Parliament was Oswald Mosely, then also a Labor Member. The wealthy and aristocratic Mosely became embittered at the Socialists' timidity when they had attained power, and asked, "What would you think of a Salvation Army which took to its heels on the day of judgment?" His disillusion with the Socialists finally drove him to break with them, and eventually he became the leader of the Fascists in England. Bevan, however, stayed with the Labor Party in spite of his frequent disappointment with its leaders. As he became a well-known Member, he was seen frequently in the luxurious home of Lord Beaverbrook, and was taunted with the title of "*Bollinger* Bolshevik." Bevan enjoyed "slumming in the West End," and even made up his own biblical verse on the subject. "Stand not too near the rich man lest he destroy thee—and not too far away lest he forget thee." However, unlike Ramsay MacDonald and Lloyd George, he never rose out of his class, but always identified himself with the poor, especially with the miners. He looked at all questions in what he called "the passion play of politics" to see if "my class will subsequently be asked to pay the price."

In July of 1932, the *Daily Express* characterized Bevan rather well as "brilliant, bitter, proud, class conscious, boastful of his ancestry and his family . . . [he has] a kind of class consciousness quite as objectionable as it is in the man who boasts of his Norman blood. . . . He can hardly enter a railway train because there is no fourth class. . . ." In his reply to this attack Bevan wrote, "my heart is full of bitterness. For when I see the well-nourished bodies of the wealthy I see also the tired, haggard faces of my own people. . . . there are better reasons for being proud of belonging to the working classes. It is better to have a future than a past." Another portrait of Bevan was his wife's comment, "Nye was born old and died young."

No single thing more outraged Bevan throughout his life than the plight of the miners and the ignoble and penurious legislation enacted supposedly to alleviate their lot, especially the so-called "Means Test." It was on the issue of the miners that he produced his most bitter invective, and sometimes it was moving as well as vitriolic. "One little collier boy fifteen years of age went home to his parents the other day and proudly announced that he had an increase of three shillings a week; the following week the Board reduced the allowance of his unemployed father. This is the modern version of 'Feed my lambs!' What satisfaction it must be to the Chancellor of the Exchequer that he is able to transmute the stunted bodies of white-faced collier boys into dreadnoughts."

His opinion of "the ruling class" in England was not a happy one: "Political toleration is a by-product of the complacency of the ruling class. When that complacency is disturbed there never was a more bloody-minded set of thugs than the British ruling class." Even during the war Bevan would say of the Conservatives that they suffered from "the deepest nostalgia for a dying order, and from nostalgia nothing comes but inertia and self-pity."

His reputation for abuse grew steadily. He said the Minister of Agriculture, Walter Elliot, was "a man walking backwards with his face to the future." When he felt that the Conservatives cared more about the problems of bankers than those of the unemployed, he said to them, "The Tories always hold the view that the State is an apparatus for the protection of the swag of the property owners. . . . Christ drove the moneychangers out of the temple, but you inscribe their title deeds on the altar cloth." His attacks on "the mandarins" of his own party could be as vitriolic as those he unleashed on the Tories, for example, when he urged, "Please don't be deterred in the fanatical application of your sterile logic." Of his fellow Socialist, Walter Citrine, who had what Michael Foot calls a "card-index mind," Bevan said, "poor fellow, he suffers from files."

Of the "juvenile lead," Anthony Eden, Bevan said early in his career, "He is more pathetic than sinister. He is utterly outmatched by his international opponents. Beneath the sophistication of his appearance and manner he has all the unplumbable stupidities and unawareness of his class and type." Bevan's early view of Eden, and the following, written for *Tribune* on January 15, 1943, now seem prophetic from the hindsight of the Suez debacle. "Attractive in the narrow, conventional sense. Always a possibility as a stopgap Prime Minister. League of Nations society at Geneva introduced him to a whole range of ideas strange to a Tory. There he acquired a progressive vocabulary, and this, allied to the amiability that flows from weakness of character, deceives many people into thinking that his political intentions are honourable. Actually there is nothing in his conduct to justify such a conclusion. His resignation from the Government of Mr. Chamberlain over our Italian diplomacy provided him with a balance at the political bank on which he has drawn generously ever since. His behavior during the civil war in Spain proves conclusively that whenever he has to choose between his Tory instincts and his progressive inclinations his instincts can be relied upon to win every time."

Bevan was also inveighed against. Young Harold Macmillan said of him, "He enjoys prophesying the imminent fall of the capitalist system and is prepared to play a part, any part, in its burial, except that of a mute." Churchill called Bevan, among other things, a "Merchant of Discourtesy," a "Minister of Disease," and in need of "psychiatrical treatment."

One of the most bitter attacks ever made on Bevan in the House was by Miss Eleanor Rathbone, who charged Bevan with "a malicious and virulent dislike of the Prime Minister." She said further, "It is with disgust and almost loathing we watch this kind of temperament, these cattish displays of feline malice." Miss Rathbone's attack had been prompted by Bevan's questioning Churchill on the propriety of the latter's son, Randolph Churchill, having written a letter to the *Evening Standard* on a political matter while he was serving with the military. Churchill at the time commented that Bevan's questions had been put "no doubt from those motives of delicacy in personal matters which are characteristic of him."

Bevan's own leaders often ridiculed him. Attlee once said in a debate in the House, "The honourable Member is so adept at pursuing lines, he pursues them so far that he generally finds himself back where he started. He is apt to become airborne in the last five minutes of his speech." "The right honourable Gentleman," Bevan replied, "is usually sunk at the end of his."

Bevan's attacks on Attlee, the leader of the Labor Party and Deputy Prime Minister, were many. "He seems determined to make a trumpet sound like a tin whistle. . . . He brings to the fierce struggle of politics the tepid enthusiasm of a lazy summer afternoon at a cricket match." Bevan characterized Attlee's attitude toward the Coalition Government as "loyal to the point of self-effacement," and when Attlee's memoirs, *As It Happened,* appeared, Bevan said, "It's a good title. Things happened to him. He never *did* anything." Bevan once characterized another leading Socialist, Gaitskell, as "a desiccated calculating machine."

Unlike so many intense politicians of both Right and Left, Bevan was not a pious, self-righteous moralist: "I have never regarded politics as the arena of morals. It is the arena of interests." "Righteous people terrify me. . . . Virtue is its own punishment."

His invective, of course, earned him many enemies, but when his friends urged caution in his attacks on both the Tories and his own Labor Party leaders, he asked, "What do you want me to be, a political gigolo?" To a fellow Member who complained of attending Rotary luncheons and Chamber of Commerce dinners, he said, ". . . you're not an M.P., you're a gastronomic pimp." He constantly criticized the timidity of his own Socialist leaders. "When Labour leaders substitute the role of courtier for that of agitator, they fail at both."

During the thirties Bevan demonstrated all too frequently that he was more frank than tactful. During the Abdication Crisis he was asked by Edward VIII what the reaction of the Socialists would be if he married Mrs. Simpson. The Welshman told the King it would be that of "a typical middle-class woman in Surbiton." Bevan recalled that same evening seeing "a single figure walking up and down under a brilliantly-lit candelabra—tears streaming down his cheeks into his whiskey—Winston Churchill." Churchill said to Bevan, "I never thought the time would come when a Churchill must desert his King." Remembering Marlborough's desertion of King James for King William, Bevan answered, "Oh, it's only the second occasion in history."

Unlike Churchill, Bevan had an unsentimental view of royalty, and saw the abdication merely as another opportunity missed by the Labor Party because of the weakness of its leaders. He wrote, "The gladiators of the parliamentary arena faced each other across the table adorned by the mace, symbol of the authority which was supposed to be in issue. The trembling accents of the Speaker fell into a well of awed silence as he read the Royal message. Surely never have sentiments so meagre been arrayed in language so ennobled by great usage and sanctioned by awful deeds. A mean wine in a goblet of old gold. Here indeed was the past mimed by the ignoble present. 'History repeats itself,' said Marx, 'first as tragedy, second as farce.' And here was farce. The pathetic can never be epic, and there was bathos affecting to speak in accents of the heroic. The Prime Minister [Stanley Baldwin], who has a natural gift for the counterfeit, surpassed himself. He spoke as a pilot who had guided the ship of State safely to harbour through stormy seas, past jagged rocks, and in the teeth of buffeting winds. The winds, indeed, were boudoir hysteria, the rocks threatened to wreck only his own career, and the official Opposition had not blown even a zephyr across his path. But what of that? He was fighting one of the great tourneys of history and he laid about him dauntlessly with his wooden sword. . . . The Labour Party missed a great opportunity. . . . Against the cant and hypocrisy of the Court scandals, the Parliamentary Labour Party should have limned its own message. . . . But from beginning to end of the monarchical crisis it revealed one grave defect. *The Labour Party has too much reverence.*"

In spite of the great wave of popularity that engulfed Churchill in 1940 when he took over as Prime Minister,

Bevan continued to view him as merely, or perhaps all too, human. The Welshman recognized Churchill's qualities, but also saw his weaknesses, and throughout the war criticized the Prime Minister, much to Churchill's annoyance. Considered by many at that time as a near traitor, Bevan now appears to have been substantially correct in many of his criticisms. The changes he recommended to the government, with all the power of his abuse and wit, when made later, proved beneficial to the war effort. The record indicates that many of the changes he demanded even before the war, which were pooh-poohed or worse when he first suggested them, were later made.

On August 24, 1939, Bevan attacked Chamberlain and the "architects of Munich," demanding Chamberlain's resignation: "The suggestion is that people of my constituency, the colliers, the steelworkers and the railwaymen, should offer their bodies as a deterrent to German aggression. There is one man over there [pointing at Prime Minister Chamberlain] you could offer—*offer him.* Let the Conservative Party if it is in earnest call a Carleton Club meeting and get rid of the Prime Minister. He is the man upon whom Hitler relies; he is the man responsible for the situation." These words were condemned and then ignored when Bevan spoke them, and yet they were no more harsh nor were they less true than those spoken nine months later by Amery and Lloyd George, which caused Chamberlain finally to resign. Indeed, they were confirmed by Churchill himself, who said of Chamberlain, "in the depths of that dusty soul there is nothing but abject surrender."

When Churchill took over and formed the Coalition Government, he kept in it men Bevan considered incompetents and Munichites. These included Sir John Anderson, Lord Halifax, Mr. Duff Cooper, Sir Kingsley Wood, and Sir John Reith. Bevan said, "It is not necessary to see the end of the race to know that some of the horses will never see the finish. We were a bit doubtful of them when they came up to the starting post. They looked broken-winded and knock-kneed and some even seemed to have the staggers. . . . The principle of coalition provides the hilt. It is the men who form the blade. We have a strong hilt, but a very blunt blade. It is Mr. Churchill's job to sharpen it quickly." Although Bevan's attack on these members of the government was treated as outrageous, within a few months all those attacked were removed from the government or to other posts in it.

On August 30, 1940, Bevan expressed what remained his point of view throughout the war: ". . . in a democracy idolatry is the first sin. Not even the supreme emergency of war justifies the abandonment of critical judgement. . . . To surrender all to one man is to risk being destroyed by him. That is why dictatorship is at the same time the strongest and the weakest of social systems, and it is one of the main reasons why the Nazis will ultimately fall and the democracies will triumph. The soul of democracy can never be fatally wounded for it is never wholly exposed." He then commented on Churchill's speeches in the late 1930's, which Bevan considered "unsurpassed in the long annals of Parliament. Towards the end of this period he started on those long series of orations about the arming of Germany, the nature of the Nazi menace, and the necessity of collective European action to meet them, which are unrivalled for prophetic insight, for colourful imagery, for felicity of expression, for sardonic humour and biting satire." But, Bevan pointed out, "although he won every debate he lost every division. All the manifold gifts of the first parliamentarian of the time could do nothing against the servile limpets of the Tory party machine." Bevan expressed fear that Churchill might have learned "a dangerous lesson" from those years, that "a party manager, no matter how stupid, was more powerful than any single individual,

no matter how brilliant and accomplished." Bevan expressed
the hope that Churchill would not be tempted "to assume
the tawdry purple [the Conservative Party leadership] now
slipping from Mr. Chamberlain's shoulders. If he does so
he will become the creature of the Tory machine. It would
be a national tragedy and a pitiful twist of personal irony if
the years of exile taught Mr. Winston Churchill the dis-
ciplines of Party obedience just at the moment when we
need the audacities of freedom."

With Churchill's approval, first Duff Cooper and later
Herbert Morrison threatened censorship of the press, including closing down newspapers. Bevan had little admiration for "the arid pages of the 'kept' press," and said, "You
don't need to muzzle sheep." But he fought for freedom of
the press whether for the *Daily Worker* or the *Daily Mirror*.
In the House of Commons he attacked Herbert Morrison,
the Labor Home Secretary, for threatening to close the
Mirror: "I do not like that form of journalism. I do not like
the strip-tease artists. But it is not because the Home Secretary is aesthetically repelled that he warns it. . . . He likes
the paper. [Bevan waved a collection of articles written for
the *Mirror* by Morrison.] He has taken its money." He
then characterized Morrison as "the witch-finder of the
Labour Party, the smeller out of evil spirits."

Both Bevan himself and Sir Stafford Cripps, who was a
member of the Coalition Cabinet, were two of the "evil
spirits" Morrison had sought to exorcise from the Labor
Party, and this attack on Morrison raised havoc in the
House. Morrison rose to defend himself, saying that the
Member for Ebbw Vale was never happier than when he
was having a shot at his friends. Thereupon, Bevan interrupted, "And you are never happier than when you are
attacking your own principles."

Later, at a mass meeting in London that criticized the
government's threats to the *Mirror*, Bevan said, "I have

never met a less judicially minded man than Morrison. He was for years the chief whipper-in of the Labour Party (laughter) and the chief whipper-out (more laughter). Our traditions are too great and too precious to be stolen from us by a little Cockney. I apologize to the rest of the Cockneys (more laughter)."

On another occasion Bevan attacked Churchill directly for calling a secret conference of a group of London newspaper editors, just before a critical debate in the House, and addressing them in "some sort of uniform or other." "I wish he would recognize that he is the civilian head of a civilian Government and not go parading around in ridiculous uniforms" but be satisfied with "ordinary fustian." Bevan maintained that Churchill continued to "rail against the representatives of the press for giving so much space to his critics" and that, considering the Prime Minister's power to suppress newspapers, this constituted "political intimidation without any precedent in the history of this country," and proof of Churchill's "increasing paranoia." But the heart of this attack was the basis of all Bevan's attacks on the Prime Minister: "The time has come when we should make this man realize that the House of Commons is his master."

Members were committed to destroy any notes they took at the secret meetings of the House during the Second World War. Churchill, nevertheless, took notes and published them after the war. We have, therefore, no Hansard against which to check the differences between the Prime Minister's notes and the recollections of his critics as to what happened. Bevan was very critical not only of secret meetings of the House or its committees but also of "the secret diplomacy of Quebec, Teheran, Cairo and Moscow." In this, he held the same point of view as the most conservative Republicans in America, proving again what strange bedfellows politics makes.

Although he had begun by distrusting Parliament, Bevan came to view it as the only possible arena in which his class could achieve its goals, and therefore he fought to uphold the power of Parliament and limit the power of the government. Bevan opposed policies and legislation arrived at in secret party or coalition sessions, and merely brought to the House of Commons for rubber-stamp approval, this to be achieved by party discipline as enforced by the whips. "In this fashion political parties become the enemies of parliamentary democracy. To allow ministers to assume that they need never face hostile criticism in the Commons would help to produce a steady and insidious undermining of the war effort. It is better that Ministers should be embarrassed than that Parliament should die. . . . In Germany democracy died by the headsman's axe. In Britain it can be by pernicious anemia." Bevan wanted to make sure that the House of Commons did not suffer the fate of the Reichstag and become merely the forum where the Prime Minister and his Cabinet announced their orders.

Often he was alone, or nearly alone, in questioning the government's methods or motives, and was characterized as a mere demagogue. This angered him, and he wrote, "apparently it was a greater offence to point out the defects in policy than to be guilty of them." Sometimes his bitterness at being alone and being called by Churchill one of "the naggers and the snarlers" showed in his invective, as when he said to a servile Under-Secretary, "Is it not time that certain members should not act as pimps to the Government every time?"

One of Churchill's greatest strategic errors was his assumption, when Germany attacked Russia, that the Soviets would be defeated in a matter of weeks or, at most, months. Churchill's view was shared by the members of his General Staff but not by Bevan, who correctly saw this as the turning point of the war and constantly called for more aid

"ELEVEN"-LEAGUE BOOTS

WINSTON CHURCHILL
(Copyright, *Punch*, London)

THE OUTCAST

ANEURIN BEVAN

(Copyright, *Punch*, London)

for the Russians and for a Second Front. He criticized
Churchill for his invasion alarmism, and accused him of
crying " 'Wolf, Wolf' at the very moment when the people
can see the wolf engaged in a life and death struggle with
the bear at the other end of the field. The general view is
that the best way to deal with the danger from the wolf is
to give the bear a hand."

Others than Bevan, General Sir Alanbrooke, for example, felt that "Winston never had the slightest doubt
that he had inherited all the military genius of his great
ancestor, Marlborough." The General, Churchill's closest
military adviser, did not share the Prime Minister's view
of himself. He wrote "Perhaps the most remarkable failing
of his is that he can never see a whole strategic problem at
once. His gaze always settles on some definite part of the
canvas and the rest of the picture is lost. It is difficult to
make him realize the influence of one theatre against another. . . . This failing is accentuated by the fact that often
he does not want to see the whole picture, especially if the
wider vision should in any way interfere with the operation
he may have temporarily set his heart on."

Emanuel Shinwell, a Jewish Labor Member, confirms
Churchill's Marlborough complex. When an aide seeking
to influence Shinwell's vote in a forthcoming defense debate said, "You must remember that the Prime Minister is
descended from Marlborough," Shinwell immediately
ended the conversation by saying, "Please be so kind as to
remind him that I am descended from an even older
military leader—Moses."

Sir Stafford Cripps, a Socialist more appreciated by Tory
Churchill than by his fellow Socialists, had been put by
Churchill in his War Cabinet when Cripps's own party os-
tracized him. When in 1942 Cripps suggested that Churchill dominated his Cabinet too strongly, and Churchill
thereupon accepted his resignation, the leaders of the

Labor Party remained silent, but Bevan wrote an article called "The Art of Political Assassination." "The Prime Minister did not take long to make full political use of the renewed prestige which came to him as a result of the victories in North Africa. He used it cynically, brutally and irresponsibly. . . . [Cripps] was . . . ripe for political assassination, and who more likely to drive the dagger home than the master in whose service he had exposed himself? . . . [Forgotten by his own Labor Party] lonely men are easiest murdered." Bevan warned the leaders of his party that if Churchill could change the composition of the Coalition Cabinet at his whim, none of them were safe. "May we suggest that the Labour leaders should read the history of John Churchill, the first Duke of Marlborough? If they do so they may then take the precaution of wearing whatever may be the modern equivalent of the medieval mailed vest."

Even admirers of Churchill can benefit from some of Bevan's insights into the great war leader. "His ear is so sensitively attuned to the bugle note of history that he is often deaf to the more raucous clamour of contemporary life, a defect which his Conservative upbringing and background tend to reinforce. The seven-league-boot tempo of his imagination hastens him on to the 'sunny uplands' of the future, but he is apt to forget that the slow steps of humanity must travel every inch of the weary road that leads there." Bevan said the Prime Minister mistook "verbal felicities for mental inspirations," and was "a man suffering from petrified adolescence." "He always refers to a defeat as a disaster as though it came from God, but to a victory as though it came from himself."

Asked during the war by his friend Archie Lush, "Why do you keep on attacking Churchill? What do you think happens if *he* goes?" Bevan answered, "All right. Suppose he fell under a bus. What should we have to do? Send a postcard to Hitler, giving in?"

Lloyd George had been dictatorial toward his Cabinet in World War I, but even he was shocked at the subservience of Churchill's Cabinet. He said to Michael Foot, "Now *my* War Cabinet was different. They were all big men. I was never able to treat *any* of my colleagues the way Churchill treats *all* of his." Then, according to Foot, he paused and his eye twinkled and he added, "Oh, yes, there was one I treated that way—Curzon."

Churchill was tremendously angered by his critics in the House, who embarrassed him when he was dealing with Roosevelt. He wrote that he pointed out to the President, ". . . we can no more control the expression of freak opinion by individual Members than he can those of Congress backwoodsmen." He ruthlessly sought to silence his critics by calling periodically for a Vote of Confidence. This forced his critics to vote for or against himself and his whole government rather than on a particular issue or Cabinet Member. He justified this by saying, "If we have handled our resources wrongly, no one is so much to blame as I," and insisted that any Member who did not go along with the government completely should be willing to vote for its overthrow, and "ought to have the manhood to testify his convictions in the lobby. . . . No one need be mealy-mouthed in debate and no one should be chicken-hearted in voting. I have voted against Governments I have been elected to support, and looking back, I have sometimes felt very glad that I did so."

Both in the House of Commons and in *Tribune* (where he now had George Orwell as editor), Bevan continued to attack Churchill's insistence on being, besides Prime Minister, his own Minister of Defence, and on his use of Captain Margesson, to enforce his authority. Now that various General Staff officers have published their memoirs, it has become evident that Bevan's accusations against Churchill of meddling with the military were correct. "The French Revolution had its Carnot; the last war produced Lloyd George; the Russian Revolution a Trotsky, and we have Captain Margesson. Could fate be more unkind? . . . We don't blame Margesson. He merely took the job Churchill gave him. Margesson's absurdity for the job is the measure of Churchill's failure as Defence Minister. The failure is costing us precious and will cost us more yet." What Bevan was seeking was a real Minister of Production and separate Defence Minister. As was the case with many of Bevan's criticisms of the government, this situation was corrected later; but, of course, no credit was given to Bevan by the government. In *The Hinge of Fate,* Churchill wrote that owing to "external pressure" he changed his government, removing Margesson from the War Office and appointing Oliver Lyttelton Minister of Production. Bevan wrote, "The political story of the war is a record of the government slowly making concessions to the critics when the latter have been proved right by events. But the loss of an army in Singapore and the sequence of disasters is too high a price to pay for the education of a government. It is no comfort to us to win the argument and to lose the war."

Churchill regarded Bevan and the few who occasionally allied themselves with the Welshman, such as Leslie Hore-Belisha and Sir John Wardlaw-Milne as "would-be profiteers of disaster." This did not stop Bevan's criticisms of what he felt were Churchill's errors, which included the Prime Minister's keeping for himself the post of Minister of Defence, the strategy at Tobruk, Churchill's miscalculations on Russia, the Norway episode, Libya, Crete, Greece, and various naval stupidities, including the loss of the *Repulse* and *Prince of Wales.* Nor did Bevan cease his criticism of Churchill's strong-arm tactics in the House:

". . . the country is beginning to say that he fights debates like a war and the war like a debate."

On no war issue were Bevan and Churchill further apart than on aid to Russia and a Second Front. Churchill continued to underestimate Russia long after others in both England and America had seen the light. In July of 1942, Bevan made his great speech in the debate on the conduct of the war and aid to Russia. "If this debate resulted in causing demoralization in the country in the slightest degree, I would have preferred to cut my tongue out. . . . The country expects and declarations have been made—I can speak freely about this, though I understand the Prime Minister cannot—that in a very short time . . . we shall launch an attack [Second Front]. . . I do beg and pray the Government when they make that decision to make it as a consequence of strategical propriety and not as a consequence of political propaganda . . . we have to do it. We cannot postpone it till next year. Stalin expects it; please do not misunderstand me, for heaven's sake, do not let us make the mistake of betraying those lion-hearted Russians. Speeches have been made, the Russians believe them and have broken the champagne bottles on them. They believe this country will act this year on what they call the second front. Molotov said so; they expect it and the British nation expects it. I say it is right, it is the correct thing to do, and the Government have practically said so. Do not in these high matters speak with a twisted tongue; do not use words with double meanings; do not use sentences with hidden purposes." Churchill dismissed the speech as a "diatribe with its bitter animosity."

We now know that there were many who agreed with Bevan and not with Marlborough's heir. President Roosevelt, urged on by the United States Joint Chiefs, wanted an attack across the Channel in 1942. He sent General Marshall, Admiral King, and Harry Hopkins to try to convince

Churchill, and their point of view was supported by General Eisenhower and General Spaatz of the Air Force. When a 1942 cross-Channel operation was nevertheless vetoed by Churchill in favor of a North African campaign, General Eisenhower said it was possibly "the blackest day in history." General MacArthur characterized the North African plan as "absolutely useless," and American Secretary of War Stimson and General Marshall also disapproved of it.

Bevan felt there was little doubt of Churchill's promise of an invasion of Europe in 1942, but absolutely none about his commitment for 1943. By now even the British General Montgomery urged an attack from Britain. Yet Churchill had been speaking with "a twisted tongue," and there was no 1943 invasion.

Bevan had always disagreed with Churchill's India policy, and when, in 1942, Gandhi, Nehru, and others were arrested, Bevan wrote with the scorn worthy of a Sheridan or Wilkes, "The Imperial Lion has roused himself. Invoking the spirits of Clive and Hastings and Dyer, he roars again. Gandhi arrested, Nehru arrested . . . and seventy-two-year-old Grandma Gandhi is also arrested lest her trembling whispers might rock the foundations of the great Raj. . . . The Kuban Cossacks gallop sword in hand in a vain endeavor to halt the Panzered invader; plea follows plea and hope battles against suspicion that Britain will sustain her Soviet Ally; military experts and Tory stooges declaim upon the practical difficulties of a Second Front; China fights on in desperate isolation. . . . Now comes our answer. Our armoured cars go into action—against Congress supporters in Bombay! Our political warfare has reached new inspiring heights. We have proclaimed A Whipping Act for the people of India. . . ."

During the war, Bevan's mind, much more than Churchill's, addressed itself to the kind of postwar world the

Allies were fighting to achieve. (He once said, "Fascism is not in itself a new order of society. It is the future refusing to be born.") He was, therefore, less tolerant than the Prime Minister of temporary expedients taken in the name of achieving victory. When in the North African invasion the Vichy Minister of Marine, Darlan, was taken on by Eisenhower as an ally, Bevan wrote, "What kind of Europe do we have in mind? One built by rats for rats?" The Darlan affair caused a tremendous stir, and even Churchill admitted that it "raised issues of a moral and sentimental character of cardinal importance" and that it was regarded by many as "a base and squalid deal with one of our most bitter enemies." In the entire North African affair, General de Gaulle had been completely ignored. He was not even told of the invasion beforehand. When he was advised of the deal with Darlan by Eden and Churchill, he said, "You invoke strategic reasons but it is a strategic error to place oneself in a situation contradictory to the moral character of this war. We are no longer in the eighteenth century when Frederick the Great paid the courtiers of Vienna in order to be able to take Silesia, nor in the Italian Renaissance when one hired the myrmidons of Milan or the mercenaries of Florence. In any case we do not put them at the head of a liberated people afterwards." The value of Darlan's help to England and America may be viewed differently now that de Gaulle ..as excluded the former from the Common Market and told the latter where to go in other respects. We are paying a great price for Churchill's having complained that the greatest cross he had to bear was the Cross of Lorraine.

Bevan's view of de Gaulle was more charitable than Churchill's. The Welshman said the "gentleman has awkward corners like we all have" and from the hindsight of history, Bevan's position in the long run would have been more beneficial to Britain than Churchill's. Bevan criticized the Prime Minister's choice of still other foreign political bedfellows. In Italy, the Prime Minister's efforts to uphold King Victor Emmanuel and Marshal Badoglio instead of the Italian underground forces enraged Bevan. "The Prime Minister has got very many virtues and when the time comes I hope to pay my tribute to them, but I am bound to say that political honesty and sagacity have never been among them." He reminded the House of Churchill's early appraisal of Mussolini as a gentle and simple statesman who deserves the gratitude of all of Europe for saving Italy from Bolshevism. Bevan went on to express his reluctance to see the House go away for the summer recess, "leaving the political architecture of Italy to a mind that reasons like that." His real view of the Tories was expressed in this same speech when he said, "There are Members in this House who have no complaint against Fascism, except when it is strong enough to threaten them. . . . But the people of Great Britain are hoping, desperately hoping, that in Italy the ordinary people of Italy will overthrow the existing regime."

In December of 1943, Bevan said in another debate, "The Italian people gave us Italy. We failed to take advantage of it"; and he asked whether Churchill planned to continue in this same course by supporting King George in Greece and refusing to recognize Marshal Tito in Yugoslavia. "The purblind adherence to reactionary forces in Europe is costing thousands of British lives." It was in this speech that Bevan made one of his most widely quoted attacks on Churchill's military ineptness. He pointed out that the Allied forces were having a terrible time in Italy, and in Bevan's view Churchill's royalist policies were responsible. In January of 1943, Bevan had challenged Churchill's description of southern Europe as "the soft underbelly of the Axis," and predicted the Allies might find there "formidable armour." "It is still for the Government and its military ex-

perts to explain how it will be more practicable to invade
Europe at the end of a three-thousand-mile supply line
across eighty miles of water than it is to do so from our
bases in this country." In December of 1943, Bevan said,
"The whole of this country wants to know what strategical
conception behind the war put the British and American
armies to fight their way right up the whole peninsula in
the autumn and winter. . . . Does anybody suggest to me
that is a wise strategy? It is nonsense. Is that the 'soft underbelly of the Axis?' We are climbing up the backbone. . . .
Indeed, I am bound to say, if the House will forgive the
metaphor, that the Allied High Command have approached
the Italian mainland like an old man approaching a young
bride, fascinated, sluggish and apprehensive."

Bevan railed against the Tories. "It is a revolutionary
Europe which confronts them, and they are frightened by
the apparition." He was equally vehement in his attacks
on his fellow Socialists who meekly acquiesced to Churchill's
policies. "It is not national unity we have now. It is a silent
conspiracy against the future." Now, twenty years later, it
is easy to see that Bevan's view was correct, and Churchill's,
unfortunate in the extreme. Stalin's disillusion over the
broken promises of a Second Front in 1942 and 1943 and
the Allied support of reactionary forces in Europe were already becoming evident by the Russian Premier's removal
of "pro-Western" diplomats such as Litvinov and Maisky
and by his replacing them with tougher men. On August
27, 1943, Bevan wrote in *Tribune* begging for an understanding with the Russians: "There is hardly a price that is
too high to attain this end. Failure will mean to lay the
foundation of a third world war."

Perhaps even more remarkably prophetic was Bevan's
analysis of the postwar world, made in October, 1943, in
which he foresaw the Cold War between America and Russia and the need (long before anyone else had visions of a

Common Market) for a united European third force in
which Britain should join. He saw that after the war, Britain would be the weakest of the Big Three, "a fact which
instinctive patriotism deters us from accepting." He foresaw the struggle between the United States and the Soviet
Union. "This polarization of international relations between
Moscow and Washington would be nothing short of world
catastrophe. It would petrify the existing systems in both
countries and make genuine cooperation between them impossible. It would make a third world war an eventual cer-
tainty. It would reduce all other nations, including Britain,
to a satellite status of depending on one or the other of the
two great Powers." Bevan recommended that Britain
should "gain the support and provide for the mutual help
of the nations of Europe." Bevan hoped for "an organic
confederation of the Western European nations, like
France, Holland, Belgium, Italy, Spain, the Scandinavian
nations, along with a sane Germany and Austria, and a
progressive Britain . . . the only solution likely to lay the
foundation for peace and prosperity in Europe."

The duel of wit and invective between Bevan and
Churchill continued after the war. Churchill said in the
House on December 6, 1945, "He will be as great a curse
to this country in peace, as he was a squalid nuisance in
time of war"; and in a speech at Blackpool on October 5,
1946, "There is, however, a poetic justice in the fact that
the most mischievous mouth in war-time has also become
in peace the most remarkable administrative failure." Perhaps the wittiest of Churchill's postwar comments was a
gratuitous insult offered on July 1, 1952, when he was
speaking in the House on the recognition of Communist
China: "As we had great interests there, and also on general
grounds, I thought that it would be a good thing to have
diplomatic representation. But if you recognize anyone it
does not mean that you like him. We all, for instance, recog-

nize the right honourable Gentleman the Member for Ebbw Vale."

So also, after the war, Bevan's invective continued, both when he was in the Labor Cabinet as Minister of Health and again as a private Member until his death on July 7, 1960. It could be savage, as it was on April 23, 1953, when Bevan said: "I do not know what the right honourable Lady the Minister of Education [Miss Florence Horsbough] is grinning at. I was told by one of my honourable Friends this afternoon that that is a face which has sunk a thousand scholarships. . . ." Or it could be hilarious, as it was at the time of the Suez disaster, when Bevan, on seeing the Prime Minister enter the Floor of the House, ceased questioning the Foreign Minister, Selwyn Lloyd, remarking, "Why should I question the monkey when I can question the organ grinder?"

It was his abuse and wit during the war, however, expressed at the cost of being called a near traitor but expressed, nevertheless, as his duty, that has given Aneurin Bevan his place in history.

The Wit of Politicians
British versus American

It [a sense of humor] always withers in the presence of
the messianic delusion, like justice and truth in front of
patriotic passion.

H. L. Mencken, *Prejudices*

In the early days of the United States, the wit and invective
of our politicians on the hustings, answering hecklers, in
after-dinner speeches, or in the legislatures, differed little
from that of British politicians. The invective of a John
Randolph, for example, is often indistinguishable from
that of a Sheridan or a Disraeli. This is understandable because, in our early days, the politicians of America differed little from their British counterparts in background,
education, and general point of view. They were a comparatively homogeneous group of well-bred, well-educated,
and usually well-to-do gentlemen, for the most part of
British extraction. But as America expanded to the West,
its politicians ceased to come in the main from such families
as the Adamses and the Randolphs and began to include
the Clays and the Jacksons, whose education, experience,
and point of view differed markedly from that of the British. As the years went by and the Irish, Italian, Jewish, German, and other immigrants who came to America began to
elect politicians to office, the homogeneity disappeared

completely, along with the similarities to English politicians.

The physical differences between the British and the American forms of government also affected both the incidence and the kind of wit heard. In Great Britain, for example, the executive branch of the government is not separated physically from the legislative as it is in the United States. Indeed, the Prime Minister must be a Member of the House of Commons, and the Members of his Cabinet are also, for the most part, Members of the Commons, and must answer in debate questions put to them by other Members.

The most extraordinary thing about "the best club in Europe," as Sir Winston Churchill called the House of Commons, is its mixture of formality and informality. To mention but a few of the formalities, each day's sitting begins with the formal procession of the bewigged and gowned Speaker from his rooms through the Central Hall and Members' Lobby preceded by the white-gloved Messenger and the Sergeant-at-Arms carrying the Mace (which embodies the authority of the House), and followed by his Train-Bearer, Chaplain, and Secretary. As this procession approaches, one hears the loud cry of "Speaker!" "Speaker!" and everyone rises and stands at attention. During the opening prayers each day, from which the public is excluded, ancient custom and tradition require that the Members turn their backs on the Speaker and his Chaplain and kneel, not on the floor, but on the benches, as in the days when Members wore swords, which precluded kneeling in any other way. In front of the Government and Opposition front benches are two red lines just far enough apart that two men with drawn swords cannot, if they stay behind the lines, reach one another. Even today, no Member addressing the House may cross these lines. A Member speaking in the House always refers to another Member not of

his own party as "the honourable Gentleman" or, if the
Member referred to is of the speaker's party, as "honourable
Friend." If, as do all ministers and former ministers, the
Member belongs to Her Majesty's Privy Council, he is referred to as "right honourable." Members who are lawyers are
referred to as "honourable and learned," and those who are
or have been soldiers as "honourable and gallant."

And yet, for all this formality, there is also an incredible
informality, not only in the dining rooms, library, smoking
rooms, and bars of the House, but in the Chamber itself.
The Chamber has room to seat only two-thirds of the six
hundred and thirty Members of Parliament. When the
Houses of Parliament were destroyed by bombing in
World War II, this was not changed in the rebuilding, so
that, today, the Chamber of the House of Commons,
though it may sometimes be crowded, never seems empty
as the two Chambers of Congress usually do. Sir Winston
said in the House on October 24, 1950:

"It excites world wonder in the Parliamentary countries
that we should build a Chamber, starting afresh, which
can only seat two-thirds of its Members. It is difficult to explain this to those who do not know our ways. They cannot
easily be made to understand why we consider that the in-
tensity, passion, intimacy, informality and spontaneity of
our Debates constitute the personality of the House of
Commons and endow it at once with its focus and
strength. . . ."

The Members, then, are all physically close to one another, and their physical deportment in the House is almost
as casual today as it was in the days when Peel used to pull
his hat over his eyes and pretend to sleep when his opponents were speaking. But it is the verbal informality, the
shouts of "Shame!" "Resign!" and "Bloody nonsense!" as
well as barnyard noises, catcalls, groans, impromptu asides,
and rude questions with which Members interrupt other

Members, that most surprise those unused to the customs of the House.

There are some rules, very few, limiting what may or may not be said in the House, such as one forbidding a Member to call another Member a liar or a fool, but even these are circumvented, as when Sir Winston Churchill replied to Aneurin Bevan in the House on December 8, 1944, "I should think it hardly possible to state the opposite of the truth with more precision." Sometimes the circumvention is a good deal more subtle, as when Sir Winston said on February 16, 1947, "I always notice that the [Socialist] Party opposite indulges in laughter which resembles crackling of thorns under a pot whenever they are confronted with any mental proposition which their intelligence forces them to resent or to reject." His reference is to Ecclesiastes 7:6, "For as the crackling of thorns under a pot, so is the laughter of the fool." Mr. Bevan also could skirt the coasts of the impermissible and still satisfy the Speaker, as when in 1949 he began his devaluation speech, "I welcome this opportunity of pricking the bloated bladder of lies with the poignard of truth."

Between Members who habitually insult one another, often a real affection grows, so that if one of the Members is not re-elected or resigns, his opponent may well miss him more than a Member of his own party. An example of this was the relationship between Dr. Dalton, when he was Socialist Chancellor of the Exchequer, and Nigel Birch, a Conservative Member, who made Dalton the object of his constant attacks. Because it is traditional that the Budget must be shown first to all the Members of the House, when Dalton leaked part of his Budget to the press prior to presenting it to the House, he was forced to resign. This caused Birch to comment, "Dammit, they've shot my fox!"

The custom of the House of Commons that most differentiates it from the American Congress, and provides much of the most brilliant wit, is Question Time. Immediately after prayers at two-thirty in the afternoon, individual Members may ask any questions they want of ministers of the Crown. These questions are submitted in advance in writing and are numbered and printed on the pale green Order Paper. Having had notice of the question to be asked, each minister has had an opportunity to prepare his answer. There is no legal requirement that these questions be answered, and for reasons of security or politics they are sometimes not answered. By tradition, however, most of them are.

Also, by tradition, no question for the Prime Minister is ever put earlier on the list than Number 45, in order that he may have time for as long a lunch as he wants. However, at 3:15 P.M. on Tuesdays and Thursdays the Prime Minister is fair game.

The earlier questions are addressed to his ministers and the Speaker calls on the Members who have submitted questions. The question is not repeated, but rather, when its number is called, the appropriate minister rises and gives his prepared answer. It is after this that the fun really begins, because the questioning Member may then ask supplementary questions supposedly on the same subject as the first question. If the original question has been broad enough in scope, the supplementaries may be questions surprising and embarrassing to the minister, and ones for which he is unprepared.

The questions asked are usually not to elicit information, but rather to embarrass the minister. One of the present stars of Question Time in the House is Sir Gerald Nabarro, who asked these questions on the Order Paper of February 13, 1958 (all written questions are reported in this form of indirect speech):

55. MR. NABARRO: "To ask the Chancellor of the Exchequer when the regulation was introduced laying down

that doorknockers five inches or more in length shall be free of tax whereas doorknockers under that length carry 30% Purchase Tax; and what has been the revenue from Purchase Tax on doorknockers for each of the past five years for which figures are available."

56. MR. NABARRO: "To ask the Chancellor of the Exchequer is he aware that in view of the fact that a nutcracker is liable to Purchase Tax at 15% whereas a doorknocker over five inches in length is free of tax, there is an increasing practice of supplying nutcrackers with screwholes so that they could theoretically be used as doorknockers, with the result that with such modification these nutcrackers become tax free; and what instructions have been issued to Customs and Excise staff with regard to this matter."

In connection with these questions and some supplementary questions, the following exchange took place in the House:

MR. NABARRO: "Why is there this invidious distinction between doorknocking nutcrackers and nutcracking doorknockers . . ."

MR. SPEAKER: "Order."

THE FINANCIAL SECRETARY TO THE TREASURY (Mr. J. E. S. Simon): "No, Sir; I do not think Customs staff need instructions to help them distinguish a nutcracker from a doorknocker."

MR. NABARRO: "Now will my hon. and learned Friend apply himself to the question I have put to him? Why is there this invidious distinction between doorknocking nutcrackers and nutcracking doorknockers? Is he aware that this is a perfectly well known device, practiced by manufacturers? I have evidence of it in my hand. Is he aware that this ridiculous position, which was mentioned in a leading article in *The Times* on 11th February, is bringing the whole matter of the Purchase Tax Schedules into disrepute?

Is it not time the matter was drastically overhauled by abolition of the Purchase Tax and substitution of a sales turnover tax at a very small and uniform rate over the whole field?"

MR. SIMON: "My hon. Friend tempts me to reply in the words of the conductor Richter to the second flute at Covent Garden—'Your damned nonsense can I stand twice or once, but sometimes always, by God, never.' "

There is today, perhaps, somewhat less wit and less bitter invective in the House of Commons than formerly; at least, there are fewer examples of the carefully prepared and polished wit of the eighteenth and nineteenth centuries and of the long classical orations full of invective that were heard in the late nineteenth and early twentieth centuries. This seems to be due to the time-consuming multiplicity of technical problems to which the House must now address itself. Parliament today is concerned with many more subjects than formerly—humdrum things such as welfare, housing, transport, electricity, and farm prices. Former Prime Minister Macmillan spoke recently on the comparative lessening of invective. "Once upon a time politics were really tough throughout—here and in America. That was before the speech writers began—when a man shot his own mouth off. For instance, John Randolph, who entered the United States House of Representatives in 1799, made his brethren sit up when he said of Edward Livingston: 'He is a man of splendid abilities but utterly corrupt. Like a rotten mackerel by moonlight, he shines and stinks.' O'Connell said of Disraeli that he must be descended from one of the thieves that hung at our Savior's side. . . . Mark Twain once wrote of a defunct politician: 'I did not attend his funeral; but I wrote a nice letter saying I approved of it.'

"Several years ago a foreign politician said to me speaking about another foreign politician that he was politically so naïve that he resented being called a crook.

"I certainly remember that in my youth politics were a good deal more rowdy in this country than they are now. There was none of the mealy-mouthed milk and water stuff that we have today. Why, you can hardly say boo to a goose in the House of Commons now without cries of 'Ungentle-manly,' 'Not fair,' and all the rest. But in those days they went at it hammer and tongs. I remember the great dock strike of 1912 and the famous chant by which Ben Tillet nightly rallied his men—a sort of litany which went: 'Oh God, strike Lord Davenport dead.' Well, nowadays we are more polite and I suppose that is a good thing. I certainly don't want to go looking for trouble myself.

"But perhaps we are about to see some revival of political vituperation. The by-election at Bolton seemed quite robust. 'Supercilious carpet bagger who, in typical big-headed fashion, says that Parliament needs him.' That's more the stuff. . . ."

Macmillan himself, however, has been both the author and the butt of a good deal of political wit and invective. Perhaps the best known example of his own wit occurred when his speech before the United Nations in New York on September 29, 1960, was interrupted by the Russian Premier, Khrushchev, who took off his shoe and pounded on the table with it. In the best tradition of British unflappability, Macmillan remarked calmly, "I'd like that translated, if I may."

Closer to home, when concern was expressed in London at the tremendous ovation given by Londoners to the Russian astronaut Major Gagarin, the former Prime Minister said, "It would have been twice as bad if they had sent the dog."

Macmillan agrees with German Chancellor Adenauer, who said, "A thick skin is a gift from God." Mr. Macmillan once said, "One newspaper, I am told, has perpetually in type the headline 'Mac at Bay.' I suggest they also keep in type 'Mac Bounces Back.' " He has been criticized by every-one, including his own son, who once wrote a letter to *The Times* very critical of the government and his father. The former Prime Minister replied in the House of Commons, "The Member for Halifax [Mr. Maurice Macmillan] has intelligence and independence. How he got them is not for me to say." And he said on another occasion, "I have never found, in a long experience of politics, that criticism is ever inhibited by ignorance."

Even a few days after the Profumo scandal, Macmillan was able to joke. He recalled his experience as Resident Minister to Allied Forces Headquarters in the Middle East when all military commanders were presented with mili-tary medals of the First Class Order of Chastity by the Bey of Tunis. With a twinkle in his eye, the former Prime Min-ister remarked, "I was rather badly treated, I did not get one. I could use it now."

The Profumo affair brought forth a good deal of invective in the House, none more cutting than Mr. Reginald Paget's comment, "From Lord Hailsham we have had a virtuoso performance in the art of kicking a fallen friend in the guts. When self-indulgence has reduced a man to the shape of Lord Hailsham, sexual continence involves no more than a sense of the ridiculous." Michael Foot, a Socialist Mem-ber, commented at the time of the Profumo affair, "The members of our Secret Service have apparently spent so much time looking under the beds for Communists, they haven't had time to look in the bed."

On infrequent occasions, British political wit is very similar in style and subject matter to the American One example occurred after Hugh Gaitskell had been asked outside the gates of an Imperial Chemical Industries fac-tory whether it would be nationalized, and replied, "We have announced plans to nationalize steel and road trans-port. We have no further plans for nationalization at the moment." Macmillan seized on this to say, "I will tell you the story of a poultry farmer who one day was wandering round his farm when up spoke a turkey, who said to him, 'Is it true that you are going to slaughter me?' The farmer replied, 'My dear fellow, you can set your mind at rest. You see that bird over there and that bird over there? They are both on the list, but I have no plans for you at present.' But it would be a very foolish bird indeed who took any comfort from that. Come Christmas, his neck will be wrung all right."

Making fun of the present leader of the Socialist Party, Harold Wilson, who, according to the Tories, had invented for himself a youth so poverty-stricken that he had no boots, Macmillian said, "If Harold Wilson ever went to school without any boots, it was merely because he was too big for them."

Wilson, when he was a loyal supporter of Aneurin Bevan, was christened by Hugh Dalton "Nye's little dog." Wilson is a student of invective, and when asked recently his favorite example, said it was John Burns's comment on Joseph Chamberlain. "To have betrayed two political leaders—to have wrecked two historic parties—reveals a depth of infamy never previously reached, compared with which the thugs of India are as faithful friends and Judas Iscariot is entitled to a crown of glory."

Wilson's own abuse is as sharp as any. It was he who first labeled Macmillan "Mac the Knife," and characterized Macmillan's initial support and subsequent desertion of Anthony Eden in the Suez crisis as a policy of "first in—first out." On November 3, 1958, Wilson said in the Debates on the Queen's Speech, "Words for the right hon. Gentleman [Prime Minister Macmillan] are like the false trail laid in a paper chase to cover up the way he is really going. It is when he has just been attacking the social services that he most likes to quote Disraeli. I always thought that Disraeli was one of his heroes until he went to Hawarden this year and made a speech about Gladstone. The right hon. Gentleman is the only statesman of this century to claim with characteristic modesty to embody all that is best in both Disraeli and Gladstone. In fact, of course, he is wrong. He has inherited the streak of charlatanry in Disraeli without his vision, and the self-righteousness of Gladstone without his dedication to principle."

On July 18, 1961, in another parliamentary debate, Wilson described Macmillan in the same words as Disraeli had used describing Lord Liverpool: "The Arch-Mediocrity who presided, rather than ruled, over a Cabinet of Mediocrities . . . not a statesman, a statemonger. . . . Peremptory in little questions, the great ones he left open."

Asked in the United States the main difference between himself and Prime Minister Macmillan, Wilson replied, "Twenty-two years." This he now quotes as an example of his invective he would rather not have uttered. Occasionally, however, Wilson is a little lighter in his attacks on Macmillan, as he was in October of 1962 at the Annual Conference of the Labor Party. "I have referred to Hugh Gaitskell's broadcast. There was another the night before —Harold Macmillan. Perhaps you saw it. He spoke, he spoke for 'those of us who are young in heart.' Macmillan, young in heart! His world is indeed a stage. As one of his admiring critics I have seen him through many roles. And I have seen him off the stage a few times in some of them. The bookmaker shouting the odds five years ago; the pawnbroker of Trinidad—and the Ford Motor Company—his valorous record of first-in first-out at Suez; the peacemaker of Moscow. Mark my words, he will be dusting the mothballs out of the old fur hat any time now with an election coming along, if Dr. Adenauer will let him. And then his other great role, the squire and his relations, most of them promoted with unfailing regularity. Right down to the Grand Guignol of July 13, Sweeney MacTodd the demon barber of Downing Street. But never, never, in my mind's eye had I cast him as Peter Pan, never had I conceived him as St. Aloysius, the patron saint of youth. Even my gullible credulity was strained. I could not forget the picture of him grouse shooting in those knickerbockers."

The above reference to July 13th was to Macmillan's firing of about a third of the members of his Cabinet on that date in 1962. Included in this wholesale bloodletting were a number of the former Prime Minister's old friends, and the most brilliant comment on Macmillan's effort to give the Tory Party a new image was made by the wittiest Member of the present House of Commons, a Liberal named Jeremy Thorpe, who said, "Greater love hath no man than this, that he lay down his friends for his life." Asked his favorite recent example of political invective, Thorpe said it was Harold Wilson's comment on the Blue Streak missile, made as the Socialist leader was looking directly at the Tory Defense Minister, Duncan Sandys. "We all know why Blue Streak was kept on although it was an obvious failure. It was to save the Minister of Defence's face. We are, in fact, looking at the most expensive face in history. Helen of Troy's face, it is true, may only have launched a thousand ships, but at least they were operational."

Two other recent favorites of Thorpe's were Lady Violet Bonham Carter's saying, "Sir Stafford [Cripps] has a brilliant mind until it is made up"; and Labor Member Leslie Lever's comment, "I have been accused of being ungenerous to this Government. Generosity is a part of my character, and I, therefore, hasten to assure this Government that I will never make an allegation of dishonesty against it wherever a simple explanation of stupidity will suffice."

There is less invective and less wit in the House of Lords

than in the Commons, but occasionally both are found in its debates. One of the stars is former Prime Minister Clement Attlee. Lord Attlee points out that the wit and invective in the British Parliament have set an example for other Parliaments of the Commonwealth. Prime Minister Billy Hughes of Australia, whom Attlee describes as a "rather eccentric and extremely deaf fellow," once watched a Member of his own party cross the floor and deliver a blistering attack on the Prime Minister from the Opposition benches. When the traitor had finished his attack, the Prime Minister simply rose and stood with his hand cupped to his ear, saying nothing. Finally, another Member asked, "What are you waiting for, Billy?" and the Prime Minister answered, "I'm waiting for the cock to crow."

Lord Attlee says, "Wit and invective do not so much affect legislation directly as they affect the standard of Ministers. A pompous Minister may be brought down by an excellent interruption. It also adds to the brightness of debate and an important point may often best be registered by a flash of wit . . . there is more wit in our Parliament than in your Congress because you tend to make orations for the *Congressional Record,* very often written out in advance and delivered from the written page, whereas, we face each other across the House and make real debating speeches, subject to interruption. There is much more point and thrust in our system. Our politicians seem to have much greater training in *ad lib* controversy and impromptu debate. We don't like great long speeches in the House. . . ."

A gratifying number of examples of wit by Members of the House of Lords still take the form of epigrams in the Disraeli and Oscar Wilde tradition. Lord Mancroft's comment, "Cricket is a game which the English, not being a spiritual people, have invented to give themselves some conception of eternity," compares favorably with Lord Altrincham's, "Autobiography is now as common as adultery and hardly less reprehensible." Lord Attlee said recently, "The idea that every nation ought to have an atomic bomb as every woman of fashion ought to have a mink coat is deplorable"; and his own wit contradicts his comment, "The House of Lords is like a glass of champagne that has stood for five days." A sounder comment, perhaps, is Lord Boothby's, "Like many other anachronisms in British public life, the House of Lords has one supreme merit. It works."

There are nearly no off-color jokes on the floor of the House of Commons, the closest thing in recent memory being the comment of Jack Jones after Nancy Astor had delivered herself of one of her temperance speeches during which she had, looking at Jones, made several pointed references to "beer bellies." Jones said, "I tell the noble and honourable lady that I will lay my stomach against hers any day."

In the Congress of the United States there are many physical differences from the British Parliament. As has already been pointed out, the executive branch does not sit in the Legislature as it does in England, and cannot, therefore, be questioned by the legislators nor take an active part in their debates. In both Houses of Congress, the floor is semicircular in shape, so that a senator or congressman is physically addressing the Chair rather than his colleagues. The Members of the House of Commons never read a speech but speak from memory, extemporaneously or, at most, from a few notes. Members of the Congress, on the other hand, often read long speeches into the *Congressional Record* and the practice is also common of having long congressional speeches inserted in the *Record* without their even having been read aloud. These speeches, really intended not for the Congress itself but for the voters back home, have added the word "bunk" to the language. In 1820, Felix Walker, a congressman from Buncombe

County, North Carolina, making a speech for the benefit of his constituents, warned his fellow members, "This is for Buncombe," and since that time "buncombe" or "bunk" has meant useless talk.

A great many speeches delivered by American politicians are written for them. In the Library of Congress there is a section called the Legislative Reference Service, whose two hundred employees are allegedly there for the purpose of doing research for members of the Congress and of the executive, but, in fact, spend a great part of their time writing speeches for them. Members of the Legislative Reference Service are suitably discreet about their clients, but say that in recent years the Washington politicians who use their services have had no interest in either wit or invective in their speeches. There is no similar speech-writing service provided for Members by the House of Commons Library.

In recent years in the Congress, there have not been the interruptions, catcalls, and impromptu asides that characterize the House of Commons. In earlier days in our Congress, there were not only interruptions and insults, but even pistols and canes brandished in the Chamber, but now there are usually only an extraordinary conformity and formality.

There is perhaps also a reflection of the differences between American and British education to be seen in the differences in the wit and invective of the legislatures of the two countries. If wit in American politics is less frequent, less subtle, and more heavy-handed, this may also be due to the higher incidence of lawyers in the American legislatures.

Occasionally the lighthearted teasing of fellow members of the club that is a constant of parliamentary dialogue is found also in the Senate of the United States. On September 2, 1960, when Senator John F. Kennedy was the Democratic candidate for President and Senator Lyndon B.

Johnson, the Democratic candidate for Vice-President, Republican Senator Everett M. Dirksen, of Illinois, said, "I extend to the Senators who are candidates the warm hand of fellowship. We want to keep them here. It would be lonesome without my distinguished friend, the Majority Leader [Senator Lyndon B. Johnson], and without my distinguished friend from Massachusetts [Senator John F. Kennedy], with whom it has been my honor and pleasure to work on the Senate Labor Committee. My affection is as high as the sky and it is as deep as the sea—and I do not want sixteen blocks to intervene."

Mr. Dirksen, the Republican Leader in the Senate, who is alleged by some of his fellow senators to confuse himself occasionally with Abraham Lincoln and who has been called "Honest Ev the Hairsplitter," is, along with Charles Halleck, the Republican Leader in the House of Representatives, a politician who believes humor is an essential in American politics today. The "Ev and Charlie" press conferences, sometimes televised, have not yet, however, produced any wit that appears destined to live as long as Lincoln's. A typical example of Dirksen's wit came during the Budget debates of 1959. "The statement made by the Majority Leader [Lyndon Johnson of Texas] on a number of occasions on the floor and in the tables he inserted in the *Record,* are quite correct so far as they go. As I said before, however, it is like the man who fell off the twentieth floor of a building. As he passed the sixth floor a friend shouted to him, 'Mike, so far you're all right.' (Laughter.) So, I believe in the interest of the whole rather than in the fraction of the story."

Occasionally in the Congress, politicians have delivered themselves of the kind of aphorism for which British politicians are known, but the style or grammar or tone or subject usually identifies the author as American, as when Senator Henry F. Ashurst said, "Silence is the best substitute for brains ever invented." There have also been in American politics flashes of bitter invective such as illuminate the dialogue of the English Parliament, but the flavor is almost always clearly American. Representative Emory Speer, of Georgia, said, "The Democratic Party is like a mule without pride of ancestry or hope of posterity"; and Senator Anselm J. McLaurin, of Mississippi, said, "The basic principle that will ultimately get the Republican Party together is the cohesive power of public plunder."

Most of the wit in the American Congress, however, has always been and still is in the form of the story, usually introduced with some form of "that reminds me of the fellow who . . ." Although most American politicians today scrupulously avoid jokes on religion, race, or liquor, these in the past have been the basis of a large percentage of American humor.

Senator Henry Wilson, of Massachusetts, once said, "I believe if we introduced the Lord's Prayer here, senators would propose a large number of amendments to it." Even Edward Everett Hale, when he was Chaplain of the Senate, made light of the subject of religion. Asked, "Do you pray for the senators, Dr. Hale?" he answered, "No, I look at the senators and pray for the country."

There has been comparatively little anti-Semitism expressed in the Congress, but just prior to the Civil War, when Senator Judah P. Benjamin, of Louisiana, was insulted by a senator of German extraction, his reply was remarkably similar to Disraeli's reply to O'Connell. "The gentleman will please remember that when his half-civilized ancestors were hunting the wild boar in the forests of Silesia, mine were the princes of the earth."

A Mississippian who achieved a great reputation as a congressional wit was John Mills Allen. He displayed his wit on the hustings when he was first running for Congress against former Confederate General Tucker, who made much of his service to the Confederacy, ending a speech one day, "Seventeen years ago last night, after a hard battle on yonder hill, I bivouacked under yonder clump of trees." Thereupon, Allen spoke, saying, "My fellow-citizens, what General Tucker says to you about sleeping under yonder clump of trees is true, for I stood guard over him whilst he slept. Now, then, all of you who were generals and had privates to stand guard over you, vote for my opponent and all of you who were privates and stood guard over the generals, vote for Johnny Allen." Allen, of course, was elected and was known forever afterward as "Private" John Allen.

Many of the stories of members of the Congress from the South and West were and are about animals, life on the farm, hunting, and fishing. Senator Tom Connally, of Texas, who so long dominated the Foreign Relations Committee, once said, "The Senator from Connecticut [Mr. Danaher] said, 'Well, just take out section 7 or 8 of the amendment proposed by the Senator from Ohio [Mr. Taft] and it will be a fine bill.' That, Mr. President, reminds me of a story which our old friend, Senator Tom Heflin of Alabama, used to tell in the cloakroom. I shall tell it on the Floor. Uncle Remus went fishing. He caught a little perch about two inches long, and took the little perch home to trim and clean it. It was slimy and still alive, and it began to flirt and flip and jerk around.

"Uncle Remus exclaimed, 'Little fish, what in the world is the matter with you? Why are you cutting up so much? I ain't going to do nothin' to you but gut you.' Mr. President, that is the situation with respect to the motion to recommit. The proponents of that motion have the complacency to say to the Senator from Texas and to the Senator from Ohio and to every other member of the Senate, 'Why are you worrying about this little bill? We want to recommit it. We ain't goin' to do a thing to it but gut it; that's all.'"

Senator Connally once said to Senator Styles Bridges, "If the Senator from New Hampshire would approach these matters with an open mind instead of an open mouth, he could understand these matters." In an argument with the bald Senator Taft, Senator Connally, whose long curls flowed down over his collar in the style of William Jennings Bryan, interrupted Taft's speech with the admonition, "Don't shake your gory locks at me!" which so convulsed the Senate that Taft's arguments were forgotten. When Henry A. Wallace was opposing ratification of the Atlantic Treaty before the Foreign Affairs Committee, saying, "If you ratify this treaty, you will turn Russia into a wild cornered beast," Chairman Connally, as though he had not understood, asked, "What's that about corned beef? What has corned beef got to do with this treaty?" and so made a laughingstock of the former Vice-President.

Connally, a great admirer of President Woodrow Wilson, and one of the unsuccessful supporters of American participation in the League of Nations, was also capable of withering invective. Having helped to draw the United Nations Charter in San Francisco, he was defending it in the Senate against the proponents of some crippling amendments when he roared, "They [the proponents] know that the League of Nations was slaughtered in this chamber," and, pausing, he pointed to the rear wall of the Senate, "Can't you see the blood? There it is on the wall." In the same speech he said, "When the history of this Republic shall be written, Woodrow Wilson's titanic figure will tower above the puny pygmies who now bark at his memory as Pike's Peak towers above the fog of an Arkansas swamp."

Sometimes in the Congress, wit has been shown in exchanges between members. When Champ Clark was Speaker of the House, he ruled that a Republican congressman, Johnson of Indiana, was out of order for calling a

Representative from Ohio a "jackass." Johnson apologized and said, "I withdraw the unfortunate word, Mr. Speaker, but I insist that the gentleman from Ohio is out of order." When the gentleman from Ohio demanded, "How am I out of order?" Johnson answered, "Probably a veterinary could tell you."

Another powerful Speaker of the House of Representatives was Thomas Brackett Reed of Maine. He once cynically replied to a Democratic member who asked, "What becomes of the rights of the minority?" "The right of the minority is to draw its salaries, and its function is to make a quorum." It was also Speaker Reed who one day remarked in a loud voice over the argument of two members, "They never open their mouths without subtracting from the sum of human knowledge." He called Representative J. Hamilton Lewis, who was rather a dandy, "a thing of beauty and a jaw forever." When the Democratic Floor Leader, William M. Springer, of Illinois, once asked for the usual "unanimous consent" to correct a statement in the House, Republican Reed remarked, "No correction needed. We didn't think it was so when you said it!" But the most famous Reed crack came when Springer said once in debate, "I'm right. I know I'm right, so I say, with Henry Clay, sir, I would rather be right than President." Reed remarked, "The gentleman from Illinois will never be either!" Knowing the reputation he had for a sharp tongue, Speaker Reed answered, when asked if the Republicans would nominate him for the Presidency, "They could look much farther and do much worse and I think they will."

Adlai Stevenson quotes another famous Speaker of the House of Representatives, "Uncle Joe" Cannon, who said, "Sometimes in politics one must duel with skunks but no one should be fool enough to allow the skunks to choose the weapons."

If one of the major uses of wit in politics is for the de-

struction of political extremism and pomposity, then one
period when it was conspicuously and regrettably absent
was during the prominence of the late Senator Joseph
McCarthy, of Wisconsin. During the period of his rise to
power, no one on the entire American political scene chose
to bell the cat with humor or in any other way. When
finally the Senate decided it must address itself to the
McCarthy problem, however, Senator Samuel J. Ervin, Jr.,
of North Carolina, told some of the stories that have earned
him his reputation as the most amusing storyteller of the
Senate in our time. These three stories, told on the Senate
Floor on November 15, 1954, during the debate on Senate
Resolution 301 to censure the junior senator from Wisconsin, are typical of the southern-parable school of political wit. "The following story is told in North Carolina: A
young lawyer went to an old lawyer for advice as to how
to try a lawsuit. The old lawyer said, 'If the evidence is
against you, talk about the law. If the law is against you,
talk about the evidence.' The young lawyer said, 'But what
do you do when both the evidence and the law are against
you?' 'In that event,' said the old lawyer, 'give somebody
hell. That will distract the attention of the judge and the
jury from the weakness of your case.' That is precisely what
Senator McCarthy is doing. . . .

"I now know that the lifting of statements out of context
is a typical McCarthy technique. The writer of Ecclesiastes
assures us that 'there is no new thing under the sun.' The
McCarthy technique of lifting statements out of context
was practiced by a preacher in North Carolina about 75
years ago. At that time the women had a habit of wearing
their hair in topknots. This preacher deplored that habit.
As a consequence he preached a rip-snorting sermon one
Sunday on the text Top Not Come Down. At the conclusion of his sermon an irate woman, wearing a very pronounced topknot, told the preacher that no such text could

This cartoon showing Governor Stevenson's reluctance to be the presidential candidate in 1952 was circulated by him to his staff. The notes—including "Notice the athletic figure"—are in his own handwriting.

(James T. Berryman in the Washington, D.C. *Evening Star*, April 17, 1952)

"HOWDY, STRANGERS!"

NIKITA KHRUSHCHEV, RICHARD NIXON, AND JOHN F. KENNEDY
(Copyright, *Punch*, London)

be found in the Bible. The preacher thereupon opened the Scriptures to the 17th verse of the 24th chapter of Matthew and pointed to the words: 'Let him which is on the house-top not come down to take anything out of his house.' [Laughter.] Any practitioner of the McCarthy technique of lifting things out of context can readily find the text 'top not come down' in this verse. . . .

"Mr. President, many years ago there was a custom in a section of my country, known as the South Mountains, to hold religious meetings at which the oldest members of the congregation were called upon to stand up and publicly testify to their religious experiences. On one such occasion they were holding such a meeting in one of the churches; and old Uncle Ephriam Swink, a South Mountaineer whose body was all bent and distorted with arthritis was present. All the older members of the congregation except Uncle Ephriam arose and gave testimony to their religious ex-periences. Uncle Ephriam kept his seat. Thereupon, the moderator said, 'Brother Ephriam, suppose you tell us what the Lord has done for you.' Uncle Ephriam arose, with his bent and distorted body, and said, 'Brother, he has mighty nigh ruint me.' Mr. President, that is about what Senator McCarthy has done to the Senate. . . ."

One of the main uses of humor by southern politicians has been to justify positions they have taken on civil rights and other issues that were unpopular with legislators from other parts of the country. Their stories have served both to lessen tensions in the Congress and its committees and to delay debate or voting. A typical example is another story of Senator Ervin's told during the debates on civil rights in 1959. "The Attorney General has a criminal statute which he can use. He has a civil statute which he can use. Yet he comes to Congress to ask us to give him a third statute. The Attorney General reminds me of the fellow who went 'a-courtin.' John was 'a-courtin' Mary and John

said to Mary, 'Mary, if you wasn't what you is, what would
you like to be?' Mary said, 'I would like to be an American
beauty rose.' And then she inquired of John, 'John, if you
wasn't what you is, what would you like to be?' And John
said, 'Mary, if I wasn't what I is, I would like to be an
octopus.' Mary said, 'John, what is an octopus?' John said,
'An octopus is a sort of a fish that has got a thousand arms.'
Mary said to John, 'Well, now, John if you was an octopus,
what would you do with those thousand arms?' And John
said to Mary, 'Mary, I would put every last one of them
around you.' Mary said to John, 'Go on away from here,
John; you ain't usin' the two arms you've already got.'
[Laughter.] The Attorney General of the United States already has two arms. I assure Senators that either one of
them is sufficient to put around any person anywhere in
the South who is willfully denying to any qualified person
of any color or race the right to register or to vote or to
have his vote counted, as cast."

There were in the United States Congress in the last
half of the nineteenth and early twentieth centuries long
oratorical flights of invective similar to those heard in the
House of Commons at the same time. Perhaps the most
famous was the reply of James G. Blaine, of Maine, to a
statement made in 1866 on the floor of the House of
Representatives by Roscoe Conkling, of New York, that he
was "profoundly indifferent . . . to his [Blaine's] opinion on
this subject, or on any subject." Blaine replied: "As to the
gentleman's cruel sarcasm, I hope he will not be too severe.
The contempt of that large-minded gentleman is so wilting,
his haughty disdain, his grandiloquent swell, his majestic
over-powering turkey-gobbler strut has been so crushing to
myself and to all members of the House, that I know it was
an act of the greatest temerity for me to venture upon a
controversy with him." Blaine then pointed out that Conkling's "extra strut" could be blamed on a satirical newspaper

article that proposed Conkling as the successor to Henry Winter Davis of Maryland. "The gentleman took it seriously," Blaine went on, "and it has given his strut additional pomposity. The resemblance is great. It is striking. Hyperion to a Satyr, Thersites to Hercules, mud to marble, dunghill to diamond, a singed cat to a Bengal tiger, a whining puppy to a roaring lion. Shade of the mighty Davis, forgive the almost profanation of that jocose satire!"

It was this speech that eighteen years later, along with his failure to repudiate the charge that the Democratic Party was the party of "Rum, Romanism and Rebellion," cost Blaine the Presidency of the United States. By then Conkling was the Republican leader of New York, and his refusal to support Blaine, the Republican presidential candidate, caused Blaine to lose New York by a mere 1,200 votes and, with it, the Presidency.

After the Civil War there was much invective exchanged between southern and northern members of the Congress. None was more moving than that of Senator Lucius Quintus Cincinnatus Lamar, of Mississippi, in reply to Senator George F. Hoar, of Massachusetts, on March 1, 1879. Hoar sought to preclude Jefferson Davis's receiving a pension proposed for veterans of the Mexican War, and an exchange between the two senators ended with Lamar's saying, "Sir, it required no courage to do that; it required no magnanimity to do it; it required hate—bitter, malignant, sectional feeling—and a sense of personal impunity. The gentleman, I believe, takes rank among Christian statesmen. He might have learned a better lesson even from the pages of mythology. When Prometheus was bound to the rock, it was not an eagle, it was a vulture, that buried his beak in the tortured vitals of the victim."

Senator William McAdoo once said about the speeches of President Warren G. Harding, "His speeches leave the impression of an army of pompous phrases moving over the landscape in search of an idea. Sometimes these meandering words would actually capture a straggling thought and bear it triumphantly a prisoner in their midst until it died of servitude and overwork." True as this is, Harding's speeches were, in the main at least, his own. The problem today with examining the wit of American politicians is that there is usually no way of knowing what is their own.

For example, Republican Senator Kenneth Keating, of New York, has some reputation as a wit, based largely on his having said, "Roosevelt proved a man could be President for life; Truman proved anybody could be President; and Eisenhower proved you don't need to have a President." An interview with Senator Keating, however, produces a vehement denial that he ever said this. It reveals that he has no spontaneous humor whatsoever, and ends with a plea from the senator that his public-relations aide be allowed to extract examples of wit from his past speeches. Members of the Washington press corps suggest that the senator's reputation for wit is based on the work of a speech writer who has recently been hired away from him by Governor Rockefeller of New York. Rockefeller aides, when questioned, delightedly admit that the speech writer in question has indeed been hired, and express the hope that he will be able to earn for the governor a reputation for wit which he is sorely lacking. And so it goes.

Many politicians in the United States who have not become known on the national scene have possessed great wit. This wit has been influenced both in style and subject matter by its locale. Some, highly regarded in its time, now seems *vieux jeu,* for example the Roaring Twenties wise-cracks of Mayor Jimmie Walker of New York. If one example of a witty local politician is given, it should be Governor Earl Long of Louisiana, the self-styled "red-hot poppa" who loved politics "better than buttermilk." Like his younger brother, Huey, Earl was performing whenever he had an audience, whether of one or of thousands. His language was profane and ungrammatical, but full of those images so dear to southern politicians, sometimes his own, sometimes from the Bible, but always in his own style. When he was at the height of his troubles in the months before his death on September 5, 1960, deserted by his former political allies and even briefly committed to a mental institution, Governor Long was asked by reporters if he thought he could still control the state legislature. He replied, "You know da Bible says dat before da end of time billy goats, tigers, rabbits and house cats are going to sleep together. My gang looks like da Biblical proposition is here."

Perhaps his most quoted remark was one he shouted in the Capitol at Leander Perez, the superracist boss of Plaquemines Parish, "Hey, Leanda, what you goin' to do now da Feds have got da atom bomb?" If the Negroes in Louisiana had a friend in political life, it was Earl Long, or, at least, he was the enemy (as was Huey) of the extreme racists. Earl used to say, for example, that Willie Rainach stirred up for his own political advantage as much trouble as the NAACP; indeed, "I suspect Rainach and the NAACP are just playing 'You goose me and I'll goose you.' "

Long was proud of Louisiana's old-age pension program, hot-lunch program, and especially its good road system, but he once joked, "What we need is a four-lane highway for drunken drivers, nuts, overloaded trucks, and come what may—and we ought to have another road for home-lovers, children, good people, and folks who don' load up on John Barleycorn before they start out on a trip." He did not often, however, condemn any of the pleasures of the flesh, which he enjoyed immensely and conspicuously. He once went so far as to say in a press conference, "A'm goin' down to get a little cush-cush. If you know anybody's got more of dat dan he can use, tell him to send it up to old Uncle Earl."

A Protestant himself (which took care of the Protestant voters), he made clear his friendship for the many Catholics in Louisiana, saying he was in their debt for his formal education. ". . . I'm not against anybody for reasons of race, creed, or any ism he might believe in except nuttism, skingameism or Communism. . . . I'm glad to see so many of my fine Catholic friends here—they've been so kind to me I sometimes say I consider myself forty percent Catholic and sixty percent Baptist. . . . I'm in favor of *every* religion with the possible exception of snake chunkin'. Anybody that so presumes on how he stands with Providence that he will let a snake bite him, I say he deserves what he's got comin' to him."

Long particularly enjoyed characterizing Mayor deLesseps S. Morrison of New Orleans as a city slicker and dude. "I hate to say this—I hate to boost old Dellasoups . . . I'd rather beat Morrison than eat any blackberry, huckleberry pie my mama ever made. . . . I want him to roll up them cuffs, and get out that little old tuppy [toupee] and pull down them shades, and make himself up [make-up for television, which Earl spurned]." "I see Dellasoups has been elected one of the ten best-dressed men in America. He has fifty-dollar neckties and four-hundred-dollar suits. A four-hundred-dollar suit on old Uncle Earl would look like socks on a rooster."

Earl had other political opponents and enemies whom he relished attacking as "stumpwormers," "grasseaters," and "sapsuckers." Sometimes they were characterized as venal, sometimes as hardhearted, closefisted enemies of the poor, the old, and the crippled, who intended to end the great Long programs instituted by Huey and expanded by Earl to "Share the wealth" and make "Every man a king." "Some sapsuckers talk about cuttin' down taxes. Where are they goin' to start cuttin' expenses? On the *spastic* school? They want to cut down on the *spastics?* On the little children enjoying the school lunches? Or on those fine *old* people, white-haired against the sunset of life. . . . We got the finest roads, finest schools, finest hospitals in the country, yet there are rich men who complain. They are so tight you can hear 'em squeak when they walk. They wouldn't give a nickel to see a earthquake. They sit there swallowin' hundred-dollar bills like a bullfrog swallows minners—if you chunked 'em as many as they want, they'd bust . . . course, I know many *fine* rich people, but most of them are like a rich old fella I knew down in Plaquemines Parish, who died one night and never done nobody no good in his life, and yet, when the Devil come to get him, he took an appeal to St. Peter. 'I done some good things on earth,' he said. 'Once, on a cold day in about 1913, I gave a blind man a nickel.' St. Peter looked all through the records, and at last, on page four hundred and seventy-one, he found the entry. 'That ain't enough to make up for a misspent life,' he said.

"'But wait,' the rich man says. 'Now I remember, in 1922 I gave five cents to a poor widow woman that had no carfare.' St. Peter's clerk checked the book again, and on page thirteen hundred and seventy-one, after pages and pages of how this old stumpwormer loan-sharked the poor, he found the record of that nickel. 'That ain't neither enough,' St. Peter said. But the mean old thing yelled, '*Don't* sentence me yet. In about 1931 I gave a nickel to the Red Cross.' The clerk found that entry, too. So he said to St. Peter, 'Your Honor, what are we going to do with him?' You know what St. Peter said?—He said, 'Give him back his fifteen cents and tell him to go to Hell!'"

Long once sued the Luce publications for libel and said, "They're going to find themselves lighter and wiser when it's over. The Luce people have been going on too long picking on people too poor to sue them, and now they're going to get it in the neck. Mr. Luce is like a man that owns a shoestore and buys all the shoes to fit himself. Then he expects other people to buy them."

A brilliantly funny view of Earl Long which also reflects a rare insight into politics is found in *The New Yorker* articles "The Great State" by A. J. Liebling, who quotes Long on voting machines. "Da voting machines won't hold me up. If I have da raight commissioners, I can make dem machines play 'Home Sweet Home.'" Liebling also quotes Long's story on another machine. "There was an important man once who had a portable mechanical-brain thinking machine dat he carried everywhere with him. Da machine was about as big as a small model of one of dose fruit machines dey have in a Elks clubhouse. When he wanted a answer: How many square feet in a room by so and so much? or, Has dat blonde a husband and is he home? he submitted his question and da machine answered it correctly. He would write out da question on a piece of paper and put it in a slot, da machine would read it, and pretty soon it would go blam, blam, blam-blam, blam, blam—dat was da brain working, and it would give him a printed slip with da correct answer. Well, finally da man got jealous of dis machine, it was such a Jim-cracker, and he thought he take it down a little for its own good.

"So he wrote out a message: 'Where is my dear father at this minute, and what is he doing?' He put it in da slot, and da machine says, 'Blam, blam, blam,' very calm, like he had asked it something easy, and it write out da answer, 'Your dear father is in a pool hall in Philadelphia, Pennsylvania, at dis moment, shooting a game of one hundred points against a man named Phil Brown. Your dear father is setting down watching, and Phil Brown has da cue stick and is about to break.'

"'Why,' da man says, 'dat's da most unmitigated libelous

slander I ever heard of. My dear father is sleeping in da Baptist cemetery on da side of da hill in Pittsburgh, Pennsylvania, and has been for da last five years. I am sure of da dates because my dear Mother who is still living reminded me of da anniversary of his death and I telegraphed ten dollars' worth of flowers to place on his grave. I demand a re-investigation and an *apology*.'

"And he writes it out and puts it in da slot. 'Dis time I got you,' he says. 'You ain't nothing but a machine anyway.'

"Da machine reads da message and gets all excited. It says, 'Blam, *Blam*' and 'Blam, *blam*,' like it was scratching its head, and den 'Blam, blam, blam, blam . . . blam, blam, blam, blam,' like it was running its thoughts through again, and den 'BLAM!' like it was mad, and out comes da message.

"Da message said, 'REPEAT,'" the Governor said. "It said 'REPEAT' and den, 'RE-REPEAT. Your dear father is in a pool hall at Philadelphia, Pennsylvania, playing a game with a man named Phil Brown. YOUR MOTHER'S LEGALLY WEDDED HUSBAND is in the Baptist cemetery on the side of the hill in Pittsburgh, Pennsylvania, and has been there these last five years, you BASTARD. The only change in the situation is that Phil Brown has run fourteen and missed, and your old man now has the cue stick. I predict he will win by a few points.'"

In both Great Britain and the United States, politicians have made use of their wit not only in the legislative halls and on the hustings, but also in that particularly Anglo-Saxon institution, the after-dinner speech.

When the Republican Senator from New York, Chauncey Depew, introduced Joseph H. Choate at a dinner, he said, "Gentlemen, permit me to introduce Ambassador Choate, America's most inveterate after-dinner speaker. All you need to do to get a speech out of Mr. Choate is to open his mouth, drop in a dinner, and up comes a speech." When

Choate rose to speak, he said, "Mr. Depew says that if you open my mouth and drop in a dinner, up will come a speech. But I warn you that, if you open your mouths and drop in one of Mr. Depew's speeches, up will come your dinners."

The late Senator Robert Kerr, of Oklahoma, whose invective was much feared by his associates, once quoted Depew in an attack Kerr made in the Senate on Senator Capehart of Indiana. "As I gaze on the ample figure of my friend from Indiana, and as I listen to him, I am reminded of Chauncey Depew, who said to the equally obese William Howard Taft at a dinner before the latter became President, 'I hope, if it is a girl, Mr. Taft will name it for his charming wife.' To which Taft responded, 'If it is a girl, I shall, of course, name it for my lovely helpmate of many years. And if it is a boy, I shall claim the father's prerogative and name it Junior. But if, as I suspect, it is only a bag of wind, I shall name it Chauncey Depew.'"

Even the late Senator Taft, who was by no stretch of the imagination a wit, felt compelled by tradition to include in his after-dinner speeches a joke. Taft's favorite concerned the debate on whether Reid Smoot of Utah should be allowed to sit in the Senate since he was a Mormon, although he had only one wife. The matter was settled in Smoot's favor, when another senator remarked, "I'd rather have a polygamist who doesn't polyg than a monogamist who doesn't monog."

When Joseph Chamberlain spoke at a dinner, he often told the story of when he was a guest of honor at a similar dinner and the mayor of the city, who was toastmaster, remarked to him just as coffee was being served, "Shall we let them enjoy themselves a little longer or had we better have your speech now?"

No dinner story surpasses that of the Chinese Ambassador, Dr. Wellington Koo, who says that early in his career he was asked by his neighbor at the table during the soup course, "Likee soupee?" Dr. Koo did not answer, and later in the evening delivered the major address of the meeting, which was reported in the press as brilliant, witty, and profound. Sitting down amidst tremendous applause after making his speech, Koo turned to the same neighbor and asked, "Likee speechee?"

Although with the increased use by politicians of radio and television and the apparently increasing premium placed upon propriety by the voters, there are fewer hecklers than formerly, the breed still exists. No study of political wit would, therefore, be complete without a few examples.

When Dominic Le Foe was supporting Ludovic Kennedy for a seat in the House of Commons, he found that a pimply-faced youth followed him from meeting to meeting in the constituency and interrupted him at every opportunity. The boy disappeared permanently, however, after Le Foe said one night in answer to an interruption, "You know, I don't mind a girly girl, but I do dislike a boily boy." Lloyd George, when he was standing for re-election in Wales, was also pursued constantly from village to village by a little fellow who delighted in heckling him. One night, Lloyd George, pretending not to see him, paused and looked around, and the little fellow jumped up shouting, "I'm here, Mr. George, I'm here." "Ah," asked Lloyd George, "but are you all there?"

Bothered at a General Election meeting in London in 1950 by a heckler with a particularly loud voice, Lord Mancroft remarked, "A man with your low intelligence should have a voice to match." And when Major Clive Bossom, a Tory candidate for the House of Commons, was repeatedly interrupted on the hustings by a Socialist heckler shouting, "Liar! Liar!" he calmly replied, "If the gentleman will be good enough to tell us his name as well as his calling, we shall be pleased to hear from him."

But perhaps the most famous riposte of an English politician came when an elector said that he would rather vote for the Devil than for John Wilkes, and Wilkes replied, "And if your friend is not standing?" Wilkes seems also to have been the originator of a witticism so often repeated it has now become a cliché in English. Offered snuff, he replied, "No, thank you, I have no *small* vices."

Raised in the rough-and-tumble of New York City politics, Al Smith handled his hecklers with ease and dispatch. Once, when Smith had paused because a heckler kept interrupting him, the man shouted, "Go ahead, Al, don't let me bother you. Tell 'em all you know. It won't take you long." Smith immediately responded, "If I tell 'em all we both know it won't take me any longer."

It sometimes happens that the heckler gets the better of the politician, as when Earl Warren was seeking re-election as Governor of California, and opened his address with, "I'm pleased to see such a dense crowd here tonight," and a voice interrupted, "Don't be too pleased, Governor, We ain't all dense." Or the congressional candidate who ended his address with, "And in conclusion, my friends, I wish to state that I was born a Democrat, have always been a Democrat, and expect to die a Democrat," whereupon a voice quipped, "Not very ambitious, are you?" Great flights of bombast seem most frequently to attract the heckler's arrow, as when William Jennings Bryan said, "I wish I had the wings of a bird to fly to every village and hamlet in America to tell you people about this silver question," and a heckler interjected, "You'd be shot for a goose before you had flown a mile."

Even as excellent a political orator as Theodore Roosevelt was occasionally bested by an unknown heckler. During one of his campaign speeches, he found himself being constantly interrupted by a drunk, who shouted, "I'm a Democrat." Roosevelt finally paused and asked, "May I ask the gentleman why he is a Democrat?" The drunk replied, "My grandfather was a Democrat; my father was a Democrat; and I am a Democrat." Roosevelt then asked, "My friend, suppose your grandfather had been a jackass and your father had been a jackass, what would you be?" and the drunk replied instantly, "A Republican!"

Adlai Stevenson's favorite story about a heckler he had from Brooks Hays, the former congressman from Arkansas, who tells about the lady temperance candidate who concluded her impassioned oration, "I would rather commit adultery than take a glass of beer." Whereupon a clear voice from the audience asked, "Who wouldn't?" But his own response to a rabid right-wing heckler during a recent speech Ambassador Stevenson made in Dallas, Texas, is an excellent example of how a witty politician can use a heckler to ingratiate himself with his audience. When the heckler had finished his nonsensical harangue, Stevenson remarked calmly to the delight of the audience, "I *still* believe in the forgiveness of sinners and the redemption of ignorance."

XI

Adlai Stevenson

> A sense of humor keen enough to show a man his own
> absurdities will keep him from the commission of all sins,
> or nearly all, save those that are worth committing.
> Samuel Butler The Younger, *Life and Habit*

In the period from Roosevelt to Kennedy, American national politics has been lamentably devoid of wit, with a single notable exception, Adlai Stevenson. Although some of his most ardent admirers have come to feel that he was martyred by his own brilliant wit, it seems more probable that his mistake was rather that he "ran against Ivory Soap." It is too early to judge, but it is possible that Stevenson will be remembered far longer in history than are most defeated presidential candidates and that it will be in large measure because of his wit.

Stevenson's wit ranges from the epigram to the sarcastic attack and on to the story. It is a happy blend of the best in both the British and American traditions. Sometimes what he says is original and sometimes it is quoted from others. His short epigrams include: "An editor is one who separates the wheat from the chaff and prints the chaff"; "Eggheads of the world, arise. You have nothing to lose but your yolks"; "An independent is a guy who wants to take the politics out of politics"; and "Someone must fill the gap between platitudes and bayonets." He characterized the Foster Dulles–Eisenhower foreign policy as "the power of positive brinking," and paraphrased Don Marquis, saying,

"The Republicans stroke platitudes until they purr like epigrams."

Stevenson, although constantly advised not to do so by those around him during his campaigns for the Presidency, attacked the Republicans generally, as well as individual Republican leaders. He said of Eisenhower and his "crusade," "The General has dedicated himself so many times, he must feel like the cornerstone of a public building"; and, "Golf is a fine release from the tensions of office, but we are a little tired of holding the bag"; "If I talk over the people's head, Ike must be talking under their feet"; and "Senator Taft is the greatest living authority on what General Eisenhower thinks. . . . The Republicans have a 'me too' candidate running on a 'yes but' platform, advised by a 'has been' staff. . . . General Eisenhower employs the three monkeys standard of campaign morality: see no evil—if it's Republican; hear no evil—unless it is Democratic; and speak no evil—unless Senator Taft says it's all right."

"Following the Great Surrender on Morningside Heights, the General was told by Senator Taft that he believed there should be a ten-billion-dollar cut next year and a twenty-five-billion-dollar cut the following year. This does not sound to me like sober intelligent formulation of the national budget. It sounds more like roulette. You have about the same chance of hitting the right number, but in this case the game is far more dangerous. These men are playing Russian Roulette with the nation's security."

"On August 30th, three New Jersey labor leaders reported after a conference with the General that he did not know the difference between Closed Shop, Open Shop, and Union Shop. When they used the term 'union security,' he said that this was the first time that he had ever heard that term used, but twelve days later, after only a two-hour breakfast with Senator Taft, the General was told, by Senator Taft, of course, that he definitely agrees with the closed shop prohibition and the limited union shop provisions of the Taft-Hartley Law. In two hours the General had become a labor expert. I wonder if Taft's school of labor relations is open to all retired Generals."

Stevenson characterized Goldwater as "a man who thinks everything will be better in the rear future," but his favorite Republican target was Richard M. Nixon: "Mr. Nixon seems to equate criticism with subversion and confuses being hard on Republicans as being soft on Communism"; "He was trained on the Republican treadmill of Republican inaction," and is "a man who believes the only thing that counts in politics is whether you win or lose"; "Nixon is the kind of politician who would cut down a redwood tree, then mount the stump for a speech on conservation"; "Nixon's farm policy is vague but he is going a long way toward solving the corn surplus by his speeches. If he continues, there may be a serious shortage by November 7th. The corn-hog ratio could reach a serious imbalance." Concerning Nixon's unhappiness with Governor Rockefeller's then rising popularity, Stevenson said, "Nothing upsets a woman like somebody's getting married she didn't even know had a beau." And: "Mr. Nixon's defenders insist that although there are certain things in his record which aren't very pretty, he has, nevertheless, shown the capacity for growth and if elected will develop the character for the job. I think it unlikely, however, that the American people will want to send Mr. Nixon to the White House just on the chance that it might do him a world of good." Prophetically, Stevenson said in 1960, "Nixon is finding out there are no tails on an Eisenhower jacket."

Unlike Franklin D. Roosevelt, who wanted voters who considered themselves Republican to vote for him and, therefore, carefully attacked only "the Republican leaders," Stevenson attacked the Republican Party itself. "I like Republicans, have grown up with them, worked with them, and would trust them with anything in the world—except public office." "The elephant has a thick skin, a head full of ivory, and as everyone who has seen a circus parade knows, proceeds best by grasping the tail of its predecessor." "The Republicans view a victory in November as a necessity, and judging by some of their campaign statements, it is obvious what necessity is the mother of." "Whenever the Republicans talk of cutting taxes first and discussing the national security second, they remind me of a very tired rich man who said to his chauffeur, 'Drive off that cliff, James, I want to commit suicide.' " "When the Republicans talk about not being able to afford our present defense buildup, I am reminded of the man who refused to put water on his burning house because his water bill was too high already."

Stevenson said about the Republican platform, "It is fine as a whodunnit, but it isn't very helpful in telling us what kind of domestic or foreign policy the Republicans are going to change to. Standing on it is a little like standing on a bushel of eels, so where is the General to stand? In some fields, he has chosen to jump on to our platform, and in broad daylight. The thing that worries me is that we can't charge him rent." "When I practised law we looked for jokers in a contract. In the Republican farm platform, it is not a question of finding the loopholes in the contract. It is a question of finding a contract in the loopholes."

Stevenson described in 1960 the rules for what he called "the Republican Shell-game": "If they criticize Eisenhower, answer, 'He's not running.' If they criticize Nixon, answer, 'Oh, but he's changed.' If they suggest being reasonable with the Russians, call them 'soft on Communism.' If they suggest getting tough with the Russians, call them 'the war party.' " He enjoyed pointing out some of the less savory members of the Republican Party. "Any similarity between the party of Lincoln and Joe McCarthy is purely coincidental. If you want to live like a Republican, you have to vote like a Democrat." Of the McCarthy-Jenner endorsement of Eisenhower, he said, "This is the first time I've heard a party campaigning on the slogan, 'Throw the rascals in.'"

Stevenson continuously pointed up the divergences of point of view within the Republican Party and the jealousies among some of its members: "Originally, the Republicans made their headquarters in Denver until they discovered it was so close to the Great Divide. The unhappy symbol of this phenomenon of nature made them so uncomfortable, they folded their tents and came East." "Governor Rockefeller says America is going too slow; Senator Goldwater says we are going too fast; Vice President Nixon says we shouldn't talk about it."

Indirectly he was criticizing Republican inconsistencies when he said, "I have not changed my views to suit my itinerary. I have not talked titles in Texas, corruption in California and love in Louisiana. I have not been a 'Sunflower' candidate, turning my face as needs be to catch the fullest rays of the voters' favor."

In both of his national campaigns, Stevenson was criticized by the Republicans both for his use of wit and for being too "highbrow." "In a recent speech in Indianapolis, Senator Taft made an attempt at his own brand of campaign humor. He said, laughingly, that he and Senator Jenner and Senator Capehart, the author of the Capehart Amendment, should get together after this speech and decide on campaign policy. If they want to make an issue of campaign humor, let's put that joke at the head of the list." "If it is a crime to trust the people's common sense and native intelligence, I gladly plead guilty." "I've just been trying to give the customers the right change. That seems to be novel and effete."

For over forty years, Stevenson has kept a notebook, putting in it not only those of his own ideas that he felt were worth preserving but quotations as well, most of which he has used in his speeches. That he equates the importance of wit with that of serious quotations could not be more clearly indicated than the fact that these notebooks contain, side by side, quotations from the Bible and Will Rogers, Lincoln and Mr. Dooley, an eleventh century Chinese sage, and Stevenson's own topical quip. (The gratitude of the author to Ambassador Stevenson for the latter's generous permission to study his notebooks is greater than can be expressed.) Some of the quotations from his notebooks will serve to illustrate Stevenson's extraordinary catholicity of taste in wit.

William Hazlitt: "Man is the only animal that laughs and weeps; for he is the only animal that is struck with the difference between what things are, and what they ought to be." John Billings: "As scare as truth is, the supply is greater than the demand."

"Alcibiades was telling Pericles how Athens should be governed, and Pericles, annoyed with the young man's manner, said, 'Alcibiades, when I was your age, I talked just the way you are talking.' Alcibiades looked him in the face and rejoined, 'How I should like to have known you, Pericles, when you were at your best'"

Dwight Morrow: "We judge ourselves by our motives and others by their actions." Stevenson: "When Republican speech makers think they are thinking, they are only rearranging their prejudices." Disraeli: "Conservatism offers no redress for the present and makes no preparation for the future." Don Marquis: "Procrastination is the art of keeping up with yesterday." "Charles V with admirable candor summed up his controversy with his cousin, Francis I, saying, 'My cousin and I are in complete agreement—we both want Milan.'" Will Rogers: "The Republican party has got only one platform. 'Elect us and maybe we can think of something to do after we get in. Up to now, we haven't

thought of it, but give us a chance and maybe we will.' "
"Mrs. Karl Marx, at the end of a long and bleak life, remarked, 'How good it would have been if Karl had made some capital instead of writing so much about it.' "

"When Evita Perón was in Barcelona and complained that she had been called 'puta' as she drove through the streets, an old general apologized, saying, 'Why, I've been retired for twelve years and they still call me General.' "
"Clemenceau was being seen off at a station by a party leader who, in his anxiety to impress the Premier, was giving him a detailed history of the political situation in France. Clemenceau, observing a man yawning on the other side of the platform, lifted his finger warningly and said in a low voice, 'I'm afraid we are overheard.' "

Stevenson, because of his Princeton background, enjoys quoting Woodrow Wilson's "I used to be a lawyer, but now I am a reformed character" and "Nothing was ever done so systematically as nothing is being done now."

Stevenson often turns the wit of other men to his own use, as when he reversed the quip of Republican Chauncey Depew into: "I will make a bargain with the Republicans. If they will stop telling lies about Democrats, we will stop telling the truth about them." In a speech such as the one quoted below, Stevenson may combine his own wit with that of others as well as brilliant epigram with a "that reminds me of the story." As Governor of Illinois welcoming the Democratic Convention to Chicago, he used the "windmill" witticism of Richard Sheridan quoted in the first chapter of this book (which was also once used by Huey Long on the floor of the Senate): ". . . In the name of more than eight million people, the people of the State of Illinois, I bring you the heartiest of greetings. As an official of the State, I was very glad to see the Republicans voting their Convention in Illinois, but as a Democrat, I am certainly pleased that the amphitheatre has a new tenant.

"The previous tenants were very boisterous and noisy and generally obstreperous. The word must have reached them that this hall is often used as a fight arena. They just didn't get along with each other at all. They behaved like people who were out of patience, out of sorts, and out of office. At intervals, they calmed down enough to talk, but then what did they say? Most of the speeches reminded me of that facetious explanation of the word 'auditorium'. It is said that the word 'auditorium' comes from two Latin words, 'audio' and 'taurus.' 'Audio,' of course, means 'I hear' and, as everybody knows, 'taurus' means 'bull.' . . . As you watched over television, did you notice the quantities of water that the speakers drank? That's the first time I've ever seen windmills run on water power. . . . I have a notion the voters are going to respond in November to those Republican promises the way a certain young lady responded to the proposal of a young farmer friend of hers. He said, 'Marry me and I'll paint the house and the barn inside and out. I'll put in electricity, I'll buy a brand new stove and refrigerator. Will you marry me?' And she said, 'Honey let's leave it this way, you *do* all those things and then ask me again.'"

Historically in the United States, much humor has been based on accent, race, color, and religion. With the increasing appointment of members of minority groups to political office, it is probable that there will be more stories of this kind than there have been in the last few years, since most members of minority groups are less shy about telling stories on their own kind than nonmembers are. For example, when Carl Thomas Rowan was appointed to replace Edward R. Murrow, the *New York Times* wrote: "An apocryphal story about Carl Thomas Rowan, the Negro former newspaperman who is slated to become Director of the United States Information Agency, goes like this: Soon after Mr. Rowan and his wife and three children moved to

Washington in 1961, they bought an old rambling house with a big front lawn in a recently integrated neighborhood. Mr. Rowan was out mowing the lawn one Saturday, in Bermuda shorts and a T-shirt, when a white man drove up to the curb and called out: 'Hey, boy, how much you get for cutting the grass?' Mr. Rowan sweating and grinning, stopped his power mower, walked to the car window and retorted: 'The lady of the house lets me live with her.'"

Formerly, Stevenson told stories of this kind. He could say, "This is a dark, dark world and that is why the Irish are always half-lit," or tell the story of the prayer of the little boy in one of Chicago's Irish wards, "Our Father, which art in Heaven, O'Halloran be Thy name." He has told the Sholom Aleichem tale of the Jewish elder whose down-to-earth stories helped amuse his fellow sufferers in the ghetto. The favorite story concerned the day the elder and his family were pursued by wolves across an icy lake and in the middle of the lake the ice gave way and the sleigh and passengers sank beneath the surface. "And what do you think God did for us in that situation?" the elder would ask, while everybody waited joyfully for the answer they had heard a dozen times before: "Thanks to Him, the whole story is a lie from beginning to end."

One of Mr. Stevenson's favorite religious stories is about the daughter of a famous divine who was busy with her crayons and whose mother asked her whose picture she was drawing. "God," she answered. "But, my dear, nobody knows how He looks," her mother admonished. Whereupon, the child answered, "They will when I'm finished." Stevenson formerly also told Negro stories, such as this one in connection with the danger of nuclear war: " 'Rastus', said his friend, who had been reading in the paper of a number of fatal accidents, 'if you had to take your choice twixt one or t'other, which had you rather be in, a collision or explosion?' 'Man, a collision,' said Rastus. 'How come?'

'Why man, if you is in a collision, there you is. But if you is in an explosion, where is you?' "

As did Lincoln, Stevenson told stories during his campaigns even on subjects about which he had very serious views. On the subject of education he quoted the prisoner who said to his cellmate, "I'm going to study and improve myself, and when you're still a common thief, I'll be an embezzler"; and in relation to taxes, Stevenson said, "There was a time when a fool and his money were soon parted, but now it happens to everybody." Perhaps Stevenson's use of wit is congenital. He enjoys telling stories of his grandfather, who, when he was to be presented to Queen Victoria, said he didn't want to be "because I have to take off my pants and wear shorts." When he returned to Bloomington, Illinois, the children asked, "What did the Queen say, father?" "Well," he said, "she leaned forward on the throne and said, 'Adlai, how's Uncle John?' "

Ambassador Stevenson believes there is more wit on the Democratic than on the Republican side. "Oh, I think there's much more on the Democratic side. I think we're much more lighthearted. I think it's probably due to the fact that our party is made up of ordinary people, for the most part, who aren't afraid of natural response—to whom it comes naturally. Actually, they aren't as self-conscious . . . the people are always more gay and lighthearted, I think, than their leaders and the people's party is more lighthearted than the party that is the party of the few."

Asked if he thought that McCarthy or the Birch Society could have been better fought with humor than with reason and could have been made ridiculous, Stevenson said: "I'm not sure that that's true. I think that they should never be spared from ridicule and humor and from the exposure of their contradictions by the use of humor and ridicule and satire. On the other hand, I'm not sure just how effective that really is. People seem to disassociate what appears to be devastating ridicule as something separate, something lighthearted and gay and amusing and funny but not serious, and unless you face a serious problem seriously, it doesn't seem to have the effect that satire and humor used to have. I don't quite understand why that should be so. I think Lincoln was effective in the use of anecdotal material, some sharp repartee, humor, satire and it seems to illuminate his dialogue and make him more effective as a political figure. I find it very difficult to understand. I think there is a certain sobriety that has overwhelmed us and I don't know whether it's a fault of our educations or whether it's because the lightheartedness of people has been submerged by a higher degree of prosperity."

Asked if humor is a more effective weapon against extremism, pomposity, and stupidity than reason, Stevenson replied: "I think it can be extremely effective, especially for Americans, because Americans are such sensitive people, responsive to humor—ordinary Americans. I couldn't really draw any comparisons. I would hate to think that humor is, in the long run, more effective than reason, but it certainly is more arresting than reason. I think ridicule, and the best of us do ridicule humorously, is effective in our political scene. Naturally, I believe that reason must prevail. If it doesn't, we're lost. Humor is no substitute for reason. On the other hand, it certainly can illustrate and enrich reason."

When asked if the American public today is less receptive to personal comments by politicians about their opponents than it was, for example, when Lincoln made fun of Douglas's love of drinking, the Ambassador said: "Yes, I think it is. I think we've lost some of the sort of lusty taste for the verbalizing assault and especially through the form of wit. I noticed in my campaigns that humor about myself and about general noncontroversial things was much more effective than sharp wit with respect to one's adversaries. While we haven't lost a certain tolerance for that sort of thing, I think we have lost a good deal of our kind of approval for it. Maybe it's a good thing. I suppose maybe it's the general quality of banality or conventionality that's crept into our political dialogue. It's become much less sharp even than it is in England today. Generally speaking, the standardization of talk, of newspaper reporting and the kind of banality of most of the television programs have created a standard of manners which is deprived of a good deal of lusty vigor, especially of the use of wit and humor that we used to have."

Stevenson was asked why, when Americans have traditionally been proud of being a pluralistic, melting-pot nation, and such a large part of our national humor once consisted of friendly jokes about foreign accents, race, religion, and the like, such jokes are now considered racist and wicked. He said:

"I agree that this change has taken place. I used to make comments that related to racial groups and religious groups and I was criticized for it, merely because of the fact that I had described groups as Jewish, as Irish, as Catholic, and so on. I would tell a story to illustrate some point I was making. But the advice in politics nowadays is to avoid anything that is controversial or that might provoke any kind of misunderstanding. I had this advice constantly and was constantly urged to err on the side of conventionality and banality rather than wit and humor and especially if it ever related to religion or race.

"I remember even having letters sharply taking me to task for having used an allusion to the Bible in my acceptance speech in 1952 when I said that I prayed that this cup might pass from me; as if this were a sacrilege, even to use a biblical phrase. It's all right, I think, if you are a Baptist and a leading Baptist like Brooks Hays and tell the kind of gentle stories that he does. I had thought that this was perfectly fair, sound, and consistent with the American tra-

dition. I know my grandfather used to tell Scotch Presbyterian stories all the time. He was a well-known Scotch
Presbyterian and married to a Scotch Presbyterian minister's
daughter and his son-in-law was a Scotch Presbyterian minister, so when you're that intimately involved, you can get
away with it. But I don't think in today's political climate
I could tell a Catholic story or Brooks a Jewish story. I think
it is too bad that we have to block out areas because we
don't have enough wit and humor to be able to enjoy them
and also some self-consciousness about it because we're
afraid of reactions from people who aren't perceptive
enough to see the humor without suspecting the barb.
We've lost a lot of our vitality and vigor. We've become
awfully bland, and awfully neutral and awfully circum-
spect in our dialogue and in our exchanges, especially in
the political arena. I used to be abused all the time for
having resorted to humor in my first election campaign on
the grounds that this was frivolous and disclosed a man
who wasn't serious rather than a man who was humorous,
if you see what I mean. To have had it diverted in that
respect seems to me to confirm what I was saying."

Asked if he thought there might be a renaissance of wit
in politics, Stevenson said: "I think everything is cyclical.
Yes, I'm a great believer in cycles. I think probably the
sense of humor in the United States, which is one of the
most precious things we have, one of the indispensable
qualities, one of the most indispensable ingredients of life,
if you please, may return. There are plenty of us, myself
included, who will, perhaps, come back and once again
enjoy the position of respect that we originally had. It can't
be forced, however. I think it has to come naturally and I
don't think there is anything more dreary than forced humor or a poor storyteller trying to tell a story or trying to be
humorous when he isn't or who doesn't have a sense of
humor. I think everybody has to be natural and has to be

what they are. It is just instinct with me to try to leaven the loaf we have to eat all the time.

"I think the people themselves have changed, tastes have changed. The old vigor and vitality of the dialogue, both private and also in the public arena, has diminished. I find even in my own case that I'm a little less unself-conscious and a little less responsive with humor than I used to be. Perhaps that's the sort of corrosiveness that comes with time or maybe age and perhaps just general exhaustion. You get your nose rubbed into this solemnity and this seriousness of our time and it begins to have its effect on you, it buries your own natural spontaneity of personality. I don't know what the answer to it is. I keep thinking it is education and, hopefully, a reversal of the pattern of conformity and standardization of thought and of reaction. If you express a view that departs from the norm nowadays, then of course, you are immediately charged with being a Communist or something or other, and this extreme form of compulsive, iron-fisted conformity, I think, is one thing that has depressed the dialogue. I've made some speeches on this theme generally, on the responsibility of our politicians as teachers. The politician is an educator, and his first responsibility is to educate the people, and one of the techniques of education is to tickle their fancy and their sense of humor. I suppose all of these wars, the First World War and Second World War and the terrible brutality of man to man and all these things have made this generation a somewhat more serious-minded generation. Now the emergence of the nuclear threat of co-extermination and all these things have combined and tend to depress the individualism which is the source of material for humor.

"I think that humor is inherent in the American heart and spirit and that we do like it. My own case is a good illustration of it, although I wasn't too successful a politician. Much of the sort of thing for which I was abused by the

Republicans (which is a confession of their own failing, you know, and this showed through) endeared me to lots of people who continue to be loyal and friendly throughout the country . . . the fact that I had a sense of humor, and didn't take myself too seriously. I remember once saying that a politician is a statesman who approaches every question with an open mouth. That kind of thing tickles the fancy of ordinary people because they've all heard the saying, 'I approach everything with an open mind,' and I was talking about these politicians who talk about everything as if they know all the answers; which always reminds me of, I think it was, Macaulay who said of some Englishman, Brougham, I believe, 'I wish I was as sure of anything as he is of everything.' Well, when you say that sort of thing, you can get a response because most of the ordinary people don't go for this self-righteous solemnity. . . . I think there is a great residue of humor and of response to humor in the ordinary people and I think somehow politicians feel it is not in fashion. I think it is too bad. Humor helps to distinguish the really bright and thoughtful, and also the humble, if you please, from the self-conscious and the self-righteous presumptuous type."

Asked who was his favorite American political wit in this century, Stevenson said it was Woodrow Wilson. "Wilson always could be extremely sharp and very funny. I suppose you remember his story about the political leader of northern New Jersey who asked him to come up to his district and make a speech. Wilson said, 'How long do you want me to talk?' And the leader said, 'Well, just as long as you care to, Governor.' Whereupon Wilson said, 'Well, I'll tell you, if you want me to talk for ten minutes, I'll come next week; if you want me to talk for an hour, I'll come tonight!' And that wonderful little jingle that he used occurs to me from time to time, 'The world is so big and I am so small. I do not like it at all, at all.' Most of Wilson's contemporaries are dead now, but of course I went to Princeton and knew some of them when they were still living and used to try to spend evenings with them to get them to talk about Wilson. I used to hear some of these sallies of his, but he was, for the most part, a pretty solemn man, too, I think. The only really great, really humorous storyteller, the really good storyteller of my political life has been Alben Barkley, who was a great raconteur in the old Kentucky tradition of my grandfather, who could go on and on telling stories like these. But the South, of course, has always been full of those people—Brooks Hays is one."

Asked why today, as in the past, the South has provided American politics with its best storytellers, Stevenson said: "I suppose because they strive to be common people. Also, they are the heirs of the storytellers of the old frontier days. You can see it in the Arab countries today. You can go into most any Arab town, and any night in the week you will see a swarm of people squatting on the ground listening to a storyteller, who, I think, must be extremely gifted if you understood Arabic. I think the tradition of the storyteller of the frontier and the pioneer period carried over into the South of today because it fell back of the rest of the country in progress, both in education and in modernization and industrialization; I think you used to see it in the bombast of the Southern orator."

Stevenson, who has been attacked not only by Republicans but also by opponents in his own party, is fond of quoting Edmund Burke's "Those who would carry on great public schemes must be proof against the worst delays, the most mortifying disappointments, the most shocking insults, and what is worst of all the presumptuous judgment of the ignorant upon their design."

Of all Ambassador Stevenson's humor, that which most delights his admirers is his wit directed against himself. The minor role assigned to him by the Kennedys, for example, in the 1960 campaign, prompted him to tell the story "about Jimmy, age eight, who went over to play with his friend, Bill. 'Let's play cops-and-robbers,' he proposed. 'I'll be the good guy and you can be the bad guy.' Bill's little brother Tommy, age four, said eagerly, 'Can I be the commercial?' "

When Stevenson was hoping to be "drafted" as the Democratic presidential candidate, he said it reminded him of "William Jennings Bryan's story when Teddy Roosevelt decided to run because of 'the public demand and pressure on him.' Miss Sally, a zealous temperance worker fell ill. Her doctor, who did not share her convictions, was called in and, fumbling around for her pulse, remarked in a sharp voice, 'Miss Sally, you've been drinking.' She reared up in bed and indignantly replied that she had signed the pledge when she was six years old and had never in her whole life tasted a drop of liquor, that she would, indeed, rather die. Whereupon the doctor said, 'Very strange indeed, Miss Sally, very strange, but your pulse is the pulse of an intoxicated person.' It turned out that he was feeling his own pulse."

After his two defeats in the race for the Presidency, Stevenson told two stories. He was reminded of Tom Watson of Indiana who had been elected to the United States Senate by an overwhelming majority but was later defeated for re-election, also by an overwhelming majority, and remarked, "I was sent to this august body with very little opposition from the people of Indiana and I leave it with none." And he said, as Lincoln had once remarked, that he felt like the boy who had stubbed his toe. "It hurts too bad to laugh, and he was too big to cry."

XII

John F. Kennedy

> Humor is the only test of gravity, and gravity of humor,
> for a subject which will not bear raillery is suspicious, and
> a jest which will not bear serious examination is false wit.
>
> Aristotle, *Rhetoric*

When Ambassador Adlai Stevenson was asked whether Abraham Lincoln could be nominated or elected President of the United States if he ran today, Stevenson said: "No, I think not. Lincoln, of course, was a genius and there is no accounting for public reaction to genius, but joking as Lincoln did about race and religion and other subjects considered 'controversial' today, I doubt it." Asked if he had noticed any revival of wit on the New Frontier, Stevenson replied, "No, indeed. It was made up of very intense young men who for the most part took themselves very seriously."

Nevertheless, in the view of this author, there has been in the last four or five years a considerable renaissance of wit in American politics. In the main the pattern was set by President John Fitzgerald Kennedy, but the use of wit in recent years can also be found frequently in the public (and private) words of as disparate a politician as Senator Barry Morris Goldwater.

Wit was as integral a part of the personality of Kennedy as courage. His style reflected both a hearty Irish wit and the urbanity of his Harvard education. It revealed his often ironic view of life and the stoicism of a man who twice nearly died, once in the Solomons and again as a result of his operation in 1954 (and also perhaps the tragedies of his brother and sister). But his humor was not bitter and did not represent a withdrawal from action and life. Rather, it was a part of his abundant vitality and courage, and reminiscent of Hemingway's description of courage, "grace under pressure." Kennedy was never in the last years of his life without the burden of physical pain, and during his three years as President he was under constant political pressure, national and international. Yet even under these pressures, Kennedy constantly displayed an irreverent and insightful wit about himself, his associates, his opponents, and the dangers of the world of which he was as aware as any living man.

Certainly no prominent politician in America today has a view of the problems of America and the world more different from Kennedy's than Senator Goldwater. Yet he, too, makes frequent use of wit. This chapter gives examples of the wit of both men on many of the same subjects. Perhaps because of their religious minority backgrounds, both men were willing to joke even on the supposedly forbidden subject of religion. Before his election disproved the theory that no Roman Catholic could ever be elected President of the United States, Kennedy joked, "I do hope that Bishop Bromley Oxnam at the PAOU will be my personal envoy to the Vatican and he's been instructed to open negotiations for that transatlantic tunnel immediately." With great courage, Kennedy opposed the inclusion of Federal aid to parochial schools in the bill for school aid which he fought hard and unsuccessfully to get through the Congress. This brought opposition from congressmen with large Catholic constituencies, and the President said, "As all of you know, some circles invented the myth that after Al Smith's defeat in 1928 he sent a one-word telegram to the Pope, 'Unpack.' After my press conference on the school bill, I received a one-word wire from the Pope myself. 'Pack.'"

Columnists such as James Reston often advised the President not to be embarrassed by his Catholicism and not to be afraid to pay a visit to the Vatican if he wanted to, but one wonders how they could feel he was anything but relaxed on the Catholic issue after he said: "I have a very grave announcement. The Soviet Union has once again recklessly embarked upon a provocative and extraordinary change in the *status quo* in an area which they know full well I regard as having a special and historic relationship. I refer to the deliberate and sudden deployment of Mr. Adzubei to the Vatican. I am told that this plot was worked out by a group of Khrushchev's advisers who have all been excommunicated from the Church. It is known as 'EX-COM.' Reliable refugee reports have also informed us that hundreds of Marxist bibles have been unloaded and are being hidden in the caves throughout the Vatican. We will now pursue the contingency plan for protecting the Vatican City which was previously prepared by the National Security Council. The plan is known as 'Vat 69.' We are, in short, eyeball to eyeball over the Holy See and the other fellow is cross-eyed. Speaking of the religious issue, I asked the Chief Justice [after the Supreme Court's no-prayer-in-school decision] tonight whether he thought our new Education Bill was constitutional and he said, 'It's clearly constitutional—it hasn't got a prayer.'"

Asked recently if he subscribed to the theory that "race" and "religious" stories should be avoided by politicians Goldwater said, "I have no qualms about kidding people. I'm half Jewish myself and make no bones about it. A politician shouldn't be afraid to tell a story because it might conceivably hurt the feelings of some hypersensitive Christians or Jews. I told this story the other night to several thousand Republican ladies, about how Mr. Khrushchev had certain problems. He found that Stalin's memory haunted him and finally he figured the best way to fix that was to get rid of Stalin's body. So he called President Kennedy and asked if he'd take the body. Kennedy explained he didn't want a Communist dead or alive in the United States, but suggested he call Macmillan. Macmillan gave Khrushchev the same line, that he would like to help him but it would cause too much political trouble, and suggested, 'Try de Gaulle. Every once in a while that fellow will help you and besides he enjoys offending the Americans.' Well, de Gaulle explained to Khrushchev that he had trouble at home and abroad, but suggested he try Ben-Gurion: 'There's a little fellow who's pretty decent, and his country has the most relaxed immigration laws. He'll probably help you.' So Khrushchev called Ben-Gurion, told him his dilemma, and said, 'We'll bring the body in the dark of night, absolutely clandestinely and you won't have anything to worry about.' Ben-Gurion answered: 'Oh, Mr. Khrushchev, don't give it a thought. We're tickled to death to help you. Just bring that body down here any time in broad daylight. We'll take care of it. But I have to remind you, Mr. Khrushchev, that my country has the highest rate of Resurrection in the world.' "

Asked if it were true that he had been black-balled by a Phoenix country club because of his background and had subsequently called the president of the country club to suggest, "Since I'm only half-Jewish can I join if I only play nine holes?" Goldwater said, "It's a damn funny story but unfortunately not true."

It was often alleged that President Kennedy was sensitive to humor directed against his family and most particularly any against his father. Actually, he took great pleasure in joking about his own family. In 1958, when it was well known that he would seek the Democratic nomination, he said to the Gridiron Club in Washington, "I just received the following wire from my generous Daddy—'Dear Jack—Don't buy a single vote more than necessary. I'll be damned if I'm going to pay for a landslide.'" During his campaign for the Presidency, Kennedy said, "On this matter of experience, I had announced earlier this year that if successful I would not consider campaign contributions as a substitute for experience in appointing ambassadors. Ever since I made that statement I have not received one single cent from my father."

Kennedy continuously kidded himself not only about his father's supposedly "buying" the Presidency for him but also about his vast unpopularity with the leaders of American business, of whom his father had been an archetype. After his election, speaking to the National Association of Manufacturers, he said, "I recognize that in the last campaign most of the members of this group supported my opponent except for a very few who were under the impression that I was my father's son." He loved kidding the businessmen (as had Roosevelt), and he said further, "I understand that President McKinley and I are the only two Presidents of the United States to ever address such an occasion [an N.A.M. convention]. I suppose that President McKinley and I are the only two that are regarded as fiscally sound enough to be qualified for admission. . . ."

When Goldwater seemed to be making fun of his own family it usually turned out that he was really taking a dig at another family. "Of course, the Goldwater clan is not as large as the Kennedy clan. And *my* brother, Bob, doesn't want to be in government—he promised Dad he'd go straight. . . . But I have a lot of uncles and cousins and in-laws whom I wouldn't mind shifting to the government payroll. Anything at all—Peace Corps, Justice Department, Senator from Massachusetts, just anything, so long as it isn't one of those dollar-a-year jobs. And I have a sister named Carolyn and a granddaughter named Carolyn which, I figure, puts me two up in that department. . . . I also have a two-year-old grandson who's too young to vote, but too old to be Attorney-General."

Senator Goldwater is a hard man to make fun of because he has a talent for taking attacks on himself and turning them humorously against his attackers. "I see my friend Herblock has coined a new word in some of his recent cartoons, 'Goldbirchers,' and I don't mind telling you that personally I think this is a pretty shabby treatment of Justice Arthur Goldberg." He is able to poke fun at himself and his policies in the very words of his opponents. "Why even back in the eighteenth century—where, as you know, I come from—we did some reading. We read the Bible—it was still legal in those days."

Kennedy had the same ability, by making what appeared to be self-deprecatory remarks, to remove the sting from attacks made against him. When he was criticized for being too young, he said, "It has recently been observed that whether I serve one or two terms in the Presidency, I will find myself at the end of that period at what might be called the awkward age—too old to begin a new career and too young to write my memoirs." Constantly attacked as being too pro-labor, he nevertheless said, addressing the AFL-CIO, "I want to express my pleasure at this invitation as one whose work and continuity of employment has depended in part on the union movement." When the Republicans sought to make an issue comparable to Roosevelt's attempt to pack the Supreme Court out of Kennedy's appointment of his youthful brother to the Cabinet as Attorney General, the President destroyed the issue with his wit. "I don't see what's wrong with giving Bobby a little experience before he starts to practice law"; and also, ". . . speaking of jobs for relatives, Master Robert Kennedy, age four, came to see me today but I told him we already had an Attorney General."

President Kennedy had no more serious and frustrating handicap in trying to get his legislative program through the Congress than the fact that he won the Presidency by so narrow a margin of votes. Yet he joked even about this.

"Some years ago in the city of Fall River, Massachusetts, the Mayor was elected by one vote, and every time he walked down the street, someone would say to him, 'Say, I put you in office.' I feel a little like that tonight here in Chicago. If all of you had voted the other way—there are about 5,500 of you here tonight—I wouldn't be President of the United States."

When wit is really a part of a politician's makeup, even his associates are not exempt from it. A good many of Goldwater's barbs are aimed at fellow Republicans, especially those who are likely competitors for the presidential nomination or who have served the Democrats. "Personally I think Nelson Rockefeller would make a wonderful President, although I don't know how the White House would look with those gas pumps out in front. And Governor Romney says he's getting tired of telling people that he's not a candidate for the Republican nomination. What's more, he's getting tired of all the traveling he has to do to tell them. . . . I believe that Secretary Dillon belongs in government—I don't think private industry could afford him."

President Kennedy was at no point in his career loath to direct his wit against members of his own party. Speaking to correspondents at the Gridiron Dinner in 1958, he said: "I dreamed about 1960 myself the other night and I told Stuart Symington and Lyndon Johnson about it in the cloakroom yesterday. I told them how the Lord came into my bedroom, anointed my head and said, 'John Kennedy, I hereby appoint you President of the United States.' Stuart Symington said, 'That's strange, Jack, because I too had a similar dream last night in which the Lord anointed me and declared me, Stuart Symington, President of the United States and Outer Space.' Lyndon Johnson said, 'That's very interesting, gentlemen, because I too had a similar dream last night and I don't remember anointing either of you.'"

At the time of his Inauguration, Kennedy said: "Clark Clifford has been invaluable in assisting me in the transition. He has been willing to do everything: appoint the Cabinet, decide on top hats or homburgs, write the inaugural address and ride a buffalo in the parade and all he's asked for is the right to advertise his law office on the back of the dollar bill." Kennedy once remarked, "I must get back to the office to meet Congressman Adam Clayton Powell. He is coming over to help me plan my trip to Europe."

Nor were even his own Cabinet members exempt from the President's wit. Of his then Secretary of Labor, Arthur Goldberg, the President said, "I was up in New York stressing physical fitness, and in line with that Arthur went over to Switzerland with a group to climb some of the mountains there. When they all came back at four o'clock in the afternoon, he didn't come back with them. So they sent out search parties and went out calling, 'Goldberg, Goldberg, it's the Red Cross.' Then this voice came down the mountain, 'I gave at the office.'"

Although Senator Goldwater does exercise his wit on fellow Republicans, his best cracks are reserved for his Democratic opponents. "I understand the President and Vice-President are out raising money to pay off the campaign debt. They could each give up one week's allowance and take care of that. I have nothing against millionaire Presidents. I'd just like to see the day return when people other than Presidents can be millionaires too." "Adlai Stevenson is mad at the Post Office—he couldn't get back the Christmas card he sent to Nehru—but it couldn't be delivered anyway, because Nehru was at a Peace Conference—that's where he spends his time between invasions." "Bobby Kennedy's finally on the right track, I think, about adequate defense. He's in favor of a large standing army—in the South, that is. How is it that our government did better against General Electric than they did against Cuba?"

The President's sharpest barbs, too, were reserved for his political opponents. During the Eisenhower regime, Kennedy said to the press: ". . . we want you to help by reporting also all Republican feuds in full. Some of them are diminishing, I must admit. Vice-President Nixon and Sherman Adams, for example, decided to bury the hatchet—in Harold Stassen. Mr. Stassen announces he will run for Governor of Pennsylvania. He has already been Governor of Minnesota. That leaves only forty-six states still in jeopardy. I do not say that Sherman Adams *alone* is responsible for these key decisions. All I say is that the Constitution will prohibit him from seeking a third term."

Kennedy made fun of both President Eisenhower and Vice-President Nixon during his presidential campaign. Of Eisenhower's answers to Candidate Kennedy's charges of recession, Kennedy said: "As I interpret the President, we're now at the end of the beginning of the upturn of the downturn. Every bright spot the White House finds in the economy is like the policeman bending over the body in the alley and saying cheerfully, 'Two wounds are fatal. The other one is not so bad.'" During a question-and-answer session, Kennedy was asked, "Senator, when does the moratorium end on Nixon's hospitalization and your ability to attack him?" and Kennedy replied, "I have said I would not mention him unless I could praise him until he got out of the hospital and I have not mentioned him." He also said: "I come from a nonagricultural state, Massachusetts, and, therefore, I am sure there are some farmers in Iowa and South Dakota and North Dakota who say, 'Why should we elect someone from New England?' Well, there is no farmer up for office this year. Whittier, California, is not one of the greater agricultural sections of the United States." "I regret the rain, but it rains, as the Bible tells us, on the just and the unjust alike, on Republicans as well as Democrats."

In a single quip, Kennedy sometimes addressed himself to several different aspects of the campaign. This one, for example, included the Republican alliance with big business, Nixon's campaign tactics, and the so-called Catholic issue: "Mr. Nixon, like the rest of us, has had his troubles in this campaign. At one point even the *Wall Street Journal* was criticizing his tactics. That is like the *Osservatore Romano* criticizing the Pope."

Of all Kennedy's wit during the 1960 campaign, many consider these words spoken at a charity dinner in New York to have been his most surprising and best. "Cardinal Spellman is the only man so widely respected in American politics that he could bring together amicably, at the same banquet table, for the first time in this campaign, two political leaders who are increasingly apprehensive about the November election, who have long eyed each other suspiciously, and who have disagreed so strongly, both publicly and privately, Vice-President Nixon and Governor Rockefeller."

Kennedy's wit manifested itself in a great variety of ways. Sometimes it could be mildly self-deprecatory, as when, after expounding seriously and at great length on the duties and glories of the American Presidency, he could lighten it all with "and besides, the pay is pretty good." At the height of the crisis, when it was learned that there were Russian missiles in Cuba, he could remark of a senator who had always advocated a hard-nosed foreign policy, "This will make Homer Capehart look like the Churchill of the sixties." He could use wit in order to avoid an ugly contretemps in his own party with another member also seeking the Democratic nomination. For example, at the 1960 Democratic Convention he refused to answer Lyndon Johnson's detailed attack on his poor record on quorum calls in the Senate made before the assembled Texas and Massachusetts delegations. Instead, Kennedy heartily agreed that all the favorable comments Johnson had made about himself and his own record in the Senate were true and that he hoped the Texan would long continue—as Majority Leader in that body.

Kennedy's wit had often a special grace and gallantry. When he had obviously bettered Nixon in a television debate, he took the opportunity, not to crow, but to explain his triumph in terms that also complimented another Democratic senator, who, like Johnson, had tilted with Kennedy for the nomination, and lost. "This week I had the opportunity to debate with Mr. Nixon. I feel that I should reveal that I had a great advantage in that debate. . . . Mr. Nixon had just debated with Khrushchev, and I had debated with Hubert Humphrey, and that gave me an edge." When Nixon tried to make former President Truman's use of profanity a campaign issue, Kennedy was able to handle even this potentially embarrassing circumstance with wit. "I would not want to give the impression that I am taking former President Truman's use of language lightly. I have sent him the following wire: 'Dear Mr. President: I have noted with interest your suggestion as to where those who vote for my opponent should go. While I understand and sympathize with your deep motivation, I think it important that our side try to refrain from raising the religious issue.'"

As the most prominent Harvard man of his own generation, his wit showed itself when he accepted an honorary degree from Yale. ". . . I am very glad to be here and as a new member of the club, I have been checking to see what earlier links existed between the institution of the Presidency and Yale. I found that a member of the class of 1878, William Howard Taft, served one term in the White House as preparation for becoming a member of this faculty. And

a graduate of 1804, John C. Calhoun, regarded the Vice
Presidency as too lowly a station for a Yale alumnus—and
became the only man in history to ever resign that office."

Senator Goldwater waxes serious on the important part
humor and wit have to play in American politics. "I think
politicians are far too staid today. I remember politicians
when I was a boy. I was brought up in this business. My
uncle founded the Democratic Party in the Territory of
Arizona. I remember the first Model-T Ford that four of
us picked cotton for two years to buy. I used to drive my
uncle around in his campaigns and he and the Republican
candidate would be sitting in the back seat. They'd have a
bottle of whiskey with them. I'd drive into a small town
and honk the horn and make a lot of noise to get a crowd
and then these two would get up and nearly tear each
other's eyes out, but they were funny. Take a crack and
make a crack and then drive home friends. That's the way
politics ought to be. . . . You rib the President, you rib the
Senator, there ought to be more of it. Not in a dirty way, but
you kid him. You'd be surprised how much good this'd do
people."

Asked if he thought we in America are too self-conscious
about what people think of us, Senator Goldwater said:
"Yes, I think we are. Again I think this is a trait of im-
maturity and we are an immature nation. We are very
young and have only been here three hundred years. Our
government is not two hundred years old yet. Many of our
states, including mine, are just passing their fiftieth birthday and some haven't passed even their second birthday.
So we are reaching this self-conscious stage, like a child. . . .
It's one of our shortcomings."

Asked if even though we are in mortal danger, our
chances of survival are not better if we laugh at our enemies
and ourselves at least occasionally, the senator replied: "I
think we should relax. Here again we get to the relative

age of our country, comparative again to a growing child.
You can remember as I can remember a period of life when
you thought you knew all about everything and you were
going around as though you had the whole world on your
shoulders and had to carry it. We Americans get that way.
I don't think we're in mortal danger any more than we've
ever been. Man is in no more danger today than he was
when they were throwing rocks at each other. . . . I don't
think a man can enjoy life without a sense of humor and
particularly he can't enjoy life in politics. It's like old Harry
Truman once said, 'If you can't stand the heat, get out of
the kitchen,' and I've never heard a better statement in my
life about this business. We have many people that have
thin skins. Lyndon Johnson is one. His skin is a millionth of
an inch thick. He just blows high and wide with you if you
kid about him. He has the only television station in Austin,
Texas. So when I was in Austin during the '60 campaign I
got up before an audience and said: 'Well, I took off from
Dallas this morning, but before I did I asked the lieutenant
on the line, "How do you get to Austin?" He said, "Well, you
head South and keep flying about an hour and fifteen minutes and then you're going to see a big city with only one
television antenna. That's Austin." ' Why the audiences just
roared, and every time I get near Texas I kid about the
television monopoly, and Lyndon goes into orbit."

Unlike Senator Goldwater, President Kennedy would
not himself discuss his point of view on the significance of
wit and humor in politics, saying that he preferred to let
his use of humor speak for itself. On the other hand, Mr.
Pierre Salinger, his press secretary, and Mr. Theodore
Sorensen, his chief speech writer, had a great deal to say
on the subject. According to "Plucky Pierre," so-christened
by the President, his boss was responsible for the rebirth of
humor in American politics. Salinger himself made a number of witty contributions to this renaissance. When

criticized by reporters for sticking to a prepared release and refusing to answer additional questions, he cracked, "I am not a textual deviate." When reporters sought details on the escape of Caroline Kennedy's pet hamsters, he said, "Our security is very tight but these were extremely intelligent hamsters." When he left the White House to seek a California Senate seat, he characterized his candidacy as a "draft . . . inspired by the candidate himself."

Sorensen said: "First of all I would say the President is at least as interested in how his humor will go over with the audience as he is in how the serious parts will go over. He thinks it's the most important way of establishing communication with the voters and that the humor, if it is successful, will create an atmosphere in which his serious thoughts will be accepted. He would not have been able to survive this job and do all he's been able to do and take all he's been able to take if he weren't able to laugh at himself and see himself in perspective."

Asked whether President Kennedy ever had started in public to tell a joke and then thought better of it and held his tongue, Sorensen said: "The President often meets with a group of us prior to his televised press conferences, especially when it centers around a controversial question that may be raised. On more than one occasion the President or someone in the group will suggest a humorous answer he would like to give but obviously does not dare give. I won't give any examples for the same reasons. Also, I remember very early in his Senate career he told a story at a Democratic gathering that caused trouble. He said: 'I was almost late here today, but I had a very good taxi driver who brought me through the traffic jam. I was going to give him a very large tip and tell him to vote Democratic and then I remembered some advice Senator Green had given me, so I gave him no tip at all and told him to vote Republican.' The AP ran that story as though it were true, as

though he had really said that to a cab driver, and he received angry letters from cab drivers about it and as a result
he had to arrange with the AP to print another story saying
it was all a joke."

Goldwater, as was Kennedy, is often at his wittiest when
addressing members of the press. The Arizona senator
shows the same extraordinary facility when dealing humorously with those areas in which the press has been most
critical. Speaking to the Editorial Cartoonists' Convention,
many of whose members caricature him unmercifully, Goldwater speculated on what he would do if they drove him
out of politics: ". . . the theatre kind of appeals to me too.
When my contract with 18th-Century-Fox runs out I
shouldn't have too much trouble. I've been offered the lead
in a production called 'Stop the World I Want To Get Off.'
Also I have been offered a job as consultant on the 'Flint-
stones' TV show. Thanks to some cartoons depicting my
political philosophy, the producers got the idea that I am
America's foremost authority on the Stone Age."

When most newspapers had been extremely critical of
President Kennedy's actions in regard to the steel industry's
decision to raise prices, the President said at the Annual
Dinner of the White House Correspondents: "I have a few
opening announcements. First, the sudden and arbitrary
action of the officials of this organization in increasing the
price of dinner tickets by $2.50 over last year constitutes a
wholly unjustified defiance of the public interest. If this
increase is not rescinded, but is imitated by the Gridiron,
Radio-TV, and other dinners, it will have a serious impact
on the entire economy of this city. In this serious hour of
our nation's history, when newsmen are awakened in the
middle of the night and given a front page story; when expense accounts are being scrutinized by the Congress;
when correspondents are required to leave their families for
long and lonely weekends at Palm Beach; the American

people will find it hard to accept this ruthless decision by a tiny handful of executives whose only interest is the pursuit of pleasure. I am hopeful that the Women's Press Club will not join this price rise and will thereby force a rescission. . . . I am sure I speak in behalf of all of us in expressing our thanks and best wishes to Mr. Benny Goodman and his group, Miss Gwen Verdon, Mr. Bob Fosse and Mr. Peter Sellers. . . . I have arranged for them to appear next week for the United States Steel Hour. Actually, I didn't do it, Bobby did it. . ."

President Kennedy on a number of occasions commented on his relations with the press. "In part, at least, I am one person who can truthfully say, 'I got my job through *The New York Times.*'" In a press conference at the time of his unfortunate cancellation of the White House subscriptions to the hostile *New York Herald Tribune,* Kennedy redeemed his act of bad temper by saying he had been reading more and enjoying it less. And when there were widespread charges against his administration of news management, he opened his address to the correspondents of the Gridiron Dinner: "Mr. President, distinguished guests, and fellow managing editors . . ." When Vice-President Johnson had been attacked in the press by Doris Fleeson, and Arthur Krock had just written a column attacking the President, Kennedy remarked, "I would rather be Fleesonized than Krocked."

While perhaps not quite so sensitive as he was characterized by Goldwater, President Johnson is much too hurt by any criticism to respond to it as wittily as Kennedy did and as Goldwater does. Nor has he the ironic view of life that quickly sees humorous analogies to the most serious and trying problems. This is not to say that President Johnson does not occasionally enjoy a joke and sometimes use one in the opening moments of a speech. One of his favorites when he was Majority Leader in the Senate he frankly admits he borrowed from Brooks Hays, former congressman from Arkansas and one of the great Washington story-tellers. It concerns a member of the Internal Revenue Service, who telephones a Baptist minister and says: "I am reviewing the tax return of one of the members of your church, Mr. ———, and he lists a donation of two hundred and sixty dollars to the church. Can you tell me if he made such a contribution?" The minister replies, "Well, I haven't got my records in front of me—but if he didn't—he will!"

According to Goldwater, President Johnson said to him at a White House dance after dancing with the Arizona senator's wife, "I have to be nice to Peggy, because I might not be here next year and I'd like to be asked to come back."

Senator Hubert H. Humphrey, of Minnesota, not only uses humor himself, but feels America should make greater use of wit and humor as political weapons against the Communists: ". . . I think, by the way, that we ought to use more humor in the cold war. I think we ought to be using it on the Voice of America programs. We should be razzing them, the leaders, not the people, subtly. For example, in Russia every block of houses has a commissar that's sort of the boss man. Now, no one likes the boss, I don't care where you are. And not only that, they don't like a boss that's a tattletale. Now this isn't a policeman—this is a sneak—the inside policeman. He's a plain-clothes man who's keeping an eye on everybody. Now we need to develop a kind of indigenous humor in which the people who occupy the apartments are getting the best of this sneak, outsmarting him, in which he is constantly being trapped and fooled. This is the best way to expose the fallacies of dictatorship. It makes the people who are listening feel better, because subconsciously they want to outsmart this no-good so-and-so, you see. Subconsciously they detest this kind of surveillance, this kind of spying and informing. This will give them a kind of relief. . . . I think we're always too serious; we're saving the world; we're pounding the table and telling about democracy . . . we're all too heavy-handed and I feel this way so much about our general politics. . . ."

President Kennedy was sparing of his wit in regard to Goldwater, though he once said of the man who might well have been his opponent in 1964: "Like Members of Congress, I have been during the last few days over the Easter holidays, back in touch with my constituents and seeing how they felt, and frankly, I've come back to Washington from Palm Beach and I'm against my entire program. I really feel that the only hope in '64 on the Republican ticket is to nominate Barry, but to be honest I thought that before I went to Palm Beach."

Goldwater, on the other hand, not only directed much of his wit against the President, but commented, before the assassination, on Kennedy's sense of humor. "Kennedy didn't really have any developed sense of humor until he found out he could take it. I remember when we served together on the Labor Committee, and we did this for nine years (he didn't know this), but the rest of the Committee, we'd just gang up on him once in a while and start needling him and the first thing you know, he's up and he wants to fight. Well, he finally realized he couldn't do this and be President, so he completely changed. I have to admire him. He overcame a great deficiency in not having a developed sense of humor. Now he has one and a good one and I think he's enjoying it."

Whether President Kennedy's sense of humor was acquired late or not, no President since Lincoln has addressed himself to so many problems with such wit. He even tried to lessen international tensions by his use of wit. When André Malraux, the French Minister of Culture, was in Washington for the loan of the "Mona Lisa," American relations with France were approaching the lowest and most tense point in our history. De Gaulle had just made another speech insisting that France must have its own independent nuclear *force de frappe*. In accepting the loan of the painting, President Kennedy said: "Mr. Minister, we in the United States are grateful for this loan from the leading artistic power in the world, France. In view of the recent meeting at Nassau, I must note further that this painting has been kept under careful French control. . . . And I want to make it clear that grateful as we are for this painting, we will continue to press ahead with the effort to develop an independent artistic force and power of our own."

There is no subject on which Goldwater is more witty than on his own qualifications for the Presidency. "I suppose I might make our finest Civil War president. . . . I'm not sure I have the necessary requirements. My wife gave up fox hunting when I bought her a fur coat—her sister is not a princess—and my brother's too busy minding the store to help me run the show. I will not deny I've thought about the presidency. Somebody ought to think about it. And I'm not afraid of the presidency. They say it's the loneliest job in the world, but those who say it have never been a Republican in the Senate. Besides there are many risks to being president—I saw that President Kennedy was *Time* magazine's Man of the Year—did you see his picture on the cover?—I didn't even know that Everett Dirksen could paint. I would not be truthful if I said I was fully qualified for the office. I do not play the piano, I seldom play golf, and I never play touch football."

At a meeting of the Alfalfa Club in Washington where he was nominated for the Presidency, Goldwater said: "Emotion chokes me when I think that you have chosen a barefoot boy from the Arizona 'valley of fear' to lead this underprivileged, undernourished, underhoused, underclothed, and over-Kennedied nation of one hundred and ninety million underlings back to the Old Frontier of

McKinley's days. . . . It takes my breath away even though I feel the White House is ready for me since Jacqueline remodelled it in an Eighteenth Century decor and I feel this is a double honor since I've never been to Harvard."

When Goldwater was asked whether his political wit was his own, he replied easily and frankly, "No, Fletcher Knebel writes most of my best stuff for me."

If a new vogue for humor by politicians has been set, however, the lion's share of the credit must go to the late President Kennedy. In Fort Worth, Texas, only a few hours before his assassination, he was in his usual form. ". . . Two years ago I . . . introduced myself in Paris by saying that— I was the man who had accompanied Mrs. Kennedy to Paris. I'm getting . . . somewhat that same sensation as I travel around Texas. Nobody wonders what Lyndon and I wear. I'm glad to be here in Jim Wright's [Fort Worth's Congressman] city. About thirty-five years ago a Congressman from California who had just been elected received a letter from an irate constituent which said: 'During your campaign you promised to have the Sierra Madre mountains reforested. You've been in office for one month and you haven't done so.' Well, no one in Fort Worth has been that unreasonable. . . ."

Kennedy was well aware of the tremendous pressures under which Americans of today live. In this same speech he said, "We would like to live as we once lived, but history will not permit it." In the speech scheduled to be delivered a few hours later in Dallas, President Kennedy had written of "a world of complex and continuing problems . . . a world of frustrations and irritations. . . ." In this same undelivered speech he had written: "There will always be dissident voices heard in the land, expressing opposition without alternatives, finding fault but never favor, perceiving gloom on every side and seeking influence without responsibility. Those voices are inevitable. But today other voices are heard in the land—voices preaching doctrines wholly unrelated to reality, wholly unsuited to the sixties, doctrines which apparently assume that words will suffice without weapons, that vituperation is as good as victory and that peace is a sign of weakness."

No man knew better than Kennedy that "our people get awfully impatient and maybe fatigued and tired . . ." and that "All this will not be finished in the first 100 days. Nor will it be finished in the first 1000 days, nor in the life of this Administration, nor even perhaps in our lifetime on this planet." No one, better than he, showed by his own example that humor helps us to bear our "frustrations and irritations" and to accept the "vituperation."

As Kennedy knew and demonstrated, what we need is patience. Humor, like courage, has with all peoples and in all centuries been an ingredient of patience. Kennedy had a great sense of history. He was a Pulitzer Prize winner in history, and enjoyed quoting in his own speeches the words of other men, as when he said: "Some 2,500 years ago the Greek historian Herodotus described Africa south of the Sahara as a land of 'horned asses, dog-faced creatures, the creatures without heads, whom the Libyans declared to have eyes in their breasts and many other far less fabulous beasts.' Apparently when Herodotus found himself short on facts, he didn't hesitate to use imagination—which may be why he is called the first historian."

Another historical quote used by Kennedy, as well as by many other politicians, was the statement of the French Leftist Liberal, Ledru-Rollin, made amid the confusion of the mobs at the barricades in Paris during the Revolution of February, 1848, "I've got to follow them, I am their leader."

Never were Kennedy's sense of history and his wit more happily combined than at a dinner honoring all the living Nobel Prize winners in the Western Hemisphere: "I think this is the most extraordinary collection of talent, of human knowledge, that has ever been gathered together at the White House—with the possible exception of when Thomas Jefferson dined alone."

Even face to face with Khrushchev, President Kennedy's wit asserted itself. At his meeting with the Communist Party Chairman in Vienna, Kennedy asked what the medal Khrushchev wore was. The Russian leader replied it was the medal for the Lenin Peace Prize and the President said, "Let's hope you keep it."

Wit and humor not only relieve the pressure and frustration of our times but also reinforce courage and, above all, support patience. President Kennedy said, at the University of California in Berkeley on March 3, 1962: "Wisdom requires the long view. . . . Beyond the drumfire of daily crisis . . . there is arising the outline of a robust and vital world community, founded on nations secure in their own independence, and united by allegiance to world peace. It would be foolish to say that this world will be won tomorrow, or the day after. The processes of history are fitful and uncertain and aggravating. There will be frustrations and setbacks. There will be times of anxiety and gloom. . . . I am reminded of the story of the great French Marshal Lyautey, who once asked his gardener to plant a tree. The gardener objected that the tree was slow-growing and would not reach maturity for a hundred years. The Marshal replied, 'In that case, there is no time to lose, plant it this afternoon.' Today a world of knowledge—a world of co-operation—a just and lasting peace—may be years away. But we have no time to lose. Let us plant our trees this afternoon."

Adams, Henry. *John Randolph.* Boston: Houghton Mifflin, 1908.

Allen, George E. *Presidents Who Have Known Me.* New York: Simon & Schuster, 1950.

Barkley, Alben. *That Reminds Me.* New York: Doubleday & Co., 1954.

Disraeli, Benjamin. *Wit and Wisdom of Benjamin Disraeli.* London: Longmans, Green, 1881.

Benton, Thomas Hart. "Duel Between Mr. Clay and Mr. Randolph." Manuscript (April 8, 1826). Houghton Library, Harvard College, Cambridge.

Bevan, Aneurin. *Why Not Trust the Tories?* London: Victor Gollancz, 1944.

———. *In Place of Fear.* New York: Simon & Schuster, 1952.

Boykin, Edward C. *The Wit and Wisdom of Congress.* New York: Funk & Wagnalls, 1961.

Bruce, William Cabell. *John Randolph of Roanoke.* 2 vols. New York: G. P. Putnam's Sons, 1922.

Busch, Noel F. *Adlai Stevenson of Illinois.* New York: Farrar, Straus and Young, 1952.

Butterfield, Roger. *The American Past.* New York: Simon & Schuster, 1947.

Cecil, David. *Melbourne.* New York: Grosset & Dunlap, n.d.

Churchill, Winston Spencer. *Lord Randolph Churchill.* New York: The Macmillan Co., 1906.

———. *The World Crisis.* 6 vols. New York: Charles Scribner's Sons, 1923–31.

———. *Great Contemporaries.* New York: G. P. Putnam's Sons, 1937.

———. *While England Slept.* New York: G. P. Putnam's Sons, 1938.

———. *Blood, Sweat, and Tears.* New York: G. P. Putnam's Sons, 1941.

———. *The Second World War.* 6 vols. Boston: Houghton Mifflin, 1948–53.

Cobbett, William. *The Political Proteus, a View of the Public Character and Conduct of R. B. Sheridan esq.* New York: Sarjeant, 1804.

Coote, Colin R. *Sir Winston Churchill, a Self-Portrait.* London: Eyre & Spottiswoode, 1954.

Foot, Michael. *Aneurin Bevan.* New York: Atheneum, 1963.

Gardner, Gerald C. *The Quotable Mr. Kennedy.* New York: Abelard-Schuman, 1962.

Garland, Hugh A. *The Life of John Randolph of Roanoke*. 2 vols. New York: Appleton, 1851.

Grossman, Richard L. *Bold Voices*. Garden City, N.Y.: Doubleday & Co., 1960.

Hall, Max. *Benjamin Franklin and Polly Baker*. Chapel Hill, N.C.: University of North Carolina Press, 1960.

Hertz, Emmanuel. *Lincoln Talks*. New York: Viking Press, 1939.

Herzberg, Max John. *Insults, a Practical Anthology of Scathing Remarks and Acid Portraits*. New York: Greystone Press, 1941.

Ismay, Hastings Lionel Ismay. *The Memoirs of General the Lord Ismay*. London: Heinemann, 1960.

James, Bessie R., and Mary Waterstreet. *Adlai's Almanac: the Wit and Wisdom of Stevenson of Illinois*. New York: Henry Schuman, 1952.

Jerrold, Walter. *Bon Mots of Sidney Smith and R. Brinsley Sheridan*. London: J. M. Dent, 1893.

Johnson, Gerald W. *Randolph of Roanoke, a Political Fantastic*. New York: Minton, Balch, 1929.

Kennedy, John F. *The Speeches of John F. Kennedy, Presidential Campaign of 1960*. Washington, D.C.: U.S. Government Printing Office, 1961.

———. *Public Papers of the Presidents, John F. Kennedy, 1961*. Washington, D.C.: U.S. Government Printing Office, 1962.

———. *Public Papers of the Presidents, John F. Kennedy, 1962*. Washington, D.C.: U.S. Government Printing Office, 1963.

Kingsmill, Hugh. *An Anthology of Invective and Abuse*. London: Eyre & Spottiswoode, 1929.

Liebling, A. J. *The Earl of Louisiana*. New York: Simon & Schuster, 1961.

Lincoln Stories. Rhodes & McClure, 1879.

Lloyd George, David. *The People's Budget*. London: Hodder & Stoughton, 1909.

———. *The People's Insurance*. London: Hodder & Stoughton, 1912.

———. *The Great War*. Toronto: Hodder & Stoughton, n.d.

———. *War Memoirs of David Lloyd George*. 6 vols. London: Nicholson & Watson, 1933–36.

———. *Memoirs of the Peace Conference*. 2 vols. New Haven: Yale University Press, 1939.

Lorant, Stefan. *Lincoln, a Picture Story of His Life*. New York: Harper & Bros., 1952.

MacNeil, Neil. *Forge of Democracy*. New York: David McKay, 1963.

Maurois, André. *Disraeli*. New York: Appleton, 1928.

Monypenny, W. F., and G. E. Buckle. *The Life of Benjamin Disraeli*. 4 vols. New York: The Macmillan Co., 1914–17.

Owen, Frank. *Tempestuous Journey, Lloyd George, His Life and Times*. London: Hutchinson, 1954.

Parker, John F. *If Elected I Promise.* . . . Garden City, N.Y.: Doubleday & Co., 1960.

Pearson, Hesketh. *Dizzy, the Life and Personality of Benjamin Disraeli*. New York: Harper & Bros., 1951.

———. *Lives of the Wits*. New York: Harper & Row, 1962.

"Mr. Punch." *Benjamin Disraeli, Earl of Beaconsfield*. London: Punch Office, 1878.

———. *Lloyd George*. London: Cassell, 1922.

Randolph, John. *Speech on the British War*. Washington, D.C., 1812.

Rosenman, Samuel I. (ed.). *The Public Papers and Addresses of Franklin D. Roosevelt*. 13 vols. New York: Random House, The Macmillan Co., Harper & Bros., 1938–50.

———. *Working with Roosevelt*. New York: Harper & Bros., 1952.

Russell, Phillips. *Benjamin Franklin, the First Civilized American*. New York: Brentano's, 1926.

Sandburg, Carl. *Abraham Lincoln: the Prairie Years*. 2 vols. New York: Harcourt, Brace, 1926.

———. *Abraham Lincoln: the War Years*. 4 vols. New York: Harcourt, Brace, 1939.

Schlesinger, Arthur M., Jr. *The Coming of the New Deal*. Boston: Houghton Mifflin, 1959.

———. *Kennedy or Nixon: Does It Make Any Difference?* New York: The Macmillan Co., 1960.

Sheridaniana: or, Anecdotes of the Life of Richard Brinsley Sheridan: His Table-talk, and Bon Mots. London: H. Colburn, 1826.

Sherwood, Robert E. *Roosevelt and Hopkins, an Intimate History*. New York: Harper & Bros., 1948.

Stevenson, Adlai E. *Major Campaign Speeches of Adlai E. Stevenson*. New York: Random House, 1952.

Van Doren, Carl. *Benjamin Franklin*. New York: Viking Press, 1938.

———. *Benjamin Franklin's Autobiographical Writings*. New York: Viking Press, 1945.

Watson, J. Steven. *The Reign of George III*. Oxford at the Clarendon Press, 1960.

Wiley, Alexander. *Laughing with Congress*. New York: Crown, 1947.

Williams, Geoffrey, and Charles Roetter. *The Wit of Winston Churchill*. London: Max Parrish, 1954.

Wilson, Rufus Rockwell. *Lincoln in Caricature*. New York: Horizon, 1953.

The Wit of Lincoln, the Wisdom of Franklin, & Other Bits of Wit. Indianapolis: Scott-Miller, 1907.

Index